D0896582

WILL THE REAL JESUS PLEASE STAND?

SEVEN RIDDLES OF ISRAEL AND MESSIAH

VENDYL M. JONES

Cassette series on this and other subjects available.

INSTITUTE OF JUDAIC-CHRISTIAN RESEARCH
Box 35 TYLER, TX. 75710

Published by

July 1983

To a generation suffering from a famine of the word of G-d, it is indeed a pleasure to commend this book. This work is so unshackled by the yoke of traditionalism, it is so different from the cold and pretentious analysis of the critic and theology, and so unalterably loyal to the original text of the scripture, that after having our mind totally blown, one rises in spirit refreshed, in faith strengthened and to new endeavor and vision encouraged.

Richard Fry
(continued inside back cover)

PREFACE

"...All this...we shall attempt to condense into a single book...We have aimed to please those who wish to read, to make it easy for those who are inclined to memorize, and to profit all readers. For us who have undertaken the toil of abridgement and abbreviating, it is no light matter but calls for sweat and loss of sleep....

"It is the duty of the original historian to occupy the ground and discuss the matters from every side and to make trouble with details, but the one who recasts the narrative should be allowed to strive for brevity of expression and forego exhaustive treatment.

"At this point therefore let us begin the narrative, adding only so much to what has already been said; for it is foolish to lengthen the preface while cutting short the story itself."

II Maccabees 2:23...-32
Revised Standard Version

ACKNOWLEDGMENTS

So many people, from so many places, for so many years, have become such a vital part of my life. I am a composite of all the souls I have met, heard or read. This book is my soul and theirs. I have had great teachers, but some of my greatest teachers were, in fact, my students. A wise man once said, "We are all a part of each other, a part of all with whom we have to do." It is with fear that I begin to acknowledge those who are a small part or a great part of this book. I fear, for fear that I might forget someone who surely should be listed, that in the pressure of the hour slipped my memory. It was with a constant prayer, I prayed for recollection, as I make these acknowledgments. Please inform me if I missed you, or someone you know, who should be added. I have restricted this list to those who I know contributed something to this particular publication. Especially I want to thank two churches who were patient with my struggles to learn and teach as I served them as Pastor. The Dungan Chapel Baptist Church, Elizabethton, Tennessee and the First Baptist Church in Lynn, North Carolina. Rabbi Henry Guttman and Rabbi Henry Barneis who began me on my course in understanding G-d, Torah and Israel, I give special Todah Rabbah!

AGRANOT, Carmel & Simon; ALLEN, Annie Laurie; BAR ADON, Pasach; BAR SELA, Mona & Dr. Ariel; BARNEIS, Ruth & Rb. Henry; BEN EZRA, Yonatan; BEN NAEH, Lidia & Emmanuel; BEN YEHUDA, Ehud & Rb. Eliezar; BERGMAN, Avraham; BERNHARDT, DeViolet; BILLINGS, Gertrude & Alex; BOBO, Virginia & Les; BONEY, Benyamin; BOREN, Shirley & Ken; BROSHI, Dr. Magen, Devorah & Dr. Ami; BYRD, Roberta & D. Harold, Jr.

CARLTON, Lila Scruggs & Max; CAUKINS, Nancy & Dave; COHEN, Dr. Gavrael, Rhoda & Rb. Jack; COLLINS, Loretta & Jack; CONNOLLY, Dr. Peter; COOPER, Dr. David L., Marilyn & Kenneth R.; DADOUN, Victor; DAN, Rb. Ephraim (Ha Falashi); DART, Jean & Harold; DEYO, Gussie Dale & Harold; DOUVERNOY, Marianna & Rv. Claude; ELLIS, Alinda & Marvin, Barbara & Don; FLUSSER, David; FREZE, Lizabeth; FRIEDMAN, Suzanna & Ben; FRY, Richard & Ida.

GLAZIER, Vera Wainscott Jones; GORDON, Sandra & Dr. Harvey; GOREN, Rav. Sholomo; GREEN, Shirley; GREGORY, Nell & Chuck, June & Joe; GRUENZNER, Norman; GUTTMAN, Rb. Henry; HAYNES, Kay & Mike; HENNEMAN, Louise & Larry; HENSLEY, Dorothy & Rv. Kenneth; HERMANN, Lois Wainscott; HILL, Bobby.

JONES, Anne & Ray, Ethelyn Marceaux, Julia Ann & Jerry Heisler, Liz & Wain Scott, Lois Richardson, Rita & Jerry, Nunnery, Sarah, Vennie, Zahava Zohara Cohen; KADAR, Lu; KAMRAD, Mordechi; KAUFMAN, Phil; KEIKAEFER, Anita; KEITH, Helen & Wayne; KEMP, Dr. Roy A.; KIRKLAND, Shirley; KNITTNER, Kalman; KYLE, Chris & Ralph; LADOR, Ehud; LANDEAU, Dina & Benny; LANDMAN, Rb. Max; LANHAM, Sherrie & Terry; LAWRENCE, John; LEE, Dr. Frank; LINDSEY, Margaret & Dr. Robert Lisle; LIPSCOMB, Nancy & Wyatt.

MACKEY, Harriet & Joseph; MALAKI, Yona; MALEV, Belle & Rb. William; MARSHALL, Dr. Mary Ann; MCAFEE, Stella & Cozell; MCGINNIS, Jean & Henry; MCKINLEY, Louise & Dr. Kenneth F.; MIER, Ruth & Israel; MINOR, Peggy & Roger; MORGAN, Louise & Jerry; MORGEN, Dr. Roy; NIDIFFER, Amelia; NORRIS, Rv. J. Frank; OKED, Yitzhak; PEAK, Wanda & Rv. Dr. Luther C.; PELET, Matti; PETTY, Cris; PHILLIP, Gertrude & Israel.

RAIMOND, Sharona & Jack; RAINEY, Dr. Anson; ROSALAR, Fannie & Mark; ROSENTHAL, Steven; ROSS, Barbara & Bob; SALEM, Beth & Joe; SAMET, Peggy & Leon; SARTAIN, Naomi & Rv. Alvin; SCHILLER, Edith & Ely; SCHIVILLI, Haim; SCHWARTZ, Rb. Samuel; SCROUPLOS, Millie & Dr. George; SHELDON, Nell & H.A.; SMITH, Eugenia & Barry; STAUBER, Rb. Max & Mrs.; STAVEY, Mr. & Mrs. Joseph; STREICHER, Sholomo; STRYKER, Pam & Bob; SUMMERLIN, Jeannie & Sheldon; TAGGER, Eva & Danny; VEAL, Rosa; VERED, Hannah & Uzi; WELLS, Grace & Rev. Dr. John R.; XIFO, Peter; YADIN, Shoshanna; ZACHERY, Glen & Oralea, Mary & children.

Special acknowledgments to my mother, Vera Leona nee Wainscott who taught me to love Israel; to Dr. Luther C. Peak who inspired me to go beyond the requirements in study; to Rabbi Henry Barneis who taught me although he did not at first trust me. To the Glen Zachary family who made place and time to write this book, to Ethelyn Marceaux who repeatedly typed the manuscript, and a double acknowledgment to Ken Cooper who helped so much with his journalistic skill.

WHY THIS BOOK?

The objective of this publication is not to make the Jew aware of the Christian view of the Messianic nature and claims of Jesus. The motive and aim of this book is to make the Christian aware of the Jewishness of Jesus and the Messianic nature of Israel. In the manner of this approach, the aim is not to prove the validity of Jesus to the Jew by rabbinic literature, but rather to attempt to show the Christian the validity of Judaism, the Jewish people and the Political State of Israel by the teachings and the person of Jesus.

The Jewish philosopher, Martin Buber, in a letter to David Cooper, said "You ask me if I believe in Jesus? Jesus who? Jesus in the arm of a stone Madonna? No! That is idolatry. The Reformation came and tore down the image and nailed up a creed. Do I believe in Jesus of the Protestant creed? No! That is fetish...I do not believe in Jesus but I believe with the Jesus of Matthew, Mark, Luke, and John."

This is not to discredit the works of others who have sought a traditional Christian interpretation of Jesus by using Jewish sources. Certainly, it is commendable to see those who have sought to remove Jesus from the pagan influences that have infiltrated Christian theology and to return him to a more authentic concept of the Jewishness of Jesus. Among these are a number of classical works.

Perhaps the most classic is the work of a German Lutheran minister, Paul Billerbeck, *Kommentar Zum Neuen Testament*. Unfortunately, the German Church and political climate were not favorable to such an approach. Luther had brought out of the Roman Church thirteen centuries of theological bigotry against the Jews. For the Teutonic and Germanic minds to identify Jesus as a Jew or with Judaism was almost an apostate step. Paul Billerbeck met with one disappointment after another and was given the silent kiss of death by his Lutheran peers. No publisher would touch his manuscript. Finally, he persuaded a Christian scholar, Hermann L. Strack, to read the manuscript. Professor Strack was very much impressed with Billerbeck's work and recommended it to C. H. Becksche Verlagsbuchundlung, of München, for publication; but his reply was, "Who is Paul Billerbeck? He is not recognized by his own church. What he is publishing is questionable by Christian scholars, and he is a man of no renown in Germany."

Because of Strack's persistence, the publisher agreed to publish the work only if Hermann Strack's name could be used jointly with the author's. The publication was printed in 1926 in five volumes and it met with condemnation before investigation. German pockets were empty from the economic recovery of the First World War which was followed by a world depression. Also, German higher criticism was at its apex in propagating the Hellenic Jesus. Billerbeck's Jewish Jesus was immediately condemned and dismissed by the new breed of philosophical theologians of the higher critical school. Greater still, the voice of Hitler was beginning to fill German ears. To consider the Jewishness of Jesus was not only unpopular, but was soon a crime against the Third Reich.

Perhaps the forerunner to Billerbeck's works were the two volumes of Alfred Edersheim, *The Life and Times of Jesus the Messiah*, London, 1886. The theme of these volumes was the political and cultural history of the Second Temple period rather than of the rabbinic nature of Jesus.

Sir Isaac Newton's writings, which stressed a literal interpretation of the Bible, brought about an awareness in seventeenth century Britain and America, of the Jew's place and role in prophetic history. In contrast to Newton, the traditional church considered the Jews as cursed, and all the prophetic literature about Israel was spiritualized and applied to the Christian church. Hence, when the prophets spoke of the restoration of Israel, it was interpreted as meaning a restoration of the Holy Roman Empire because Rome was considered to be spiritual Israel. There is no statement or allusion in the Scriptures of any such concept as a Holy Roman Empire. Yet, many evangelical writers today propagate such an imposition. Furthermore, the Treaty of Versailles spelled out clearly that the Holy Roman Empire was neither holy nor Roman nor an empire, and no nation was thereafter permitted to herald that banner name. This and many other misconceptions of Christian theology are a result of spiritualizing the Scripture.

Sir Isaac Newton wrote in 1693: "About the time of the end, a body of men will be raised up who will turn their attention to the prophecies and insist on their literal interpretation in the midst of much clamor and opposition."

Slowly, a sprinkling of writers began to do as Newton had predicted. It should not be a surprise to note that most of these writers were converts from Judaism: Alfred Edersheim, Andrew Jukes, Arno C. Gaebelein, David Baron, Jacob Levi Bartholdy, Paul Cassel, Isaac Solkinson, David Ginzburg, Adolph Saphir, the list goes on. It is important to note that it was not the Reformation, but the Jewish influence within the church which brought Christian theology out of the Dark Ages. Dr. Luther Peak gave an interesting analogy of the role of the Jew in the Christian Church: "At the point where the wild olive branch [the Gentile Christian church] is grafted into the good olive tree [Israel's spiritual economy], the graft imbeds itself into the tree and a part of the tree imbeds itself into the graft. The origin of the Church was Jewish; also, the major return of the Church to its origin has been of the Jews."

These writers, from their Jewish backgrounds, began to show the imperative need for a literal interpretation of a few basics: namely, the assertions that Israel was Israel and the Church was the Church. It was this influence which brought about the Plymouth Brethren movement and the publication of the Scofield Bible. The Brethren and its sister movements, Pre-millennialism and Dispensationalism, insisted on the validity of National Israel and the Jewish people in a community sense. However, these movements still maintained the old church tradition toward the individual Jew, Judaism and the rabbis. By some rape of lbgic, these organizations, institutions, or schools of thought treat Israel and the Jew collectively as a chosen people and the elect of G-d. But the individual Jew and Judaism are treated as apostate and damned. In all that has been written heretofore, there are certain common traits: "The Jews are judicially blinded and lost"; "Judaism is the antithesis of Christianity." There is a certain sneer and distrust toward rabbinic authority unless it can be used to prove Jesus as Savior to the Jew. In dispensationalism, the Jews are singled out as a prime objective for conversion.

Drs. W. A. Sampey, A. T. Robertson, and David L. Cooper at Louisville Seminary, initiated a research entitled, "Jesus in the Talmud, Targums, and Rabbinic Writings." This work was comparable in time to Billerbeck's work in Germany following the First World War. The project died for lack of denominational support by the Southern Baptist Convention. Dr. David L. Cooper, however, carried the project forward as his life's work. Doctor Cooper was very warm toward the Jew and did not swing a missionary ax. He was highly commended by Jewish and Christian scholars for his seven-volume publication, *Messianic Series*. Cooper had lengthy discourse with Joseph Klausner, Martin Buber, and other Jewish scholars. Yet, as in all other works, Cooper's objective was still to prove the validity of Jesus to the Jew. Without argument to the value of these books and writers—and they certainly have a vital place in Christian Apologetic literature—no book has been written from the other point of view. This publication is intended to state that other point of view.

Christians have created Jesus in their own image. Christian art seems always to reflect the theology of the day. Take, for example, the paintings of the Spanish Renaissance. The pictures of Jesus are always backgrounded with the topography of Spain; the architecture is Moorish, not Middle Eastern. All the pictures of Jesus and his disciples are Spanish.

In Italian painting, he was always a tall, beautiful Roman. However, the Italians did know how to paint Jews. Scenes of the crucifixion at Passover portrayed rabbis in their Yom Kippur attire around the base of the Cross while they executed the Roman Jesus. Leonardo da Vinci's "Last Supper," posed as the Passover, had fish on the table rather than a lamb. It was Friday night, was it not? Da Vinci's Jesus and his disciples were all distinctly Roman except for the one holding the purse, Jew-das Iscariot. Matzos? Hardly. It was a loaf of Italian bread. Of several hundred madonnas and the Christ child where the innocent babe is unclothed, never will you see a circumcised Jesus. That would be too Jewish; substitute instead a halo! Have you ever seen a painting of Jesus that makes him appear Jewish? Except for Rembrandt, everyone has chiseled out his own image of Jesus in one manner or another. One prominent rabbi, Menachem Schneerson, the Rebbe of the Lubavitch Chabad Chassidim, asked, "What does Jesus of Nazareth have to do with Christianity today?" Martin Buber, in his book, *Two Types of Faith*, stated the problem thusly:

> For nearly fifty years the New Testament has been a main concern in my studies, and I think I am a good reader who listens impartially to what is said.
>
> From my youth onward I have found in Jesus my great brother. That Christianity has regarded and does regard him as G-d and Savior has always appeared to me a fact of highest importance which for his sake and my own, I must endeavor to understand.... .My own fraternally open relationship to him has grown ever stronger and clearer, and today I see him more strongly and clearly than ever before.
>
> I am more than ever certain that a great place belongs to him in Israel's history of faith and that this place cannot be described by any of the usual categories. Under history of faith I understand the history of the human part, as far as known to us, in that which has taken place between G-d and Israel. There is something in Israel's history of faith which is to be understood by Israel, just as there is something in the Christian history of faith which is to be understood from Christianity. The latter I have touched only with the unbiased respect of one who hears the Word.

Higher critics, philosophers, and cynics have sought to make a "quest for the historical Jesus." Unfortunately, they searched in the plains of Macedonia rather than in the mountains of Israel. Naturally, they found what they sought: the "Hellenized" Jesus. In the Jewish Midrash commentary, *Bere'shit-Rabah*, on Genesis 11:2..."they found a plain in the land of Shinar," the rabbis point out that they found a plain of Shinar because they were

Martin Buber

looking for a plain in Shinar. One always finds what he is looking for. You seek a Hellenic Jesus, you will find a Hellenic Jesus. You seek a theological Jesus, you will find a theological Jesus. If anyone ever dared to seek a Jewish Jesus, no doubt he would have found one. This book is a search for that Jesus of the Galilean hills, the Judaean mountains, and the Temple and synagogues of his day.

Jesus of Nazareth was a Jew religiously, he was of Israeli nationality, and he was a native Sabra from *Beit-Lehem* of Judaea. To miss that in only a casual reading of the New Testament would require a great deal of effort. Yet, if one takes a verse here and another there to prove his own theological position, ignoring those verses that might say otherwise, he will find what he is looking for and any other will be hidden from him.

Abba Eban, in his book, *My People*, points out: "Early Christianity is closer to Judaism than the adherents of either religion have usually wished to admit. Both Christian theologians and Orthodox Jews have underestimated the original Judeo-Christian affinity. It was only gradually that Christianity severed its connection with the Jewish community and became transformed to a Gentile religion."

Abba Eban

Judaism and Christianity have many common denominators. They also have many irreconcilable differences. The primary problem between the two is a difference of semantics. The Jew and the Christian have many identical words in their vocabulary of faith, such as: G-d, Messiah, Bible, Salvation, Redemption, Sin, and Kingdom. Yet, the definition, connotation and denotation of each by the Jew and Christian are variant and sometimes opposite in meaning. At the same time, both the Jew and the Christian have many words which are totally alien to the ears of the other and yet may have the same meaning. The first step in understanding each other is to overcome the higher strata of the linguistic problems.

Yet greater than the linguistic problem is the basic problem of the traditional Christian attitude toward the Jews. As long as the Christian does all the preaching and expects the Jew to do all the listening, there is no chance for communication. So long as the Christian looks down on the Jew as blind, lost, ignorant, and inferior, there is no basis for sharing. So long as the Christian fails to recognize that the Jew does have a vital relationship with G-d through faith in the Abrahamic Covenant, he cannot identify with the Jew spiritually. So long as the Christian fails to understand that the Hebrew language is *Leshon ha-Qodesh*, the Holy Tongue, the linguistic problem will remain. Until the Christian acknowledges that Jesus was of the same Jewish religion as traditional Jews are today and that they are indeed his brethren, there is no common denominator. Until the Christian recognizes the validity of Judaism and the Jew there is no basis for dialogue. When he does recognize the validity of Judaism and the Jew, there is no need for dialogue.

Christian unawareness is a greater enemy to Jewish-Christian relations than raw prejudice. This unconsciousness on the part of the traditional Christian toward his Jewish neighbor is the lubricant on the hinges, if not indeed the very hand, that slammed shut the doors on the gas chambers.

The chasm between Judaism and Christianity is haunted by the echo of silence and unconcern. Even worse, this apathy toward the Jew is esteemed as a Christian virtue. As Edmund Burke said, "The only thing necessary for the triumph of evil is for good men to do nothing."

The Jews are not always without guilt in their attitudes toward Christians. A Jew can be just as sinister in his snarling of the word *goyim* as a Ku Klux Klansman is when he projects his lower jaw fully forward to say, "The Jews!"

History will almost pardon the Jew for his reaction toward the Christian. Yet, that does not justify his painting every Christian with a brush imported from Auschwitz and paint from Dachau. Many Christians died there, also, for the crime of Jewish sympathy. If a Christian feels a coldness or even rudeness from a Jew who is using an Auschwitz brush and Dachau paint, he must remember that the slime and mortar that built the gas chambers and crematoriums were traditional Christian theological attitudes and dogmas toward the Jews. What happened in Germany had happened before; it can happen again, as long as the theological dogmas continue.

The Talmud, in Makot VII, states: "A Sanhedrin that sentenced a man to death once in seven years was called *Hablanoot,* or a destructive court of killers." David Flusser pointed out that the Sanhedrin of Jesus' day was called *Sanhedrin Dam*, or a bloody Sanhedrin, because it sentenced two righteous men to death in seven years. In the Talmud, Gittin ha-Nazikin LVII, and following, are lengthy discourses against the Sanhedrin of the latter Second Temple period. (cf. Mhkut 1:10, Danby's translation of Mishna, p. 403)

Herod the Great had the legitimate High Priest of the Sons of Zadok assassinated and replaced him with his own appointee, one Simeon. After that, the true lineage of priests stopped, and the office became a bid to anyone for money or political favors.

Herod also eliminated forty-seven of the Pharisees on the Sanhedrin and replaced them with his own stooges from among the Sadducees. The court was under so much political pressure from the Herodians and the Romans that they never convened in the House of Judgment or the Marble Hall from forty years before the destruction of the Temple. Herod murdered his wife and two sons along with the entire Hashmonean house of the Maccabean dynasty. He sought also to murder all the Regal descendants of the throne of King David. Many of them fled the land of Judaea—some to the Golan and others to the Galilee. Why do you suppose that Joseph and Mary lived in Nazareth rather than their native Bethlehem?

Traditional Judaism abhors the corrupt priests who were appointed by the Romans and Herod. Among them were Annas and Caiaphas. Yet, many Christians today associate all Israel, and even modern Jews, only with the destructive Sanhedrin and the apostate priests of the Herodian era.

Many Christians read their Old Testament and glean all the beautiful promises made to Israel and apply them to themselves; all the curses of the Law they leave for the Jew. The change in attitude on the part of the Christian can only be brought about when he begins to identify Jesus as a traditional Jew. Once the Christian sees Jesus in the light of traditional Judaism, he will begin to see the Jew as a brother.

This book will attempt to initiate a study of the Jewishness of Jesus. It will attempt to answer questions that have never been answered, and ask questions that have never been asked.

The premise of this discourse is in the framework of Traditional Orthodox Jewish thought. Therefore, the English spelling of the name of God will appear in form of G-d for the sanctity of the Holy Name. "LORD" will be "The Eternal One".

TABLE OF CONTENTS

I. Riddle of the Messiah 1-1

II. Riddle of Israel 2-1

III. Riddle of the Languages 3-1

IV. Riddle of Interpretation 4-1

V. Riddle of the Sequence of Events 5-1

VI. Riddle of the Plural Covenants 6-1

VII. Riddle of the Rejection 7-1

Epilogue E-1

Bibliography B-1

Chapter I
RIDDLE OF THE MESSIAH

Rabbi Leo Baeck, in his book, *Judaism and Christianity*, said, "The unreconcilable difference between Judaism and Christianity is the question of the Messiah. Any compromise on that question would mean the destruction of either one or the other institution, and in the final analysis, probably the destruction of both."

Who is the Messiah? Who is really qualified to say? Those of whom Jesus was say he is not! While those of whom he was not say he is!

The first and most sensitive question the Christian will ask a Jew is, "Why don't you Jews accept Jesus as the Messiah?" The Jew, on the other hand, though he may not say it, is equally in wonder as to what the Gentile Christian finds in accepting Jesus that generates such a dynamic force and change in his life.

This question of "accepting Jesus" is to the Jew more than a mere inquiry. He has not forgotten that throughout his history, this issue was the prick of the Crusader's lance, the lash of the Spanish Inquisition and the peril of the Russian pogroms. The Jew is very sensitive about this question because it is the phantom of harassment that haunts his entire history among the Gentile Christian nations. The historic walls of the house of Israel are lined with the shadowing ghosts of his ancestors who chose death rather than compromise on this question.

The Christian, on the other hand, also has a certain ghostly haunting in his mind as to why the Jew does not see in Jesus that same image he himself sees. If anyone should know what a Messiah should be, certainly the people who prophesied and produced that Messiah and wrote all the Books in the Christian's Bible should. The fact that the Jew does not *accept Jesus* as the Gentile

Christian does is, in itself, a haunting thought to the Christian. Subconsciously, the thinking Christian is deeply bothered by this issue. While on the surface he may project blame on the Jews for not accepting his message of Good News, deep inside, the Jew's "rejection" of Jesus creates a gnawing doubt in his own faith in Jesus. The impelling mission to convert a Jew, on the part of many Christians, is in reality an attempt to fill the vacancy and void that shrouds the validity of what they have themselves experienced in Jesus. "Why," they ask, "does not the Jew feel the need of Jesus as we do? Why does Jesus not qualify to them for their expected Messiah?"

To the Jew, Israel is the Messiah, the Messianic Nation, the Messianic People, and the Messianic Hope. The Christian finds this Jewish concept of Messiah as alien and foreign to his own experience as the Jew finds Jesus alien to his own experience. The Christian also finds it as difficult and strange to accept Israel as Messiah. Apart from this issue, Judaism and Christianity have many common denominators.

The question, "Who is the Messiah?" is indeed a riddle. Logically speaking, Leo Baeck was correct in naming it "the unreconcilable difference. . . ." Yet, if we do not bind ourselves to logistics and get back to the primal foundation of both Judaism and Christianity, there is an approach, that both the Christian and the Jew can take, and each have an appreciation for the other's Messianic faith, without a compromise of either on the issue of the Messiah.

Monotheism, the belief in one true and living G-d, is the basic common denominator of both Judaism and Christianity. There is nothing logical about the G-d of Israel. He is the ETERNAL ONE. He is the uncaused cause of all things. He is the ESSENCE which pre-existed both Creator and Creation. He is the INCOMPREHENSIBLE. Before the beginning, He is not subject to matter, energy, space or time. He is the invisible G-d who can neither be seen nor be reduced to material expression in an image. He dwells both inside and outside the sphere of creation, yet his place is unapproachable by mortal creature. His Name, though written YHVH, is totally UNUTTERABLE. It cannot be pronounced because the four letters of the tetragrammaton, יְהֹוָה, YHVH, are merely an abbreviation of the

Name of seventy-two letters. The G-d of Israel is a G-d of mystery who does not respond to the laws of logic but to the act of faith. There is also no such thing as Jewish theology in the traditional sense of the word, for Judaism is a mystical faith.

In this sphere of the mystical monotheistic concept of G-d, Judaism and Christianity find their common denominator. However, since Judaism has been around twice as long as Christianity, the Jews have had more time to develop mystical thought than have the Christians. At the same time, Jewish mysticism must not in any way be confused with pagan, secular, or even Christian mystical philosophy. The Jewish kind is always subjected to the texts of their scripture. Only the ESSENCE of Jewish mysticism is experienced by the Christian. "The Gentiles who turned to G-d from serving idols" found, through faith in Jesus, that they could have a vital relationship with the G-d of Israel. Somewhere, in the perimeter of turning to G-d (at what particular degree between 0° and 180°, we cannot say), the Gentile Christian zeros in on the genuine mystical quality of the ESSENCE of the Jewish faith. Although Christian and Jew alike experience this ESSENCE, neither can explain it; if it could be explained, it would not be mystical— it would be logical; it would not be experience of faith, it would be philosophy. Going beyond the allegorical, let us glimpse at the mystical!

Jewish mysticism is the work of the Kabbalists. The name Kabbalah comes from the idea of the mystical or secret meanings of the words of the texts. The word *QiBeL* means "received." Hence, those who "*receive*" the "*secret*" meanings are called Kabbalists. The Kabbalist will be discussed more fully under the "Riddle of Interpretation."

The Kabbalistic level of interpretation deals extensively with the higher sphere concerned with the PARADISE of G-d, that sphere from which angels ascended and descended on Jacob's ladder (Gen. 28:10-12). This PARADISE of G-d is synonymous, in Jewish thought, with the Eternal Garden of Eden, called GaN-EhDeN. The Greek word PARADISE comes from the Hebrew word, *Pardes*, which means "an orchard." *Pardes* is symbolic of the four levels of interpretation known to Jewish hermeneutics. Hence, to go into PARADISE, or PARDES, means to go into the mystical level of interpretation, to enter the eternal Garden of Eden.

If a person in this temporal world ascends into that Paradise of G-d, the Garden of Eden, he will discover that all the things that this temporal world calls "mystical" will become "realities" and all the material things of this temporal world will become only models, symbols, and facsimiles of the world to come. "While we look not at the things which are seen, but at the things which are not seen: for the things which are seen are temporal; but the things which are not seen are eternal." (II Cor. 4:18) Does this suggest perhaps that Paul himself may have been a Kabbalistic rabbi? Does this suggest that he may have gone into the Garden?

According to tradition, one should never go alone into the secret orchard. He should go with one who has been there before and knows his way back out. We are not forbidden to enter that mystical garden, neither are we encouraged to go in.

In the Talmud, Moed or Hagigah, is the story of four sages who entered this garden: Rabbis Akiba, Ben'Azai, Ben Zoma', and "Aher," Elisha' Ben Abuyah. Ben'Azai died. Ben Zoma' went insane. Elisha' Ben Abuyah went apostate. Only Rabbi Akiba came out of the garden unharmed.

Despite the wisdom of Rabbi Akiba in being able to come from Paradise unharmed, he made a very grave mistake about the Messiah. Rabbi Akiba declared that Bar Kochba was the Messiah. Bar Kochba overthrew the Romans in Israel during Hadrian's time of 134-137 C. E. Since Bar Kochba's name means "Son of the Star," and he had done much of what the Messiah is expected to do, Rabbi Akiba interpreted Balaam's prophecy in Numbers 24: 17 of "the star [כוכב, Koh hKV] out of Jacob" as being Messiah Bar Kochba. Strange, is it not, that the only one to return from that secret garden unharmed should make such a mistake about "who is the Messiah."

Yet, in this garden may be found the clue to his identity. Would you like to go into that garden to find it? Would you dare to go?

The apostle Paul himself dared to enter that secret level in the orchard. Listen to his account in II Cor. 12:2-4: "I knew a man in Christ above fourteen years ago, (whether in the body, I cannot tell; or whether out of the body, I cannot tell: G-d knoweth;) such a one caught up to the third heaven. And I knew how such a man, (whether in the body, or out of the body, I cannot tell: G-d knoweth:) How that he was caught up into *Paradise*, [in Hebrew, *Pardes*], and heard unspeakable words, which it is not lawful for a man to utter."

If you have the desire and the courage to go there also, come with me. My teacher took me there several times. You, too, will see things that may frighten you; but I promise to return you unharmed.

Lend me your mind (whether in the body you cannot tell; or whether out of the body you cannot tell: G-d knoweth). Only lend your mind. I will return it unharmed. Dream a dream of dreams with me in a riddle of riddles.

Your thoughts always arrive in this Garden ahead of your mind. The mind is hindered by having to leave the shackles of logic and reason by the gate. Unless they are left there, your mind can never enter the gate. Think with me, but not without caution. Think with me, but think unshackled by reason.

We are in the Garden now. In here there is neither a synagogue nor a church nor a mosque. There is no creed, no dogma, no tradition. Since there is no law in this Garden, hence it will be "unlawful to utter" what you might chance to see when you return. Here in this Garden, riddles are born. Here, parable and allegory breed their young, which wing their flight to the world of reality outside this Garden. It is sad, but when outside this Garden, many of them fall prey to the snare of creed and dogma. Inside, they are safe from such, for here there are no institutions.

My thoughts are trees in this secret Garden. On each tree the leaves of words are blown by winds which utter a myriad of meanings. As the breeze blows the rustling leaves, lend me your mind and I will give you a riddle about the Messiah. Yea, I will give you the riddle, but the breeze-blown leaves will speak the interpretation.

The riddle of the Messiah is a riddle of seven lines:

1. I am thinking about someone in history. He left his indelible imprint on mankind. Without a biological miracle on the womb of his mother, his birth would have been impossible.
2. As an infant, he was called the Son of G-d.
3. He was taken into Egypt to preserve his life.

4. He returned to the land of Israel, hated by all those about him, despised and rejected of men—a man of sorrow and acquainted with grief.
5. He was hated so greatly that he was executed by the Romans.
6. At the third day, he came out of the tomb.
7. He will never die again!

These are the seven lines to the riddle. About whom do you think I speak? Simple! You think that I speak about the only one who could have ever possibly done those seven things—Jesus of Nazareth, of course!

Listen! You can hear the laughter of the angels. Cherubim and seraphim muse at the subtlety of this riddle! I was not speaking about Jesus of Nazareth! No! Not one second, not one thought, not one word was meant for Jesus! Had I been thinking of Jesus, it would not have been a riddle; it would have been a sermon, a liturgy, a homily. No! I was not thinking of Jesus of Nazareth!

Although I was not thinking of Jesus, I was thinking of someone in history who fulfilled line upon line, precept upon precept, of each word of the seven lines of this riddle. Every word, and every letter of every word...even the white spaces between the letters...are light symphonies of the Messiah. Yes! I was thinking about the Messiah, but I was not thinking about Jesus of Nazareth. If not Jesus, then whom? Who else could have fulfilled such a dynamic role and yet been kept "secret" until the end of the age? Let us listen again carefully to each line of the riddle. Let the tender, rustling leaves whisper who else might have been the secret Messiah.

First Hint

I am thinking about someone in history...
He left an indelible mark upon mankind...
Without a biological miracle on the womb of
his mother, his birth would have been impossible.

Your mind went back to the hills of Beit-Lehem (Bethlehem); yet, my mind went back to the plains of Mamre. Your mind stopped twenty centuries ago; mine doubled your years in time to forty centuries. Your mind stopped at a cave, at a manger, at the shelter for the flocks, while mine went in space only twelve miles farther. At Mamre I stopped at a Bedouin tent, the shelter for the shepherd. In your cave were two people, the same as in my tent. Yours were a middle-aged carpenter and his fourteen-year-old betrothed maiden. Mine were a centenarian, the patriarch, and his ninety-year-old matriarch wife. You thought of Joseph and Mary; I thought of Abraham and Sarah.

Look at your Mary. Did she need a miracle on her womb? She was a virgin of youth in the virility of passion. Her womb was ripe. Her fountain flowed with the vibrance of life. There was nothing malfunctional about Mary's womb. Every gland, cell, vital fluid and hormone was in perfect balance. Her womb yearned for the opportunity of procreation. All systems were "go" in Mary's womb. The miraculous element of her conception of Jesus was not *on* her womb but rather *in* her womb...and that only one single cell.

Now come with me from your cave of Beit-Lehem, a space of twelve miles farther, to the tent in the plains of Mamre. A dominant parallel between your cave and my tent is that they were both attended by the same Angel of His Presence. I hear that Angel of His Presence speaking to Abraham in front of the veil of the tent door.

"Sarah, thy wife, the Princess, I will bless her: Yea! I will bless her and her name shall be called blessed! She will be called the Mother Blessed of all nations! Abraham, by aged Sarah will I give thee a son." (Gen. 17:15-16)

Abraham was stunned. "Why?" thought he. "Why not Eliezer of Damascus? Why not Ishmael?" Aged Abraham, now ninety-nine years old, leaning on his shepherd's staff, slowly turned and looked backward to the tent door. There, behind the veil, he saw the profile of his old wife, only a decade younger than himself, with her weathered skin, withering from time and the cruel desert sun and wind. Though well preserved for her age, her face had begun to erode with wrinkles of time, as often happens to an old adobe house. In a muse, Abraham turned back to the Angel.

"Sarah?...Sarah, the daughter of Terah? No! Not Sarah! As a child, my Lord, I spent much time jesting with the young men of the mountains of Uratu. Yes, played I satire with the men of Ur. Indeed, there was some ironic folly in me the day I crushed all the idols in my father Terah's idol shop and told him they had gotten in a war and destroyed each other. But, my Lord, since you appeared to me I have been a sober prince. What are these words about this old woman being with child? Surely, Lord, you are jesting; what kind of joke is this?"

"At the space of a year," replied the Angel of His Presence, "I shall return unto thee and Sarah shall bear thee a son in her old age."

"Yits-hak! Yits-hak! Yits-hak!" Abraham broke into a cackling, oriental laughter, falling on his face before the Angel of His Presence.

Yits-hak! Yits-hak! Yits-hak! Aye, But Lord, she is ninety years old! Her fountain is dry! Her womb is withered! The way of women is not with her! Even in the virginity of her youth, her womb was crippled that it could not bear! In puberty, her gates were shut that she could not conceive. Yits-hak! Yits-hak! Yits-hak! Hagar? Yes! Sarah? No!"

Inside the tent, aged Sarah laughed inside herself in muffled tones.

Yits-hak! Yits-hak! Yits-hak! What can that old centenarian do for me? He too is at the threshold of a hundred years. Were my youth returned and my crippled womb healed, what could he do about it? And the arrogant conceit of that old shepherd! What *chutzpah* for him to speak of my withered womb! My womb is not the only secret in this tent that is withered! His circumcision will be an autopsy! The only erect thing in his hand is his shepherd's staff...Yits-hak! Yits-hak! Yits-hak! His name should not be *Av-ra-ham*, the father of many nations, but *Sab-a-ham*, the grandfather of many nations! Yits-hak! Yits-hak! Yits-hak! If I am made fertile, who will sire me? Not this old stone!"

The Angel of His Presence in scorn spoke to Sarah, "You laugh inside yourself, Sarah!"

"No, my Lord, I laughed not!"

"Yes, you laughed inside yourself, Sarah, even as Abraham laughed outside himself. Now shall I also laugh forever! Yea, I shall laugh at you, and I shall laugh with you. For when in about the space of a year, I shall return, Sarah, you will bear a son by Abraham, even in your old age. I shall return the way of women unto you. I shall again open your fountain and rejuvenate your withered womb. I shall make you a green tree and open the gates that barred your conception. I shall heal your crippled womb which did not bear. Thou shall bring forth a first born son, even a son of Abraham, and thou shall call his name Yits-hak [Isaac] because you *laughed*."

TSaKhahQ, צחק, is the Hebrew verb for laugh. YiTs-KhahQ, יצחק, means "he will laugh." The birth of Isaac was G-d's "divine comedy" on the Gentile nations. The Creator took from the wrecking yard of mankind, two old dilapidated wrecks of humanity. He refurbished their powers of procreation. By that biological miracle on the womb of Sarah, He created the miraculous nation of Israel. Without that miracle, there would have been no Joseph, Mary, and Jesus.

The case of Mary was only one cell in her perfect womb. The case of Sarah was of much greater magnitude. For Sarah's conception, it took multiplied billions of cells in the rejuvenation and healing of her aged, withered, dry, barren system. "Without a Biological Miracle on the Womb of Sarah, the Birth of Isaac Would Have Been Impossible."

Adam was created without man and without woman. Eve's formation was with man, but without woman. Natural humanity is with man and woman. Jesus' birth was with woman but without man. Isaac's birth is yet unique in itself.

Second Hint

As an Infant, He Was Called the Son of G-d.

The phrase, "Son of G-d," is not exclusively a Christian term. Yet, like so many other words of Jewish origin, the term first became Hellenized, then Christianized to the point that Judaism shies away from its usage. In Genesis 6:2, "...the Sons of G-d, saw the daughters of men...." In Job 2:1, "...the Sons of G-d came to present themselves before the Eternal One." Again, in Job 38:7, "...all the Sons of G-d shouted for joy." David in Psalms 2:7, "Thou art *my son*, this day have I begotten thee." The prophecy of Agur in Proverbs 30:4, speaking of the Creator, "...what is his name, and what is *his son's* name, if thou canst know it." In Daniel 3:25, the King Nebuchadnezzar had cast the three Hebrew children into the furnace, and yet there appeared four men in the flames, "the fourth being like to the *Son of G-d*." The point of these quotations is to demonstrate that the concept of "the Son of G-d" is not an exclusive of Christianity but rather finds its roots in Judaism.

Who is the Son of G-d? Of whom was I speaking? The Eternal One commissioned Moses to deliver a message to

Pharaoh, "and thou shalt say unto Pharoah: 'Thus saith the Eternal One, Israel is *my son* even my *firstborn*: I say unto thee, Let *my son* go that he may serve me: and if thou will refuse to let him go, behold I will slay thy son even thy firstborn.'" (Ex. 4:22-23)

Israel is called "the Son of G-d." Again in Hosea 11:1, the Eternal One said: "When Israel was a child, I loved him, and called *my Son* out of Egypt."

"I speak about someone in history. He left his indelible imprint upon mankind. Without a biological miracle on the womb of his mother, his birth would have been impossible. As An Infant He Was Called The Son of G-d." Israel is the Son of G-d in a national sense.

Third Hint

He Was Taken into Egypt to Preserve His Life

"And the famine was sore in the Land." (Gen. 43:1) Joseph had been sold by his brothers to the Ishmaelite merchants, who in turn sold him as a slave into the house of Potiphar in Egypt. Joseph was an *avant garde* of seventy souls who went into Egypt as the "House of Jacob." When Joseph weepingly revealed himself to his brothers, he said: "G-d hath sent me before you TO PRESERVE you a posterity in the earth, and to save your lives by a great deliverance." (Gen. 45:7)

His "flight into Egypt" to preserve Israel's embryonic life occurred exactly 3,500 years before the modern State of Israel celebrated its thirtieth anniversary in their Third Commonwealth. Israel went into Egypt in the Jewish year 2238; Israel celebrated the year of its priesthood, the thirtieth year, in 1977-78, which is the Jewish year 5738. "Of the House of Jacob, seventy souls went into Egypt. Into the Land of Egypt they came." In the matrix of Egypt the seed of Israel was gestated into a mighty nation. That nation was received into the bosom of Egypt by a pharaoh's love; it was delivered out of the womb of Egypt by the travail of a pharaoh who knew not Joseph.

Egypt, מצרים, *MiTS'RaYiM*, or *Misr* in Arabic, comes from the root "metser," מצר, which means "to persecute." As pointed out by Dr. Ariel Bar-Sela, "Egypt, in Hebrew, is מצרים; *MiTS'RaYiM* is a dual form meaning the two Egypts. That is, the upper and lower levels of the *MiTSRS*. The Chosen Seed, the House of Jacob, were ejected from their promised land by the providence of a famine into the nourishing womb of the persecutor to produce a nation which could survive more than three and a half millennia of persecution and, in fact, actually has survived it.

Each year the Jews commemorate the deliverance from the *metser*, or persecutor, of Egyptian bondage by the celebration of Passover. This liberation feast ends in the solemn reminder of Israel's perpetual suffering and repeated triumph. This conclusive reminder is the "Khad Gad Ya," meaning One Kid. Apparently a childish lilt, it goes as follows:

1. One kid, one kid, which my father bought for two zuziim. KHAD GAD-YA, KHAD GAD-YA.
2. Then came a cat and devoured the kid, which my father bought for two zuziim.
   KHAD GAD-YA, KHAD GAD-YA.
3. Then came a dog and bit the cat, which devoured the kid, which my father bought for two zuziim.
   KHAD GAD-YA, KHAD GAD-YA.
4. Then came a staff and beat the dog, which bit the cat, which devoured the kid, which my father bought for two zuziim.
   KHAD GAD-YA, KHAD GAD-YA.
5. Then came a fire and burned the staff, which beat the dog, which bit the cat, which devoured the kid, which my father bought for two zuziim.
   KHAD GAD-YA, KHAD GAD-YA.
6. Then came the water and extinguished the fire, which burned the staff, which beat the dog, which bit the cat, which devoured the kid, which my father bought for two zuziim.
   KHAD GAD-YA, KHAD GAD-YA.
7. Then came the ox and drank the water, which extinguished the fire, which burned the staff, which beat the dog, which bit the cat, which devoured the kid, which my father bought for two zuziim.
   KHAD GAD-YA, KHAD GAD-YA.
8. Then came the Shochet and slaughtered the ox, which drank the water, which extinguished the fire, which burned the staff, which beat the

dog, which bit the cat, which devoured the kid, which my father bought for two zuziim.
KHAD GAD-YA, KHAD GAD-YA.

9. Then came the angel of death and killed the Shochet, who slaughtered the ox, which drank the water, which extinguished the fire, which burned the staff, which beat the dog, which bit the cat, which devoured the kid, which my father bought for two zuziim.
KHAD GAD-YA, KHAD GAD-YA.

10. Then came the Holy One, Blessed by He, and slew the angel of death, who killed the Shochet, who slaughtered the ox, which drank the water, which extinguished the fire, which burned the staff, which beat the dog, which bit the cat, which devoured the kid, which my father bought for two zuziim.
KHAD GAD-YA, KHAD GAD-YA.

The Kabbalistic interpretation of *Khad Gad Ya* is that each name in the successive lines of the lilt is a prophetic symbol for a Gentile empire. Each not only destroyed the former empire but was destroyed by the succeeding empire. The One Kid, being Israel, was always the one who suffered the pain in each era of Gentile history. Each of the symbols was associated with some sort of pagan deity worshipped by that particular Gentile empire.

One kid—one kid which Father bought for two *zuziim*—is interpreted as being the dual nature of suffering Israel. On *Yom Kippurim*, two kid goats were brought for the sacrifice. Lots were cast upon them (Leviticus 16) and one kid of the goats was called *Azazel*, or the scapegoat, while the other was called the goat of the Eternal One. The latter was killed as a sacrifice. The other one, *Azazel Yisrael*, was the goat for Israel. He was the scapegoat and was driven out into the wilderness. Somehow, the *Yom Kippurim* sacrifices were typical of Israel's suffering history . . . the goat of the Eternal One—the one sacrificed, and *Azazel Israel*, the one driven out—this is what holocaust and pogrom mean. The one kid that the father bought for two *zuziim* is the stretched-out suffering history of Israel.

Then came the Cat of Egypt and bit the Kid that Father bought for two *zuziim*. The cat was an animal deity of Egypt. The pyramids contained countless mummified cats. The Cat of Egypt made the first attempt to annihilate Israel by the pharaoh who knew not Joseph. Pharaoh said: "Lest Israel become more and mightier than we...Lest they join our enemy..." This chiché of Pharaoh's has followed Israel throughout history. The Cat of Egypt bit the Kid of Israel. He wasted him, but could not consume him.

Then came the Dog of Assyria and bit the Cat of Egypt. In biting the Cat of Egypt, the Assyrian Dog laid waste a path of destruction in the land of Israel. These Assyrian kings, Tiglath-Pileser, Shalmaneser, Sargon, Sennacherib and Esar-Haddon, plundered Israel. Sennacherib's army of 185,000 had Judah under siege during the reign of Hezekiah (II Kings 18-19). "That night...the *Angel of His Presence* went out and smote in the camp of the Assyrians 185,000; and when they arose early in the morning, they beheld all the dead corpses." (19:35) The Dog of Assyria which bit the Cat of Egypt could not consume the one Kid of Israel.

When the Stick of Babylon hit the Dog of Assyria and slew it, Nebuchadnezzar led the children of Israel away in chains. One child in chains, Daniel, would one day stand as prime minister in the courts in Babylon. He it was who interpreted the solemn decree: *"Me'ne, Me'ne, Te'kel, Uphar-sin,* God hath numbered thy Kingdom and finished it. Thou art weighed in the balances, and art found wanting, Thy Kingdom is divided and given to the Persians."

The Babylonian empire, the Stick which had hit the Dog of Assyria, had afflicted Israel in the furnace of fire (Daniel 3:23) and was that night burned by the Fire of Persia.

The book of Esther relates the story of wicked Haman, the Agagite or Syrian, who organized the Ku Klux Klan of Persia. King Ahasuerus ignorantly signed a law for the execution of all the Jews on a given day. Esther, the Jewish queen, interceded for her people. "The law of the Medes and Persians which altered not" could not be changed, nor could it be annulled. However, King Ahasuerus issued a new decree that permitted the Jews of Persia to defend themselves from the fiery hatred of wicked Haman. On the night before the day appointed for the slaughter of the Jews in the 127 provinces of Persia, the Persian Ku Klux Klan, with their disguise of hoods and veils, gathered for a drunken carnival celebration. It was to be the final solution to the Jewish problem.

The Jews also attended the carnival in masquerade. Since everyone was in a masquerade costume, who would know "who's who?"

When the klansmen were drunken in their folly, the king's latest order was executed. So was the Ku Klux Klan of Persia! Haman had erected a gallows seventy-five feet high on which to hang Mordecai the Jew. "The king ordered Haman hanged on the gallows Haman had prepared for Mordecai." Today the Jews still celebrate the feast of Purim in masquerade, commemorating G-d's deliverance of Israel from the fire of the Persian inquisition and holocaust.

Then came the Water and quenched the Fire. The flooding victory of Alexander the Great over Darius III put out the Fire of Persia in 333 B.C.E. Alexander treated the Jews with kindness. After his death, Antiochus Epiphanes attempted to drown the Jewish soul by forcing them to Hellenize. His oppression was overthrown by the Maccabean revolt. The Maccabees' dynasty fully reestablished the kingdom of Judah in the Second Commonwealth.

Then came the Ox of Rome and drank the Water of Greece. Within a few years the Roman Ox gored Israel out of the land in the second and great Diaspora. After stretched out centuries, The First and Second Reich of Wilhelm I and Kaiser Bill, Wilhelm II, attempted to restore the Holy Roman Empire. Their failure brought about the Balfour Declaration which decreed the return of the Land of Israel to the people of Israel.

The First and Second reichs of the two Wilhelms of Germany lacked one quality. There was not the *metser* of a pharaoh who knew not Joseph, nor a Sennacherib, nor Haman, nor Antiochus, nor a Titus. What the first two reichs lacked, the Third Reich personified in the "Slaughterer" who slaughtered the Ox. Adolph Hitler was the epitome of all that were before him. He was the "*metser* of Pharaoh," "the systematic conqueror of Sennacherib," "the Tsar of Nebuchadnezzar," "the Fire of Haman," "the antagonist Antiochus Epiphanes," and "the goring horn of Titus," all in one. Yet, with the travail of the holocaust, the "Angel of Death" slew the Slaughterer who slaughtered the Ox, that drank the Water, that quenched the Fire, that burned the Stick, that hit the Dog, that bit the Cat, that ate the Kid that Father bought for two *zuziim.*

The travail of Egypt established Israel's First Commonwealth. The travail of Persia brought forth Israel's Second Commonwealth. From the ashes of the crematoriums of the holocaust came the rebirth of National Israel in their Third Commonwealth. There is a sad note in that it took World War I to get the land ready for the Jews, but a World War II to get Europe's Jews ready for the land. Rude as it may sound, had there not been a strange pharaoh who knew not Joseph, there would not have been a Mordecai. Had there not been an Antiochus Epiphanes, there would have been no Maccabeans. Had there not been a Hitler, there would not have been an Israel today. The House of Jacob had to suffer famine to go into Egypt to preserve his life. Israel will continue at Passover to sing Khad Gad Ya till the coming of the Holy One, the Messiah who shall destroy the Angel of Death and forever deliver Suffering Israel.

Israel Was Taken Into The Land of Egypt to Preserve His Life. From the matrix of the *metser*, Egypt, came the nation of Israel, which was born to survive all persecutions. A nation reborn from destruction after destruction always survives not only his persecutions but also his persecutors.

Fourth Hint

He Returned to the Land of Israel, Hated by All Those About Him, Despised and Rejected of Men, A Man of Sorrow and Acquainted with Grief

Who hated Israel in his First Commonwealth? Amalek tried to destroy him by the sword. Edom tried to destroy him by forbidding him passage to the Promise Land, thus forcing him to die in the wilderness. The Ammonites and the Moabites fought against his establishment in the land when Sihon, king of Heshbon, and Og, king of Bashan, made war with him. The Agagites never ceased to plague Israel and its national existence. Who are these? Who are the sons of Amalek and Edom? Who are the descendants of the Ammonites and the Moabites? Who are the posterity of Agag? If we translate ethnic names into modern vernacular, Misr is still Egypt. Hadad, the king of Amalek, joined himself to the king of Edom.

Today they are known as the country and people of Saudi Arabia. Ammon and Moab is Jordan, whose capital is Amman. Agag is today Syria. The current events of the Middle East are a rerun of an old story. The Holy Land is a stage where the world today is seeing Act III in the drama of Israel's Third Commonwealth. The actors have the same names: the script and the plot are identical; the story is all a part of that drama that is forty centuries old. The drama is like Abraham who came into the land, then went out because of famine. He returned a second time only to be forced again to leave, but the third time he returned, he was never to depart again. Israel today, back in their Third Commonwealth, have demonstrated their determination never to depart again.

Abraham was hated because of his distinctively different faith and relationship with One G-d. As Abraham was persecuted because of his distinctive, uncompromising religious differences, Isaac was hated because of his prosperity. He was the well digger who never sank a dry shaft; yet, his jealous enemies would fill his wells with stones. Jacob was hated because of his personality. He just did not fit into the mold of those about him—not even when he tried. His values were different; his purpose was more noble. Jacob never sacrificed the eternal on the alter of the temporal—no, not even with his own brother.

Israel, like the Patriarch, is hated by all those about him. He is rejected because of his religion, because of his prosperity and because of his personality. The Israelis are not known for trying to "win friends and influence people." Their long history has taught them the vanity of such applause. The people of Israel have again returned to the land of Israel, hated by all those about them; Egypt, Saudi Arabia, Jordan, and Syria, the United Nations, Russia, and UNESCO. Why not? If "Israel should dwell alone and not be reckoned among the nations," (Numbers 23:9) why then is Israel in the U. N.?

The riddle would not apply if Israel's history were any different. "He returned to the land of Israel hated by all those about him, a man of sorrow and acquainted with grief." Who has suffered as Israel has suffered? Who can justify such treatment of any people? A people who have given so much good to the world and yet have not only gone unrewarded, but have been rewarded evil for good? No people have ever suffered so wrongly as Israel. No people have survived to suffer so long as Israel. We read David's cry in Psalms 22:1, "Ali, Ali, *Lama Azavtani,*" which is "My G-d! My G-d! Why has thou forsaken me?" Israel's history is triumphant out of tragedy—hated, despised, rejected, driven out, wandering Jews, rejected of men. Living, Israel suffers. Suffering, Israel lives. He Has Returned to the Land of Israel, Hated by All Those About Him, Despised and Rejected of Men, A Man of Sorrows and Acquainted with Grief.

Fifth Hint
A Hatred So Great He Was Put to Death by the Romans

How can this be applied to Israel? The direction of thought now is inverted. As in the first hint, you thought of Bethlehem twenty centuries ago; I thought of the plains of Mamre, only twelve miles away from Bethlehem in distance, but forty centuries away in time. The woman of your thoughts was a young woman; in the woman of my thoughts, she was an aged woman.

In the second hint you thought of a man who came from Israel; I thought of Israel from whence that man came. Without Israel he could not have come.

In the third hint, in the flight into Egypt, you thought of a Joseph and his wife and her son. I thought of a Joseph too; not the later Joseph, but the greater Joseph; not a carpenter, but the prime minister of Egypt.

Now in the fifth hint, you thought of a hatred and execution by the Romans in the Jewish year 3790, or the year 30 of the Common Era. The execution I thought of was exactly forty years later. The Jewish year 3830, or the year 70 of the Common Era, when the same Roman government which had executed Jesus as the Messiah, King of Judaea, in exact manner executed the Kingdom of Judaea as the Messianic nation. Josephus relates that the Romans crucified until there was no more wood with which to make crosses, nor yet another hill to place them on. The same Roman government which crucified Jesus in the year 30 C. E. crucified Israel in the year 70 C. E. Yes, A Hatred So Great That He Was Put to Death by the Romans.

Sixth Hint
At the Third Day He Came Out of the Tomb

How could this apply to Israel? Hosea the prophet provides an answer. In Chapter Five, he prophesied the great diaspora of Israel. "Ephraim is smitten, Judah is wounded." (Hosea 5:11-14) He prophesied in another place, dispersed Israel "shall abide many days without a king, and without a prince, and without a sacrifice, and without an image, and without an ephod, and without teraphim: Afterward shall the children of Israel return, and seek after the Eternal One their G-d, and David their king. . .in the latter days." (Hosea 3:4-5) In this prophecy, he does not stop with judgment but goes on to answer the questions: Who can regather the outcast people whom G-d called *Lo Ammi* (not my people), and *Lo Ruhamah* (a people who received not mercy)? Yea, in the sovereign provision of G-d, Jezreel is born (Hosea 1:4, 10-11), meaning a remnant shall return from the sowing (Jezreel, Yizr'ael, in Hebrew, means seed sown of G-d; in Greek, it means diaspora or scattering of the seed). In Hosea 6, Israel replies to the Eternal One: "Come let us return to the Eternal One: for he hath torn, and he will heal us; he has smitten, and he will bind us up. After [toward the end of] two days, will he revive us: in the third day he will raise us up, and we shall live in his sight [before him]."

The regathering of Israel was promised by Hosea the prophet at the end of two days and before the third day. How long is a day with G-d? David said in Psalms 90:4: "A thousand years in thy sight are but as yesterday when it is past, and as a watch in the night." Again, Simon Peter quotes this in II Peter 3:8: ". . .be not ignorant of this one thing, that one day is with the Lord as a thousand years, and a thousand years as one day."

"At the end of two days will he revive us, and the third day we will stand before him." Two days, or two thousand years from the scattering, Israel shall return; that is, toward the end of two thousand years from the great diaspora in the year 70 C.E., National Israel would be revived. One thousand nine hundred and forty-eight years is at the end of the second day from Israel's dispersion. May 15, 1948, National Israel was revived.

Jerusalem was under siege by the Romans in the Jewish year 3838 (68 C. E.). That siege filled the tombs of

Israel and scattered the remains. On Rosh Hashanah, in the Jewish New Year 5728 (or 1967-68), Jerusalem had just been under siege again. This siege brought life and hope to Israel. The Holy City, for the first time in 1,900 years, was liberated. For the first time since King Solomon 2,500 years before, Jerusalem was the solo-rex capital of united Israel, and the Star of David on the Israeli flag fluttered over liberated Jerusalem. From Suez to Mount Hermon, from the Jordan River to the Red Sea and Sharm El-Sheikh, Israel has arisen—alive forevermore.

"At the third day he came out of the tomb." Ezekiel 37, in the vision of the valley of the dry bones, the prophet interpreted thusly: "These bones are the whole house of Israel: behold, they say, our bones are dried and our hope is lost: we are cut off from our parts. Therefore prophesy and say unto them: Thus saith the Eternal One the creator; Behold, O My People, I will open your tombs, and cause you to come out of your tombs, and bring you into the land of Israel. And ye shall know that I am the Eternal One, when I have opened your tombs, O my people, and brought you out of your tombs." At the Third Day He Came Out of the Tomb.

Seventh Hint
He Shall Never Die Again

How does this apply to Israel? Will the Jewish State of Israel again be destroyed? The Arab neighbors have avowed Israel's destruction. By present calculations there are over 250 million Arabs against three million Israelis—yet Israel lives! Many Christian theologians would clap their hands to see the literal Israel erased from the face of the earth. Yet Israel lives to defy the theology which teaches that Israel no longer exists. According to prophetic expectation, however, all these forces will someday unite to attempt the final destruction of Israel. Will they succeed?

The events between Hosea's "at the end of two days...and the third day" are vividly described by the prophet Ezekiel. The "last days," the "time of the end" and the "end of the world [actually end of the age]" are phrases appropriately fitting the period of Israel's Third Commonwealth. It is interesting to observe the particular details that occur in the prophetic sequence of Ezekiel, Chapters 33-48.

In ancient Israel there were watchmen on the walls of Jerusalem who warned of coming destruction. On the Eastern Wall stood a tower in which a watchman was to look Eastward for the coming Messiah who would appear in the last days. In Judaism the term "days of the Messiah" also is applied to the "last days." Ezekiel 33:7 reads: "So thou, O Son of Man, I have set thee (as) a watchman upon the house of Israel." In the role of the watchman upon the walls, Ezekiel foresaw those events which would occur, not in his lifetime, but at the "end of days," "the time of the end," or that period of history preceding and involving Israel's Third Commonwealth before the appearance of the Messiah or Messianic age.

These visions of the "watchman" concerning the last days, the end also of the "times of the Gentiles," are recorded in a particular sequence from the 34th to the 48th chapters of Ezekiel. Broadly this is their scope:

Chapter 34: Against the lazy shepherds of Israel who fail to lead Israel back to the land

35: Against Mt. Seir or Saudi Arabia for resisting Israel's return

36: Promise to restore the Land of Israel to the people of Israel

37: Promise to restore the people of Israel to the Land of Israel by the two visions of "dry bones" and "two sticks"

38: Russia's (Gog and Magog of Rosh) first invasion of Israel with conventional weapons to drive them back out of the land

39: Russia's second invasion of Israel with ancient weapons of wood, again to dispossess them

40-48: Rebuilding of future Temple and Messianic Kingdom, establishing them firmly in the land

In Ezekiel's general view, Israel will never die again. The general view is not nearly so dramatic as the detail of the particulars in each of the chapters. A mere skimming of the surface of a few statements and observations the prophet made 2,500 years ago uncovers much that has become history since the turn of the twentieth century of the Common Era.

Chapter 34 is against the slothful shepherds of Israel who forestalled the opportunity to regather the scattered flock of Israel once it was possible for them to return. The Balfour Declaration had made the land available for the Jews; but, on the whole, world Jewish leadership was not prone to make the Jewish people available for the land.

Even the World Zionist Organization, which had been instrumental in bringing about the Balfour Declaration through Chaim Weizmann, had become a mutual admiration society of idealists who were all exhaust and no horsepower. As far as the Zionist leadership was concerned, Zionists themselves were the big boys who wanted to encourage the little guys to return to Israel to drain the swamps and to make the desert bloom. The Zionists at this time, however, became slothful shepherds and promoted the placing of Palestine under British Mandate after World War I. As far as Zionist leadership was concerned, business was too good and life too easy among the Gentiles to think about returning to Israel. Chaos and schism so plagued the World Zionist Organization that by 1921, the American Zionist Organization broke affiliation with the World Organization. The reestablishment of the Jewish state came about in spite of and not as a result of the World Zionist Organization.

An interesting story concerning this is that of the late Mr. Ben Avi, who was publisher and editor of *The Palestinian Post*, which later became *The Jerusalem Post*.

Ben Avi's name had a double meaning. Ben Avi means "son of my father." However, A.V.I. were also the initials in Hebrew of his father, Eliezar Ben-Yehuda, the linguist who revived the Hebrew language. The Ben-Yehudas, in opposition to the Zionists at this time, led the Palestinian Jews in their movement for immediate independence for Israel.

In 1917, Ben Avi made a trip to America representing the Jews of Palestine who, against the World Zionist Organization, wanted the immediate establishment of the Jewish state in Palestine. The Arabs were agreeable, as Weizmann and King Abdulla of Jordan had drawn up an agreement for the co-existence of Jewish and Arab states. Transjordan on the east of the Jordan River was to be the Arab state, the west bank to the sea was to be the Jewish state. The Arab hostility came several years later

Ben Avi

as a maneuver of the British to prevent the establishment of the Jewish state.

The purpose of Ben Avi's trip was twofold. First, he wanted to represent Israel at the conference of oppressed nations in Philadelphia; and second, to get President Wilson to help him get appointed as the Palestinian Jewish representative to the League of Nations. There was a body at the League of Nations made up of representatives of those countries who had lost their sovereignty to larger nations in previous wars. Mr. Avi contended that Israel's right to sovereignty was a priority even over the other countries after the defeat of the so-called Holy Roman Empire of Kaiser Bill because their claim to statehood was oldest.

Providence had made good provision as far as the Zionists were concerned. Because the Zionist Organization of America had just severed ties with the World Organization, Ben Avi hoped to get help from the Z. O. A., whose spokesman was Rabbi Stephen Wise.

When Ben Avi approached Rabbi Wise concerning his mission, the rabbi scorned him. "Who are the Jews of Palestine to dictate policy to the Zionist Organization? Who is Ben Avi? Ah! So you are the publisher of a small newspaper in Palestine! So what? You have to be somebody to get an appointment with the President of the United States. You can't see the President unless you are a person of notoriety."

"All right," replied Ben Avi. "What do I have to do to be famous in America? Tell me and I will do it the first thing tomorrow morning."

"You can begin by getting your name in some newspapers. People have to know you and know what you are doing. You bring me the news articles and I will see that the President sees them, but I can't guarantee he will see you."

Disappointed but not discouraged, Ben Avi went to his hotel room and was reading the newspaper. A full page advertisement caught his eye. "Hear Evangelist Billy Sunday. . . ." Ben Avi immediately inquired as to where Reverend Sunday was staying. Unannounced and unexpected, Ben Avi knocked on Billy Sunday's door. Barefooted and shirtless, the country boy evangelist walked to the door with one suspender holding up his pants.

The frail-framed caller at the door looked little better than the half-dressed evangelist. Perhaps his very casual dress lent urgency to his being there unannounced.

"Reverend Sunday," blurted Ben Avi, "I am Mr. Saturday, a Jew from Palestine. My name is Ben Avi. I am in America to ask help from President Wilson in establishing a Jewish state in the land of Israel. Right now, Mr. Sunday, I need your help more than I need the help of the President of the United States. May I come in and tell you my problem?"

It was not an everyday occurrence for a Jew to call on Billy Sunday, especially a Jew from Palestine. The evangelist was bewildered by this zealous man from the land of Israel. As Ben Avi shared with Billy Sunday his enthusiasm, his burden, and the problems of the Jews of Palestine, he found to his surprise a Christian Zionist in the evangelist. Having stated his problem as Rabbi Wise had put it to him, he asked for only five minutes on Reverend Sunday's platform with pre-arranged news coverage to give him exposure and publicity.

The renowned evangelist, having heard him out, replied, "Mr. Avi, I am one of many Christians who believe that the return of the Jews to their land is a sign of the Second Advent of Jesus. I have announced that I will preach on the Second Coming Sunday afternoon. Now if you don't think you will be offended by hearing me preach on the Second Coming of Jesus Christ, and that He will destroy the enemies of Israel, restore the Kingdom of David and sit on His throne in Jerusalem, I will not only give you five minutes but at least one hour to

Ben Avi (far right) at the League of Nations.

present your cause. As for the news coverage, let's get your picture with mine in tomorrow's paper."

"Mr. Sunday, not only do I not object to your preaching that Jesus will do all you expect him to do, but for heaven's sake and ours too, please tell him to hurry back and be on with it. I am sure he will do a much better job of it than the Zionist Organization."

The novelty of a Jew from Palestine and the evangelist on the same platform packed the meeting to capacity. Ben Avi did not disappoint himself, the evangelist, or the crowds. Nor was he disappointed in the results. The appointment was scheduled with the President by Billy Sunday himself. President Wilson granted Ben Avi's request, and he was off to Paris for the meeting of the League of Nations.

When Ben Avi arrived in Paris, he was met by a delegation from the World Zionist Organization with the red carpet treatment. When he prepared to go on to the league meeting, however, he found himself a kidnapped prisoner of the World Zionist Organization. They could not let him blow up their plans to put Palestine under the British Mandate Protectorate. After three days, Ben Avi did manage to escape his Zionist captors and make it to the League of Nations to represent Israel, and to accomplish his mission.

Historically, the Jewish people survived more in spite of themselves than because of themselves. Israel came into existence more in spite of the Zionists than because of the World Zionist Organization. The miracle of all miracles today is not so much the feats of the Israeli army as it is the defeats of Israeli government. The Israeli government seems in such a total state of confusion that neither G-d nor the Israelis understand it. Israel will survive, not because of itself but in spite of itself. "He shall never die again," not because of the army, or the government, or anything else humanly speaking, but rather: "Had it not been for the Eternal One, Now may Israel say, Had it not been for the Eternal One. . . ."

The slothful shepherds failed to respond when the door was opened for Israel to return after the First World War. Ezekiel 34:11 answers the slothful shepherds thusly: "For thus saith the Eternal One the Creator, Behold, I, even I, will both search my sheep, and seek them out. As a shepherd seeketh out his flock the day that he is among his sheep that are scattered, so will I seek out my sheep, and will deliver them out of all the places where I have scattered them in the cloudy and dark day. I will bring them from the Gentiles and gather them from the countries, and will bring them into their own land. And I will feed them on the mountain of Israel. . . ."

In Ezekiel 35:11-36:5, we see the prophetic opposition to the return of the Jews and to the establishment of the nation. This opposition is Mount Seir, or Saudi Arabia, Transjordan and the Arab league. They are cursed in verse 5: "Because thou hast had a perpetual hatred, and hast shed the blood of the children of Israel."

The Arabs say in 36:2: "Aha, even the ancient high places are ours in possession. . . ." What the Arabs mean by "justice in the Middle East" is "just-us," and no Jews; "just-us," and no Israel!

In spite of world political opinion against the idea of a Jewish state, and regardless of British ambition to colonialize the Middle East, and despite Arab opposition, Israel was reborn. They have survived each attempt to annihilate them and have become the conqueror rather than the conquered. "The people of Israel live." Even despite the overt efforts of the "slothful shepherds of Israel" (Ez. 36), the World Zionist Organization, Israel was there to be represented at the League of Nations by Ben Avi.

Chapter 37 of Ezekiel contains two visions of Israel's rebirth: the vision of the valley of "dry bones," the revival of Israel to life, and the vision of the "two sticks," portraying the reuniting of ancient Israel and Judah. There are some details we shall explore in these visions and their relations to the particulars of Israel's rebirth and endless life. However, observe quickly the 38th and 39th chapters which predict Israel's invasion by Russia and the satellite countries of Europe and Africa. Without comment on the detail of this invasion of Israel by Russia and the Gentile hordes, one conclusion is clear. All the enemies will be destroyed and Israel will live.

These words of Ezekiel hardly imply that Israel will die nationally again. Furthermore, Chapters 40-48 describe in detail the future Temple of Israel which shall never be destroyed, world without end.

Now that we have observed the broad and general proposition that "He will never die again," let us look back at the vision of the dry bones for some detailed particulars.

The vision of the "Valley of Dry Bones" has its own interpretation in the eleventh verse of Chapter 37: "...these bones are the whole house of Israel."

The following chart illustrates the reading of Ezekiel 37:7, which is translated from the original text.

I. *And We Regathered Together Again.* The first observation we note is the sixth word of the text, "and we regathered together again." Notice in Figure 1, that the Hebrew text is numbered word by word from right to left. The transliteration is numbered accordingly from left to right. The lower line is the translation of each word from the transliteration. The sixth verb, ותקרבו, *VaT'Q'R'VoU,* is in the *hitpa'el house*, meaning a repeated or reflective action. Not simply "coming together" but a "regathering together again."

This word, *TiKRaVoU*, is also translated "restore" or "restored again," "reformation," "restitution," "regeneration," "rebuilding," "rejuvenate," and "refresh." In modern Hebrew the word תקרובת, *TiQ'RoVehT,* is a refreshment as a snack or drink.

The word תקרבו, *TiQ'R'VoU,* in a prophetic or an eschatological sense, means: the "*refreshment* of National Israel"; "the *restoration* of the land to the Jews"; "the *return* of the Jews to their land"; "the *reestablishment* of the political state"; "the *recovery* of the Ashes of the Red Heifer"; "the *re-instatement* of the Sanhedrin Court"; "the *return* of the Tabernacle"; "the *rebuilding* of the Temple"; and the "*reinstitution* of the sacrificial system." In the traditional Jewish sense of the word, *TiQ'R'VoU* means literally that.

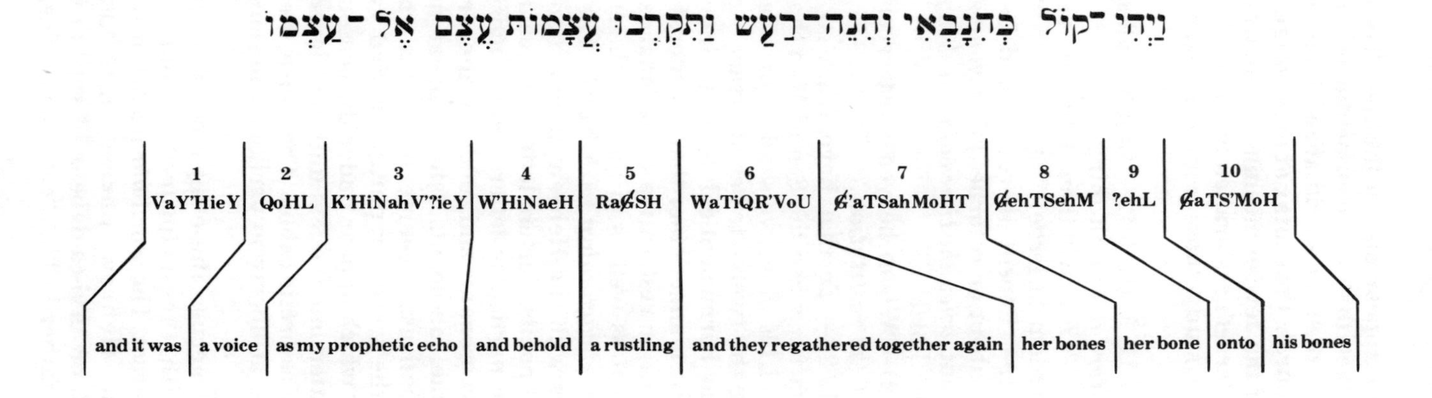

10 9 8 7 6 5 4 3 2 1
וַיְהִי־קוֹל כְּהִנָּבְאִי וְהִנֵּה־רַעַשׁ וַתִּקְרְבוּ עֲצָמוֹת עֶצֶם אֶל־עַצְמוֹ
1 VaY'HieY
2 QoHL
3 K'HiNahV'?ieY
4 W'HiNaeH
5 RaȻSH
6 WaTiQR'VoU
7 Ȼ'aTSahMoHT
8 ȻehTSehM
9 ?ehL
10 ȻaTS'MoH
and it was
a voice
as my prophetic echo
and behold
a rustling
and they regathered together again
her bones
her bone
onto
his bones

These words appear also in the New Testament text. Despite the fact that the commentaries have usually either ignored them or spiritualized them and applied them to the church, the syntax of their usage is always in the context of the Jewish meaning of the words. That is, as applied to Israel's restoration literally. For those who would like to study those contexts, here are a few examples:

1. Matt. 17:11, Mark 9:12—"Elijah shall surely come and *restore again* all things."
2. Acts 1:6—"Lord, wilt thou at this time *restore again* the Kingdom to Israel?"
3. Acts 3:19—"Repent therefore and be converted [turned about or returned] that your sins may be blotted out, *when the times of refreshing* shall come from the Lord."
4. Acts 3:21—"Whom heaven must receive until *the times of the restitution*. . . ."
5. Matt. 19:28—"Ye that have followed me, *in the regeneration* when the Son of Man shall sit on the throne of his glory, ye shall sit on twelve thrones judging the twelve tribes of Israel."

There is no hermeneutical basis to interpret these passages in any manner other than the literal meaning of the *TiK-RaVU*, or restoration of national Israel, in the New Testament as well as in the Jewish scriptures.

II. *Playing Abracadabra with Words*. The Kabbalists played games with the Hebrew alphabet and punctuation, or vowel points. Certain letters in the language can replace other particular letters. Some invisible vowels can become consonants and suddenly appear in a word. Likewise, some consonants can disappear and become vowel punctuations; of course, when this was done, the meaning of the words or phrases varied greatly. The vowel points, which appear under the consonant letters, were not written into the text until the eleventh century C. E. by the Massoretic rabbis. Therefore, the Kabbalists were and are at liberty to vacillate the sounds accordingly.

You might accuse these mystics of playing "abracadabra" with the scriptures. If you do, you are absolutely correct. The word *abracadabra* is an English form of the Hebrew phrase, אבי כדבר, ?ahViY hK'DahBehR, or "Avi-ca-dabehr." "Avi," in the phrase, means "my father." The "ca" means "as," and the "dahBehR" means "he said it." Therefore, *abracadabra* means "*my father, as he said it.*" By such manipulations, the Kabbalists were not seeking to invent something new. They were only trying to determine fully "what the fathers said and meant."

III. *The Regrouping of our Exceeding Great Army.* To illustrate a little Kabbalistic abracadabra, notice what can be done with word No. 6 and word No. 7 in the verse. Word 6 is תקרבו, *TiQ'R'VoU,* and word 7 is עֲצָמוֹת, *Ȼa'TSah MohT.* Aṣ it is here punctuated, it translates to "and we regathered together again her bones."

Now, let us observe what happens with an application of the abracadabra: The letter צָ, *TSah,* is repunctuated with a vowel change from צָ, *TSah,* to צוּ, *TSu,* and it would read, תִקְרְבוּ עֲצוּמוֹת, *TiQ'R'VoU ȻahTSoUMohT,* which would translate: "Regrouping our military re-enforcements," with this modification, the regrouping of our military re-enforcement becomes cognate to the following words in verse 10: "And they stood up an exceeding great army." Slaves of Egypt became soldiers after the Exodus and lambs led to slaughter in the holocaust became a world renown army after the Third Exodus.

IV. *Israel's Independence Day* is the final observation we shall make in this context. What appears to some to be a grammatical mistake in the texts is actually a hidden prophecy. The phrase, "her bones, her bone on his bone," is not good Hebrew grammar. Notice that the gender changes from feminine to masculine ". . .her bone on his bone." In proper Hebrew it would be "her bone on her bone." According to traditional Judaism there are no mistakes in the scripture. Where there is an apparent mistake, it is a hint of a deeper meaning than could appear in the normal construction.

Let us play a little abracadabra again with the gender. Earlier, we changed the צָ, *TSah,* to צוּ, *TSoU,* or צֻ; now, let us change the *camatz* vowel "ah" to the consonant *aleph,* א. The phrase would then change from "the regathering together again her bones," to "we regathered together again our independence—" תִקְרְבוּ עַצְמָאוּת *TiQ'R'VoU ȻaTS' MAh?oUT.*

The "noise and shaking" (Ez. 37:7) of World War II regathered the bones of Israel from the tombs of the nations "in a cloudy and dark day." (Ez. 34:12) On the fifth day of the month Iyyar in the Jewish year 5708, or

May 15, 1948, Israel declared its "independence." On that date each year, Jews around the world celebrate יום העצמאות, YoHM HahǾaTS'Mah?oHT, Independence Day for Israel's Third Commonwealth. Ezekiel foretold not only the regathering of Israel's dry bones but also the "establishment" and "framework" of their *"national independence."* The words עצומה argument, defense and להיתעצם means "to become great and strong and possess substance" come from the same עצם root.

Twenty-five centuries ago, Ezekiel foresaw and foretold Israel's national resurrection from the tombs of the Gentile nations. He prophesied the *regathering, restoration* and *rebuilding* of the Third Commonwealth. He foresaw the military *re-enforcement* of an exceedingly great army of Israel. He saw their establishment and framework which was expressed on their independence day. He also saw Russia and the United Nations of Europe and Africa invading Israel. He foresaw the *return* of Israel's ancient worship in the Tabernacle and Temple. His vision of the Third Commonwealth of Israel was like that of his colleague Daniel in the Babylonian captivity: "...in the days of these kings shall the G-d of heaven set up a Kingdom which shall not be destroyed: and the Kingdom shall not be left to other people, but it shall break in pieces and consume all these kingdoms and it shall stand forever." (Daniel 2:44)

The Israeli army has excelled far beyond expectations. What the prophet plainly foresaw 2,500 years ago is the very thing the military academies of the world today are trying to figure out. Ezekiel's prophetic definitions are very particular. His terminology is not in expression of generalities but in specifying particulars.

If Israel is doomed for national destruction, as its many enemies would like to think, they surely missed some grand opportunities in 1948, 1956, 1967, and 1973. No, Israel was not destroyed because "He shall never die again."

This national resurrection of Israel from the tombs of the Gentile nations is as important to the hope of Israel and the historic Jewish community of faith as is the resurrection of Jesus to the Christian's personal faith. So vitalizing is this national resurrection to Israel's hope that not only those living in the land, but also the Jews in the diaspora, have taken on a new living dimension in their faith, in their religion, in their relationship to themselves and to the world about them. What could be more appropriate to express this hope than the Israeli national anthem, "Ha-Tiqvah," "The Hope"—"all what's in our hearts inside the Jewish soul still lives. . . ."

At the end of two days, 2,000 years, Israel was revived from their international sepulchres. Now in the Third Commonwealth, the "standing up of an exceeding great army" (Ezekiel 37:10) has brought Israel over halfway through the first jubilee of fifty years. At the end of this period, about the year 2000, Israel will "stand before Him" in the third day from the Roman crucifixion of Israel.

"Why seek ye the living from among the dead, he is not here—he is risen, and lo, he is alive forevermore." The day after Israel is destroyed again will be the day the cynics find the bones of Jesus Christ. . .or vice versa.

In 1948 half a million Israelis stood up against 150 million enemies who had sworn their destruction. Military experts around the world predicted the conflict to be the shortest war in history. Israel was doomed to be the shortest-lived nation in modern times. Virtually unarmed and greatly outnumbered, the Jews, for the first time since 70 C. E. and Bar Kochba, were fighting for their survival both as a nation and as individuals. The war went on; weeks of fighting became months. Legion after legion of Arab forces fell before the advance of the Israelis. Six months and all Arab aggression crumbled to a defensive war, and finally there was a surrender in the form of a ceasefire.

At that time in 1948, Jews in Rome gathered at the Arch of Titus. The graven image on the arch depicted the Jews being led to Rome in chains with the Temple Menorah. Now, almost 2,000 years later, Jews danced the circular "Horah" around the Arch of Titus, singing "David, David, King of Israel, He lives, He lives forever." One of the joyful dancers ran to the arch depicting the IUDAEA CAPTA and painted in Hebrew that ancient adage, עם ישראל חי,, GahM YiS'RahAael KHiY, meaning, "the people of Israel live!"

In 1956, the Great White Bear of Russia slashed his claws into the Middle East by arming Nasser's Egypt with unlimited military arsenal. Israel again was in jeopardy, and the world asked, "What will Nasser do to Israel?" The answer came quickly, with a typical Jewish style of answering a question with a question: "What will

Israel do with Nasser?" Egypt's army folded and fled as the sands of Sinai as before a *hamseen* wind. Again, "the people of Israel lived."

In 1967, the angry Russian bear came up with a strategy for the conquest of Israel. Now the armies of Syria, Jordan, and Egypt were under the direct command of Russian officers. The Arabs were armed in an astronomical proportion against Israel. The bear hug of death was squeezed tightly around the tiny Jewish state. Political and military prognosticators world wide prophesied the final doom of young Israel. After those six dynamic days, Israel's major problem was what to do with the hundreds of Russian officers they had captured in their defensive liberation of all the lands from Suez to Mt. Hermon.

October 1973, was the Jewish year 5734. Written in Hebrew letter characters, ה'תשל"ד, it means שנה התשלד, or Sh'NahH Ha-TiSH LaD, the "year of the skeleton." Under U. S. pressure, Israel was forced to refrain from attacking and suffered heavy defeats and losses so as not to be called the aggressor in the conflict. The result of this decision certainly spelled out the significance of the year of the skeleton as far as Israel was concerned. For the first time since 1948, Israel actually looked defeated as they engaged in a confrontation of heavy weaponry hitherto unparalleled in the annals of world military history. All the tank battles in history combined did not equal the armament crushing into Israel. The sands of Sinai drank the blood while the rocks of Golan ate the flesh of thousands of Israel's youth. Israel was defeated, alas! Russian vodka flowed in toast to Israel's imminent destruction. Yet, out of the haze of smoke and fire, Israel recoiled in valiant force. Suddenly division after division of Egyptian and Syrian forces folded before the Israeli army. Despite it all, the howling cry of the defeated Russians and their friends was "Israeli aggression!" Israel's regathered bones survived the year of the skeleton. Again the Russian bear's claws were crushed in another defeat that will someday bring Gog from the land of Gog of Rosh (or Russia) against Israel in final confrontation of Ezekiel's visions of chapters thirty-eight and thirty-nine. So...Israel lives! The Third Commonwealth, according to prophetic expectations, will never be uprooted or left to another Gentile people. In the Midrash, which teaches that Abraham's life was a profile of Israel's history, we see another point. Abraham came into the land and sojourned but went out to the land of Egypt because of famine. Abraham then re-entered the land a second time, but again he was forced to leave. However, when Abraham returned the third time, he never departed again. Likewise, Israel entered the land in the First Commonwealth, or First Temple period, under Joshua until the Babylonian captivity. They returned and established the Second Commonwealth, or the Second Temple period, from Ezra until Titus. "After many days," Israel is returned again in the *times of refreshing* for the third time, like Abraham, never again to be uprooted. "Never to Die Again!"

Israel's regathering and restoration in their Third Commonwealth was predicted to be in a period of world crises and accompanied by unexplainable signs in the heavens. The world crises are for sure. Now we must ask if there have been unexplainable signs in the heavens. There have been over 15,000 UFOs sighted since the rebirth of Israel's Third Commonwealth.

Yet, after a quarter century, the sudden appearance and disappearance of unidentified flying objects, the UFOs, remain a phenomenon. A phenomenon, by the very nature of the word, denotes the quality of a phantom, the Greek word for a ghost. All that one recent observer of a UFO in an air control center could say in describing the speed of the object which left a three-inch streak across the radar screen was, "Fantastic . . . fantastic . . . absolutely fantastic," or, as a Greek would have said it, "Phantasma!" The only thing more fantastic than these mystical phantoms themselves are the efforts by those of us who try to make a logical explanation of the phenomena.

A phenomenon is not in the parameter of logical explanation; therefore, this explanation makes no attempt to deal logically, but rather eschatologically with the matter. We shall think in the bounds of the mystical while dealing with the phantoms. Admittedly, it is more hypothetical—a mere observation—yet, an earnest effort to be objective while dealing with a subject matter too "other-worldish" to approach logically.

Just assume that the UFOs might possibly be one of the wonders in the heavens of the credentials of Israel's Third Commonwealth. Perhaps the late Eliezer Ben-Yehuda, father of modern Hebrew, would have named them מרכבה-מופתים, "MehRKahVahH MoHFTiYM." This name best describes the UFO's indescribable nature, meaning "vehicles of wonder."

First, let us note the pattern sequence. In late 1947 through the following year, "flying saucers," described as being disc-shaped, or viewed from the side as cigar-shaped, brought much speculation. At first, they were suspected of being a Russian secret weapon, or an invasion from another planet. After about a year, the objects vanished as suddenly as they had appeared, not to be seen in a verified report for a decade. Then, again, they were sighted in massive reports for a few days, and again, disappeared. Such happenings inspired the hit song, entitled, "The Red-Eyed, One-Horned, Flying Purple People Eater."

After a few years, there was another brief appearance of the UFOs in 1961. Their absence had made their memory sort of "ho-hum." Again, they appeared over Europe, Africa, Australia, the U. S. S. R. and the U. S. A. This time, the Federal Government financed a research program on the UFOs from 1967 to 1969. Tens of thousands of supposed sightings were analyzed the world over and about 10 percent were verified. In 1969, the research project was concluded; the report simply stated three points: 1. There are UFOs; they are not ours. 2. They are not from another planet or nation. 3. They offer no threat to our national or earthly security.

Again, for the fourth time in twenty-five years, in October 1973, the UFOs came out of their eclipse and made a more vivid apocalypse than ever before. By mid-November there was another phase-out of the reported sightings. "Most fantastic" is not a trite statement relative to the sequence of their apocalypse and eclipse in correlation to Israel's military and political crises.

UFOs made their first dramatic appearance in the Jewish year 5708. This was 1947-1948 in the Christian calendar. That was the year of the rebirth of the Jewish State. In the rebirth of the State of Israel were the wars of Liberation and Independence. Upon the close of those conflicts, verified reports of the UFOs were gradually phased out.

A decade later, in early October, in the Jewish year 5717, 1956-1957, came the Sinai campaign. It brought repeated massive sightings of the Merkavah. In the precise sequence of that conflict, the UFOs made their appearance and disappearance. During Israel's political war in the United Nations over the Eichmann affair, there was another brief appearance of the UFOs.

Then, in the Jewish year 5727, 1966-67, this time in the late spring of 1967, the Six-Day War erupted. With that conflict, the recurrence of Merkavah Mophate was sighted in magnitude. Edmund Wilson, in his latest edition of *The Dead Sea Scrolls,* relates the account in the Israeli newspapers, *Ha Eretz* and the *Jerusalem Post,* of such a phenomenon occurring south of Elat over the Gulf of Tiran between the Sinai (then Egypt) and Saudi Arabia during the week preceding the Six Day War.

The UFO's exodus after 1967 was half the time of their two previous absences. No sooner had the High Holy Days begun in September and October of 1973, the Jewish year 5734, but the sightings were again reported in greater number and detail. Approximately 80 percent of the verified sightings of UFOs have been in a radius of twelve months of the pivotal years of Israel's military and political crises, namely 5708, 5717, 5721, 5727, and 5734, or 1948, 1956, 1961, 1967, and 1973.

With these latest sightings came the surprise Syrian-Egyptian invasion of Israel, exploding the War of Yom Kippur. In the annals of military confrontation, this battle was of the greatest magnitude.

The name *merkavaht mophteem* for the UFOs is no new coinage; neither is the historic reports of their sightings. the name *merkavah* means "a chariot of fire," and the word *mophet* means "a wonder," or, the plural *merkavaht mophteem.*

Many Hebrew words are close in meaning; yet, the exact connotation and denotation show a marked differentiation. Two examples related to the word *mophet* are *"nes"* and *"seeman."* The word *nes* means a miracle such as has to do with the aversion of natural law, but within the framework of natural elements. A *nes* has no allegorical significance beyond the event or action itself. For example, the healing of King Hezekiah's incurable sore was a *nes.* The king, however, was not satisfied with the *nes* of his promised healing, so he requested of the Prophet Isaiah a sign, or *seeman.* The *seeman* differs from the *nes* in that, while it is an aversion of natural law, it also has an allegorical meaning superimposed over the event or action itself. Hence, the moving of the sundial backwards ten degrees was the *seeman*, or sign, required of the king. This violation of nature, while involved with the elements of nature, was a *nes* in itself. However, since it conveyed an allegorical meaning, it was a *seeman*, or sign. *Mophet* differs from nes and *seeman* in that it has a quality of "other worldness," a phenomenon outside the sphere of nature and physical comprehension. *Mophet* is usually translated "wonder" in English.

The history of Israel is well punctuated by the appearance of the Wondrous Chariots of Fire. The Apocryphal writings, as well as those of Flavius Josephus, describe the Exodus from Egypt as being accompanied by the *merkavaht mophteem*. The assumption of Enoch and Elijah was executed by a *merkavah mophet*. Elisha and Israel were delivered from a Syrian invasion by the UFOs as an invisible force (II Kings 2:11, 6:17). Tradition relates that as Alexander the Great led his armies against Jerusalem, he, too, saw *merkavaht mophteem*, or chariots of fire.

Surprisingly, Christianity is, despite her Judeo-heritage, devoid of any concept of the *Merkavah*. The concept is totally Jewish in character. The Merkavah was so forcefully impressive upon the traditional Jewish community that the rabbis who collected, arranged, and inspired the Jewish Prayer Book were called "The Yorde Merkavah," or the descenders of the Chariots of Fire. These mystic rabbis made mammoth contributions to Mishnah, Gemora, Midrash, and especially to the Zohar. Dr. Gershom G. Sholem, Israel's leading authority on the academic studies of Kabballah and Jewish mysticism, dates the period of the organized groups of the Yorde Merkavah rabbis from the Jewish years 3650 to 4850, roughly from the first century before the Common Era until about the tenth century A. D.

The practice of the *Merkavah* tradition, however, goes back to Abraham's time, as reflected in Genesis 15:17. The major premise for the *Merkavah* tradition is based on the vivid description of the first chapter of Ezekiel. Since the first sighting of UFOs in the mid 1940s, there have been several who have called attention to their similar description as compared to *Merkavah* of Ezekiel, chapter 1. As in Ezekiel's description, there have been rare reports of nondescript creatures attending the appearance of the vehicles of the *Merkavaht*.

Ezekiel had two descriptions of the Merkavah in his discourse. The first description, which was rather vague, seemed to be made at a distance in the opening verses; the second description later in the chapter was evidently from a close perspective. The size, shape, texture, proportion, hue, sound, and action of these unearthly objects are translated by the prophet, with some difficulty, into earthly metaphors and materials. Some of the Hebrew words are very difficult to structure linguistically. For example, the prophet's vision of these flying wheels, "ophanaim," in modern Hebrew, means bicycles, which is hardly what the prophet was describing. In size, the vehicle's description is vague; but comparable to the size of a horse and a chariot, it was approximately twenty-five to thirty feet in diameter. The shape (verses 15-16) was like wheels or discs. The discs were four in one. The three inner discs telescoped inside the outer, forming one unit. Each of the inner telescoped discs had the ability to expand and contract inside the outer wheel, thus making a variable proportion to the belly and the back of the vehicle. The texture (verse 4b) is described at a distance as having the appearance of a cloud of fire enfolding the flames inside itself. This cloud was translucent and semi-transparent, radiating a brilliant aura about it. At a closer perspective (verse 16), the texture was described as "tarshish," a tin metallic or pearl-like gloss as of chrysolite. The hue is described (verse 4) as the color of amber out of the midst of the fire; in essence, it was the hues of the primary spectrum: yellow, red, and blue, in vacillating brilliance of aura into the secondary spectrum of green, orange and purple. The distant sound (verse 4) is described as that of a whirlwind, whereas the closer sound was that of a waterfall (verse 24). The motion (verse 12) indicates that the vehicle was uninhibited by the natural forces of gravity and principles of physics. Their movement cannot be explained by the laws of aerodynamics. They moved vertically in their ascent and descent. They hovered or meandered, but never turned in flight. The flight was always straight forward, by self-determined speed (verse 13), at a velocity compared to lightning, and leaving an electro vapor in its trail. The comparison of the character of Ezekiel's *Merkavaht Mophteem* and the reports of the witnesses of UFOs have striking parallels, especially if we allow for the communication gap in language and materials knowledgeable to Ezekiel's day.

If the UFOs are the *Merkavaht Mophteem*, the Russians and Arabs have failed to calculate the factor in their strategy against Israel. This might explain why the world has witnessed a modern demonstration of what historians formerly called "Maccabean exaggerations" in modern Israel.

The prophet Joel in chapter 3:3 describes the last days, or Israel's Third Commonwealth, with the words, "*V Nahtati MoHFTiYm B'Shah MieYM,*" or "I will show wonders in the heavens and in the land [of Israel] blood, fire and pillars of smoke." From the Golan Heights to Sinai, Israel today has well dramatized Joel's vision of blood, fire and pillars of smoke. For the thousands who have been witnesses of the UFOs in this quarter century, the unexplainable wonders in the heavens are just as vivid a reality as are the Middle East wars.

Two things are certain: Israel's regathering did come about as a result of world crisis, the Holocaust; the Third Commonwealth is accompanied by signs in the heavens as predicted by the holy prophets of Israel.

...Awake now from your dream of dreams, and depart from hence where riddles of riddles are born! Come out of the Garden called Paradise and return to the outside world of logic and reason. The mind you lent me, I return well exercised but unharmed. Your mind is now your own, and mine is mine! In my riddle of riddles and dream of dreams, you thought not what I thought. Your mind is your own and mine is mine! Who is the Messiah? Again your choice is yours, and mine is mine!

In reality, the seven hints of the Messiah apply both to Israel and to Jesus. The Christians believe Jesus is the Messiah. Jews believe Israel is the Messiah. Who is right? Who is wrong? Perhaps if we look at the issue as one being right and the other being wrong, we may both be wrong. Then "that unreconcilable difference between Judaism and Christianity, the question of the Messiah," will always exist. Why not look at the common denominators rather than at the differentials? Why can't the Jew, in the historic experience of his faith, be allowed to share that heritage of the suffering Messiah in the character of his people with full privilege? After all, the prophets who wrote the Bible were his own.

At the same time, let the Christian who is "alien to the covenants and stranger to the commonwealth of Israel" (Eph. 2), who shares no part or parcel of Israel's historic character, be likewise privileged to find in Jesus that Messianic character of the Messiah to the Gentile world. The question of the unreconcilable difference in Judaism and Christianity in the question of who is the Messiah is not so much the person of the Messiah as it is the people of each community.

A Jew who reads in Isaiah 53 "the suffering Messiah," experiences the whole history of his people, a suffering Messianic nation. There is no way a Christian can conjure up such an emotion or relationship because he has no share in that history, suffering or tradition of Israel. In this respect, it is the Christian who is judicially blinded to Israel's Messianic character. Likewise, the Jew can never, by the fondest extrapolation, even by conversion to Christianity, know the span of distance a Gentile Christian is speaking of in "being translated from the kingdom of darkness to the kingdom of his dear Son." Neither can the Jew describe what a Christian means by being "lost," (that is, not knowing from whence one came, where he is, or where he is going). No Jew can honestly say he is or was "without G-d, without hope and without consciousness of a Messiah in the world." The Jew is likewise judicially blinded to the meaning of "Good News!" There is no Good News to one Jew about another Jew being executed by the Romans. He is as alien to that gospel as the Christian is to Israel's Messianic character.

As Rabbi Samuel Schwartz said, "The Bible in reality is not a Jewish scripture nor is it a Christian scripture. The Bible is the Oracle of G-d. The interpretation is oriented to each in his own community of faith."

The Bible plainly states that Israel is the product of a Supernatural Birth, the Son of G-d who made a Flight to Egypt and Returned to the Land Where He Was Hated by all Those about Him. History attests that Israel is Despised and Rejected of Men, acquainted with Sorrow and Grief. The Romans Crucified Israel, and at the end of two millennial days, at the threshold or twilight of the Third Millennial Day, Israel was Brought Out of his state of national death. Out of the archaeological cemetery of so-called Palestine, Israel Arose in a National Resurrection, Never to Die Again.

If all seven hints be true of Israel, and the Bible and history witness to such, is it necessary for the Gentile to accept Israel as a personal Savior? The Jew has never taught such because he recognizes the Christian's right and access to G-d through his faith and relationship through Jesus Christ. The RaMBaM, or Maimonides, and many other Jewish writers, attest to this. Traditional Judaism has always recognized the Christian's right to be a Christian without challenge. Unfortunately, the Christian has been slow to come to the realization that the Jew has a vital relationship with G-d through faith in the Abrahamic Covenant.

Israel is the Messiah! The Messiah is Israel! The Gentiles had no access to G-d through the covenants of Israel but were strangers to them, and aliens to the commonwealth of Israel. In the economy of G-d, it was never intended that there should be competition between Judaism and Christianity. Each community is complementary to the other. Where does Jesus fit into the picture? Simple! About 1,948 years after the creation of Adam, Abraham was born. About 1,948 anno domini, Israel was reborn. Then, about midway between the birth of Abraham and the rebirth of national Israel came the birth and life of Jesus of Nazareth. With respect to time, there is where Jesus fits into the picture.

Let us be a bit more precise. Let us step in for a little closer look. The year of the Exodus when Israel was nationally born out of the matrix of the Egyptian travail was the Jewish year of 2448 (from Adam). Israel was reborn in its Third Commonwealth in the Jewish year 5708 (or 1948 C.E.). Now, at the end of the present Jewish century, the nation of Israel will be thirty-three and a half centuries old. Where does Jesus of Nazareth fit into that picture? Tsk! Tsk! Simple! Right in the middle of all that time, he wrapped up in his own thirty-three and one-half years all of Israel's thirty-three and one-half centuries of national life.

He personified Israel's suffering Messianic history, wrapped it up in himself and extended that personified Messianic image to the Gentiles in the Good News of the Gospel. That Gospel was not intended to be to Israel from the Gentiles; it was in all prophetic expectation to be from Israel to the Gentiles.

The evangelical Christian might see this as a point of irrefutable proof of the Messianic claims of Jesus. He must not overlook, however, that the same argument also established the absolute irrefutable proof of the Messianic claims of Israel.

The Jew does not feel that urgency to accept Jesus as his suffering Messiah. The Christian cannot understand why the Jew feels himself exempt from that obedience to the faith. Many evangelicals admit that when they share the Gospel with other Gentiles, they witness the energy of the Holy Spirit in their own utterances and in the responses of their audiences.

However, the same words drop dead when spoken to a Jew. The evangelist becomes nervous, words do not flow properly; and he vainly forces his argument into the air. Strangely, the same Holy Spirit that so energizes him in his witness to the Gentiles fails to energize him in his attempt to witness to the Jews.

The Jew does not feel a need to accept the Messiah, because he is a part of that Messiah. The Messiah that the Gentiles accept is the epitome of the suffering of Israel. The suffering of Jesus was the suffering of Israel! The suffering of Israel is the suffering of Jesus! For the Jew to be expected to accept Jesus as the alien Gentile does would not only be redundancy to the point of hyperbole, it would be double jeopardy! Should a father say to his son, "Son, I accept you as my son"? One does not need to accept what he is or what is his.

The suffering and death of Jesus at the hands of the Gentiles, Herod and Pilate, cannot be divorced from the historical suffering of Israel at the hands of the Gentile nations. What Jesus suffered that day, Israel has suffered in the stretched-out centuries. Israel is the Messiah and the Messiah is Israel.

"The preaching of the cross is to the Jews an offense. . . ." Why? Christians wear crosses dangling from their necks as pious symbols of the faith. To the Jew, the cross, the electric chair, the gas chamber, the guillotine, and the hangman's noose are all symbols of indignity and execution. The Jews have too often been the objects of those applications to glory in them. The perspective of the cross is different to the Jews than it is to the Christians. The difference is that the Christian's cross dangles from his neck; but the Jew has too often found himself dangling from the neck of the cross.

One might ask why Paul said in Romans 1:16, ". . .to the Jew first. . ." if the Jew is not the object of the preaching of the cross. But a closer analysis indicates that the subject of the syntax in Romans 1:14-16 is not "salvation" but "the preaching of the Gospel." Since there is no indirect object in the text, the *dative* translation "*to* the Jew first" is incorrect. The Greek case is instrumental and should be translated by syntax: the preaching of the Gospel was *by* the Jew first, even the Greeks.

Some years ago a fable became very popular: the Jews had a prefabricated temple cut from Indiana limestone, and it was secretly hidden in a New York warehouse. At the right moment, they were going to ship it to Jerusalem for rebuilding their Third Temple.

Can you imagine shipping limestone to Jerusalem from Indiana? Jerusalem has enough limestone to build a forty-foot wall around the whole state of Indiana. Shipping Indiana limestone to Jerusalem is a more humorous simile than shipping coal to Newcastle or snowballs to the Eskimos. The only thing more futile than limestone, coal, and snowballs is to send missionaries to the Jews. All the church history since Nicaea has proved that the most non-productive missionary effort is that directed toward Jewish evangelism. Nowhere in the New Testament, by word or deed, was a Gentile ever commissioned to take or send the Good News back to Jerusalem or to the Jews abroad. The "preaching of the Gospel" in Romans 1:14-16 was from the Jews to the Gentiles, never from the Gentiles to the Jews. The Jews have not responded to the Gospel for the same reason—limestone, coal and snowballs!

This conclusion may not agree with evangelical theology, but it agrees with history and the New Testament texts. Certainly, it is a sour note to those who are professionally involved in Jewish evangelism or who are mi$$ionarie$ to the Jews. Admittedly, Jewish evangelism is a very lucrative work.

This principle of the Jew's purpose as the origin rather than the objective of the Gospel was aptly stated by Martin Buber: "G-d who gave himself to Israel by Moses at Sinai...gave himself to the world by Jesus at Calvary."

There is some phenomenon in the observation that the Good News of the Gospel to the Gentiles has been most effective in those areas of the world where the Jewish community is strongest. The effectiveness of the message of Jesus Christ to the pagan world can be measured in direct proportion to the strength of the Jewish community in that particular area. In all places where the Jews were indigenous, Christian churches sprang up almost spontaneously. In the places where the Jews were not present, Christianity has been maintained only by perpetual missionary efforts, supported from those other areas where the Jews were present.

The British Isles were fertile to the Christian message until the expulsion of the Jews in the twelfth century. Afterward, the church suffered great decadence and apostasy. After Cromwell let the Jews back into England, the great revivals of the Christian church occurred.

Lithuania was the last European country to receive the Jews, and there the Jewish community produced some of its greatest sages and scholars. There the depth of Judaism became its strongest. Only after the coming of the Jews did the Lithuanians embrace Christianity. In Lithuania today is the strongest expression of courage of the Christian church in the U. S. S. R. and perhaps in the world. The Russians have imprisoned over 35,000 Lithuanian Catholics who refused to let their children be taught the atheism of Marxist dialectic materialism. The Lithuanian church has defied and defeated the Russians in the triumph of their faith. Their example was the exhibit of the Lithuanian Jews.

Not only in quantity, but also in quality and stability, the church's success is in direct proportion to the quantity and quality of the Jews in a given area. The Jews' presence in a land is the fertility of the land to the seed of the message of Christ to the Gentiles.

Rome and Istanbul, later Constantinople, became strong Christian centers because they were first strong Jewish centers. Colonial America was an extension of Europe's stale, prejudiced, parochial church states or state churches. The Jews came to America first in 1641 and were granted religious tolerance by Roger Williams and the Duke of York. This marked the beginning of the then unique freedom of religion and worship, unharassed by ecclesiastical or state authority. Where the Jew was treated with equality by the Christians, the Christians soon became more tolerant of each other. As goes the welfare of the Jews and Judaism, so goes the welfare of the Christians and Christianity. Where go the Jews and Judaism, so go the church and Christianity. Where the Jewish minority suffers, so suffers the Christian minority. Without the reading of Moses, the preaching of Jesus has no dimension. The Jews are the "salt and savor" of the earth. Without the Light of Torah, the preaching of the cross is meaningless. Judaism is the necessary catalyst to the function of Christianity.

The degree to which the church in any given space or time has divorced itself from Judaism is the same degree to which the church has introduced paganism or philosophy. Without the Messianic people of Israel, the message of the Messianic person of Jesus is vague and obscure.

Much issue is made today in evangelical circles about the *New Testament church.* There were two things the church of the New Testament did not have—one was the New Testament and the other was a church. Every book of the Bible, not only the Jewish scripture of the so called Old Testament but also the twenty-seven books of the Christian's New Testament, was written by Jews. That includes the books of Luke and Acts. Hence, as to its origin, the Christian's New Testament is also Jewish scriptures. But the influence did not stop there. It was carried on into the first two centuries when the major proponents of the message of the Good News were propagated primarily by the Jews themselves to the Gentiles. After the Council of Nicaea in 325 C. E., the Jews were excluded by the Bulls from participation unless they denied Judaism and converted to Christianity. Persecution after persecution of the Jews by Christendom drove the two complementary communities worlds apart. Yet, even now, the very presence of the Jew is necessary for effective Christianity. The nation today that has the most Christian churches, the most missionary programs, the most Christian schools, the most widely represented denominational scope and the most tolerance of worship in coexistence per capita and per square mile is the nation of Israel. The Israeli government is the only government in the world that furnishes free Christmas trees to all its Christian citizens. If that is not the Christian spirit, what could be? Just think, the Jewish National Fund could adapt "Jingle Bells" as its theme song to "Plant a Tree in Israel."

Too long, too long has Christianity looked at the Jew and Judaism through the over-tinted theological bifocals of Christian theology whose upper lenses are plus prejudice, and lower frames are minus investigation.

Therefore, the Christian's view of the Jew and his religion is vague and distorted. Not only are the spectacles mis-prescribed and faultily ground, but the only hope is critical eye surgery. Theological cataracts must be amputated! As Irving Fisher said, "To unlearn the taken-for-granted is harder than to learn the hitherto unsuspected."

It is just as important for the Christian to recognize and accept Israel as the Messianic nation as it is for the Jew to recognize and accept Jesus as the Messianic Savior of the Gentiles. The answer to that riddle is that it is really not essential that either accept or recognize the other for each economy to function in its own purpose. Yet, a lot of problems might be solved if each did.

In the Riddle of the Messiah, there is a certain mystique, both on the part of the Jewish attitude toward the Messianic character of Jesus and the Christian attitude toward the Messianic character of Israel. Paul addressed this "mystery" on the former as "*blindness in part hath happened to Israel....*" but to the Gentile Christians, "*I would not, brethren, that you be ignorant....*" The blindness of Israel "happened" as a judicial act. The word "happened" occurs in the passive voice as an action that happened from outside their own effort or control and is restricted only to the aspect of the Gospel of death, burial, and resurrection of Jesus so that salvation could come to the Gentiles. If the Jew is called "judicially blinded in part" by Paul for not seeing the Messianic character of Jesus, the Christian who does not see the Messianic character of Israel he called an "ignoramus." And that "ignorance" occurs in the middle voice indicating an action imposed upon one's self. John Lawrence has said, "Ignorance can be cured, but there is no hope for stupidity." If you meet a man who is blind or ignorant, don't accuse him. Just take him into the Garden. You now know the way so you can bring him back safely.

Chapter II
RIDDLE OF ISRAEL

"In 1899, Mark Twain wrote an essay which he entitled 'Concerning the Jews', and brought it to a remarkable conclusion. We must remember that this was long before the Balfour Declaration of 1917, let alone the re-creation of the State of Israel in 1948. He wrote:

'If the statistics are right, the Jews constitute but one per cent of the human race. It suggests a nebulous dim puff of star dust lost in the blaze of the Milky Way. Properly the Jew ought hardly to be heard of; but he is heard of, has always been heard of. He is as prominent on the planet as any other people, and his commercial importance is extravagantly out of proportion to the smallness of his bulk. His contributions to the world's list of great names in literature, science, art, music, finance, medicine and abstruse learning are also way out of proportion to the weakness of his numbers. He has made a marvelous fight in this world, in all the ages; and has done it with his hands tied behind him. He could be vain of himself, and be excused for it. The Egyptian, the Babylonian and the Persian rose, filled the planet with sound and splendour, then faded to dream-stuff and passed away; the Greek and the Roman followed, and made a vast noise, and they are gone; other peoples have sprung up and held their torch high for a time, but it burned out, and they sit in twilight now, or have vanished. The Jew saw them all, beat them all, and is now what he always was, exhibiting no decadence, no infirmities of age, no weakening of his parts, no slowing of his energies, no dulling of his alert and aggressive mind. All things are mortal but the Jew; all other forces pass, but he remains. What is the secret of his immortality?'"

As is the riddle of the Messiah, so is the riddle of Israel. There is again an unreconcilable difference, this time between Jacob and Israel. The latter is a "chosen people"; the former is a "suffering people." The paradox of this riddle lies in their identity: they are both the same people.

Here, in this paradox, also lies the antithesis of the Christian and the Jew. In spite of all the common denominators, this one unreconcilable difference makes any compromise between Judaism and Christianity forever impossible. Orthodoxy is what makes a Christian a Christian, while paradoxy is what makes a Jew a Jew.

The tap root of what makes a Christian a Christian is a matter of making an active choice. One is called a

Christian when he sees the facts and makes that decision to choose the facts for himself.

The tap root of what makes a Jew a Jew is the opposite. The Jew does not make an active choice to be a Jew, but rather, the Jew is in the most passive sense "the chosen." The facts are that: first, his mother is a Jewess—he had no choice in that; and second, on the eighth day he was circumcised—again he had no choice in that either. Yet, that is what makes a Jew a Jew.

As Menachem Dayan put it: "The Christian chooses the facts, but the facts choose the Jew and that's what all this being a chosen people means." Perhaps to this Jesus alluded when he said "many are called but few are chosen."

The ethnic family from the Patriarchs have a religious bond and unity that is unique when compared to all other nations. That religious bond is faith, the very fiber of the Jewish soul. This soul faith is expressed in a language which is the oldest and youngest language spoken by men. Through this speech is communicated the oracle of G-d to mankind. It was the Holy Tongue of the prophets. It was the sacred script of Moses, and the poetic song of the Psalmists. It is the Hebrew language. The chosen language for the chosen people.

In this language, the Jews gave the world the Bible. "Unto them were committed the oracles of G-d." Not only did they give mankind that Sacred Library upon which the three major world religions are based, but they have also made more major contributions in the fields of art and science than all other nations combined. Proportionate to their number, no people have contributed more to humanity than have the Jews. They have to some degree enjoyed a temporal prosperity in spite of all the adversity that has railed against them. Israel enjoys a special character in his prophetic history. At the same time no people have been more ravishly raped of honor than the people of Israel. Despite a perpetual crucifixion, Israel lives...a perpetual resurrection!

This is the riddle of Israel: "What is the secret of his immortality?" How is Israel different from all other nations?

Israel is distinctively different from all other nations in its ethnic origin. The progeny of all other nations was by natural descent through the three sons of Noah. Their rapid decadence of G-d consciousness degenerated from mere ingratitude to idolatry and then to total rebellion against G-d at the Tower of Babel. Humanity soon became "junked-out" so far as an awareness of a monotheistic relationship was concerned.

The Eternal One went into the wrecking yard of humanity and "chose" two old, antique, non-functional, obsolete people. He removed them from that environment and refurbished their reproductive systems. Through his "chosen couple," the patriarch Abraham and the matriarch Sarah, he created a "chosen nation." The very existence and survival of Israel *excuses* any Jew from having to explain being "chosen." That he exists *excuses* any further explanation.

So unique is Israel in his national origin that no nation or people can say, "Israel descended from us!" No! Quite to the contrary, many peoples falsely claim to be the descendants of Israel.

Jesus levied words of judgment, fierce and harsh, against those who falsely claim to be Israel or to be spiritual Jews: "...I know the blasphemy of them which say they are Jews, and are not, but are of the synagogue of Satan." (Rev. 2:9)

If some say they are Jews but are not, who are the *true Jews*? Paul defined them as the circumcision in Romans 3:1, "to whom were committed the oracles of G-d." Again in Romans 9:3-5, he defined "Israel" as being synonymous with the *true Jews* and gave eight marks of their identification:

1. They have the *adoption*.
2. They have the *Shekinah Glory*.
3. They have the *covenants*.
4. They have the *giving of the Law*. (Torah)
5. They have the *service of G-d*. (Temple or synagogue worship)
6. They have the *promises*. (The Land of Israel)
7. They have the *Fathers*. (Patriarchs)
8. They produced the Messiah.

These are the *true Jews*—this is the *true Israel*. Others who say they are Jews and are not, or say they are true Israel or spiritual Israel in *any sense* of the term, Jesus himself accuses of being "liars and blasphemers."

British Israelism teaches that the British people, namely England and the United States, are the "ten lost tribes of Israel." But there is no such group either in the Bible or in history as the ten lost tribes. As far as the Jews are concerned, they have always known where they are and have kept a detailed history of their whereabouts. They have never lost their identity. There are no ten lost tribes of Israel.

Replacement theology teaches that the Church is the heir of Israel's posterity. This differs very little from the misnomer of British Israelism. Every cult of Christendom lays emphasis on its being the "true Israel." If replacement theology is correct and the Church is spiritual Israel, the most consistent theology is that of the Jehovah's Witnesses and the Mormons. The degree to which cultism can be measured is the depth to which they claim to be spiritual Israel or to be Israel genetically. Many try to imitate Israel, but none can claim to be their progenitors. None yet can say "Israel descended from us." Israel is distinctively different in his origin.

Israel is the indelible nation that defies definition. Their sages wrestled with the questions "who is a Jew?" and "what is a Jew?" The Supreme Court of Israel is still struggling with the issue. Israel, the Jewish people, are distinctly different in the mystique of their identity. There is a Jewish identity, but the very nature of it defies description and explanation. How can they be indelible, yet undefined?

Like the "ten lost tribes," the "Jewish race" is a misnomer. There is no such thing as a Jewish race. A Gentile may be pure German or Polish or English. He may be part of each with a little Spanish, Indian, or African thrown in. He may be half Japanese and half Portuguese. Never is he one-half Jewish! While there is no Jewish race, yet there is an ethnic quality to Israel.

The ethnic value lies in the traditional aspect that being Jewish is a family matter. The determining factor of the issue whether or not one is in the family is not whether his father is Jewish, but rather his mother. Ishmael and Isaac had the same father. The determination was made in the matriarch Sarah, not the patriarch Abraham. No Gentile nation determines its descendants by the mother. Again Israel is unique in this matter. By the "seed of the woman" the redeemer was to come into the world (Gen. 3:15). If the mother is Jewish, the child is Jewish. If the mother is not Jewish, the child is a Gentile regardless of the "kosher" pedigree of the father.

As in any other family, one can be adopted into the Jewish family by conversion. The adoptee is then a *guayer*, or "stranger within the gates," but he is not at all a part of the ethnic family, he is still *not* Jewish. In the case of a woman convert, her children would be Jewish if their birth was after conversion. Intermarriage accounts for the greater part of the conversions to Judaism. Hence, like any other family, there are three ways to enter: by birth, by marriage, or by adoption. Marriage alone does not constitute conversion. Doctor Flusser points out that Gal. 4:4 "...made of woman, made under the Law [Torah]..." is Paul's certificate of Jesus' Jewish pedigree.

Israel, the Jewish people, have not only a unique ethnic entity but also a unique family religion. Judaism is the only religion of this family. Judaism is the only religion in the world that was ordained by G-d directly. Jesus did not say he had come to give mankind a new or better religion. He said, "I am come that men might have life, and life more abundantly." There is nothing more dead than mere religion. The Christian religion is an invention of man. The Christian faith is life and truth. These cannot be institutionalized. The Church or Body of Jesus Christ is a living organism, not an organization.

Judaism is the exercise of the Abrahamic faith as prescribed by G-d in the Torah, or Law he gave Moses at Sinai. Moses received the Written Law on stone. He was given the Oral Law verbally. He gave the Written Law to Joshua and Eliezer, then rehearsed in their ears all the words of the Law. That rehearsal was the Oral Law. The official interpretation of the Written Law, or Torah, by the rabbis is totally subject to the principles of interpretation given to Moses in the Oral Law. This oral tradition, or Massorah, is as binding on an observant Jew as is the Written Law. They are both the "Word of G-d."

Because of this Word of G-d, Israel, the Jewish people, though scattered among all nations, have proven themselves most patriotic to each country in which they live. Yet they have a national identity with the Land of Israel, for there is also a national quality to the Jewish faith. The promise of the Abrahamic Covenant is a real estate arrangement which is the eschatological hope of Israel. The subject of "heaven" is not mentioned in the Jewish scripture in an eschatological sense. Life in the world to come is a life in the Promised Land. The land of Israel is the hope of the people of Israel.

Judaism has a Holy Trinity of its own! G-d, Torah, and Israel are one! This tri-unity is inseparable. To subtract any one from the others would destroy the whole. This triad in human history is a paradox and riddle which cannot be explained.

To understand why this Trinity of Judaism cannot be explained is relatively easy when one is vaguely acquainted with the Jewish people, the Jewish religion, and the Jewish state. To be Jewish, one must have a Yiddisha mamma; to be Jewish, one must adhere to the Jewish religion; to be Jewish, one must have an affinity for the Jewish state. If it were as simple as that, the Jew or Israel could easily be explained. It is not all so simple!

There are many in the ethnic family of Israel who are in no way in affinity with either the Jewish religion or the State of Israel. There are many Israelis who are not only non-religious but are anti-religious as far as Judaism is concerned. There are some in the Jewish religion who are equally anti-Israel. They do not recognize the political or the religious validity of the State of Israel. On the other hand, the State of Israel does not recognize the validity of many who profess the Jewish religion: for example, the Conservative or Reform rabbinates. Even more paradoxical, the Israel government recognizes those of the Orthodox who oppose the government's validity, but does not recognize the Jewishness of the others who do support the validity of the present government. Some of the most devout people in Judaism are converts who are no part of the family of Israel in an ethnic sense. This is only to explain why the Trinity of Judaism—G-d, Torah, and Israel—defies explanation.

The principle might be stated again: "Some of it, plus the rest of it, equals all of it." The sum of it is that G-d, Torah, and Israel are one. This is the riddle of the mystique. Explain Israel and you have explained the G-d of Israel. Explain the G-d of Israel and you have explained the people of Israel. Then Israel will be no different from any other people, and their G-d will be no different from any other god.

The sum of that mystique is that Israel was a man named Jacob. The same night his name was changed from Jacob to Israel, he was "blessed," but he was also "crippled." (Gen. 32:24-32)

There is a certain dual paradox in the story. The name "Jacob" means "the one who takes the heel." He, the younger, would rule the elder Esau. Thus his name was changed to "Israel," meaning "G-d will rule," or "a prince with G-d."

"Crippled" and "blessed" in the same night, the patriarch Jacob had twelve sons who had families which became tribes and finally grew into the nation of Israel, the House of Jacob. The entire history of that nation, like the patriarch, lives in paradox. They are blessed as Israel, the "chosen people," but at the same time, they are "crippled" and cursed by the Gentile nations as the "suffering people."

The history of Israel staggers between the "blessed chosen people" and the "crippled suffering people." The Jew is much too close and too personally involved to give an objective definition of this paradox. The non-Jew is much too distant even to be sympathetic to Israel's suffering. Worse than the apathy of the Gentiles is the attitude that Israel deserves the suffering. From Pharaoh's Egypt to the present, all Israel's sufferings are from man, not from G-d!

As for the glory or honor due the Jew as the Chosen People and benefactor of man through many inventions, the Jew is seldom credited as a Jewish contributor but rather as an American, Russian, German, or English scientist.

Albert Einstein said: "If my theory of relativity is proven correct, Germany will claim me as a German and France will declare I am a citizen of the world. Should my theory prove untrue, France will say that I am a German and Germany will declare that I am a Jew."

Inseparable from the Jewish religion is the Hebrew language. Hebrew never died. It could never have become a dead language because it was necessary in Jewish worship. It ceased to be a language of the street, but it never ceased to be the language of worship. Hebrew is the oldest spoken language in the world. Yet today it is the street language of Israel and can therefore be called the newest (youngest) language in the world. Were an ancient prophet of Israel brought back and put on the streets of Jerusalem today, he could converse with

Albert Einstein

the people. No other nation can make that claim. The Hebrew language is as mystical as the people who speak it. It has survived as they have survived.

The Romans destroyed Judaea, the Temple, and the national state of Israel in the year 70 C. E. They were sure the Jews would vanish without their country or their Temple. The Jews were stronger in unity sixty years later than they were when they had the State and Temple. Hadrian, the Roman emperor, decided that to destroy the Jew, he had to destroy Judaism. The simple way to destroy Judaism was to destroy the Hebrew language. Therefore, he made it punishable by death for the Jews to speak, read, or teach the Holy Tongue. Destroy the Hebrew language and the Jewish soul would die. This decree brought about the Bar-Kochba revolt which led to the defeat of the Romans in Israel from 134-137 C. E. Hadrian could not stand the shame of that defeat, so he bankrupted Rome in quelling the Bar-Kochba rebellion. Though the Bar-Kochba forces were defeated in the land, they left Rome too weak to enforce the law against the Hebrew language. The tongue of the prophets survived with the sons of the prophets. The real victory was that Bar-Kochba's Hebrew lived on as the people of Israel lived on.

Like the people of Israel, the language of Israel is the eternal language. Rashi, the greatest of Talmudic commentators, who lived in the twelfth century, wrote a book on the Hebrew language proving that Hebrew was the original language of Adam. Linguists have discovered that many primitive languages have the same structure and many times similar words to the Hebrew. Israel is distinctively different from other nations in their historic language.

Through the vehicle of that holy language, the Jews gave the world the Bible. The Jewish scripture is the premise for both Christianity and the Islam as well as Judaism. Many other religions use it also to some degree. The language of Jesus and the original gospels was Hebrew. Except for Paul's writings to the Gentiles, the Greek testaments are full of Hebrew words and structure. Why is this so? What other nation on earth could say, "We gave you the work of G-d."? "What advantage then hath the Jew? Or what profit is there of circumcision? Much in every way: chiefly, because that unto them were committed the oracles of G-d." (Rom. 3:1-2)

Is it not ironic, then, that the nation that gave the world the Bible was put out of UNESCO in 1974 for desecrating the Holy City with their archaeological excavations? Was it not Israel which made the city holy from the beginning? Israel was expelled from the United Nations Educational, Scientific, and Cultural Organization for cleaning up an accumulation of twenty centuries of Arab and Christian Crusader garbage over the places that Jews had made holy through the conversations with G-d and acts of obedience to his Word.

Almost half of the scientific papers presented at UNESCO each year come from Jewish scientists. In 1968, over 12,000 papers were issued by UNESCO and over 4,000 of those were given by the state of Israel alone, not counting those by Jewish scientists elsewhere. Look at the leaders in the scientific, cultural and educational world. An astounding majority of them are Jewish. Israel demonstrates that to make enemies all one must do is have more, know more, or do more than those about them.

Israel is distinctively different from all other nations in that under the most severe oppression, the Jews have not only survived but have enjoyed much prosperity in the most adverse circumstances. "How do the Jews get ahead?" is a stock question by many non-Jews. Isaiah, the prophet, gave the answer: "Thus saith the Eternal One, thy Redeemer, the Holy One of Israel; I *am* the Eternal One thy Creator which teacheth thee to profit. . . ." (Is. 48:17) The ability of the Jew to profit has always been in spite of and not because of the circumstances that surround him. There has never been the need of a national association for the advancement of the Jews. Like Abraham's words to the king of Sodom: "...I will not take a thread even to a shoelatchet, and I will not take anything that is thine, lest thou shouldest say, 'I have made Abraham rich.'" (Gen. 14:23-24)

Those who try to play the wit of Laban against the Sons of Jacob learn as did Laban that the Jew is not to be outwitted. Like Shakespeare's Jew, Shylock, in the *Merchant of Venice*: "The villainy you teach me I will execute; and it shall go hard but I will better the instruction."

The mighty British provoked the Arabs to act in terrorism against the Jews during the British Mandate of Palestine. The "Stern Gang" and the Irgun slashed back at the British with their own methods of treachery. The British forces, of 80,000 and finally 200,000 strong, could not maintain control of their ambitious colonial Palestine. The British hoped to invoke a phobia upon the Jews that would force them to leave Palestine. It was, however, the British who left. If Chamberlain and Bevin did not know the Bible and the story of Laban, they should have known Shakespeare's Shylock.

No people have contributed more to mankind than have the Jews. Even in the adversity of circumstances, the G-d of Israel turns each defeat into a victory for his people. He shall transform each dishonor into a glory.

The corrupt government of France at the end of the nineteenth century sought to make a scapegoat out of a Jew in the Alfred Dreyfus case. That single Jew, though dishonored, exiled and imprisoned, made a full exposure of the debauchery of the French government. Alfred Dreyfus was in the end triumphant over those who sought to destroy him. At the very lowest ebb of the Dreyfus affair, another Jew, observing the Dreyfus situation, saw the necessity of a Jewish state. The Dreyfus tragedy inspired Theodor Herzl to begin the Zionist movement. Unlike any other nation, the wings of protective providence are spread always over the House of Israel.

Above all other distinctive differences, which are innumerable, the most important characteristic to remember is that Israel is singled out by the Almighty Eternal One as being totally separate from all other peoples: "Israel shall dwell alone and not be reckoned [thought of] as among the [Gentile] nations." (Num. 23:9)

If Israel should dwell alone and not be reckoned or thought of among the other Gentile nations, why then is Israel in the United Nations? Perhaps one weakness of modern Israel is that they are far too anxious to be like other nations.

Why are the people of Israel not to be reckoned among the other peoples of the world? In the Holy Tongue, עם-ישראל, ǤahM YisRahAL, is the people of Israel, while עמי העלם, ǤahMieY HaǤoHLahM, is the people of this world or age. The distinction between the two is lost in translation. The contrast of the *people of Israel* and the *people of this age or this world* is defined by Paul in II Corinthians 4:3-4. Here Paul refers to Satan as the "god of this world or age." The Gentile nations wear the brand of Satan. The "kingdoms of this world" that Satan made to pass before Jesus in the story of the temptation were truly Satan's to give. All nations are branded by Satan as his own except one. The maverick nation of Israel, unbranded, is Yis-RA-EL, which means "G-d will rule." Until the kingdoms of this age or world become the kingdoms of the Eternal One and his Messiah, Israel will remain a maverick nation among the Gentile nations. The Christian dispensation did not terminate the separateness of Israel. Israel continues to be distinctively different from all other nations in that "he shall dwell alone and not be reckoned [thought of] as among the Gentiles," is a timeless principle.

Israel is distinctively different from all other nations in that it is the only nation whose history was written before it happened. That is the Spirit of Prophecy. Israel's history is foretold, not in vague or general terms, but in minute detail description that defies human imagination. Other nations were spoken of by the prophets, but *only* as they related to Israel.

> Remember the days of old [study history]. Consider the years of many generations. Ask thy father, and he will show thee—thy elders and they will tell thee: When the MOST HIGH divided to the [Gentile] nations their inheritance, when he separated the sons of Adam [mankind], He set the bounds of the [Gentile] peoples [in space and time] according to the

number [chronological history] of the children of Israel. For the Eternal One's portion is his people [Israel]. Jacob is the lot of his inheritance. (Deut. 32:7-9)

Remember the former things of old [study history]: For I am G-d [the Creator] and there is none else [no other]; I am G-d [the Creator of time and space, matter and energy], and there is none like me, Declaring the end from the beginning and from ancient times the things that are not yet done. Saying, My Counsel shall stand, and I will do my pleasure. (Is. 46:9-10)

...The Holy One hath created Israel...[ye Gentile pagans] produce your cause saith the Eternal One, bring forth your strong arguments saith the King of Israel. Let them bring forth and show us what shall happen: Let them show the former things [from history] what they be [historically] that we may consider them; [much less] to know the latter end of them [the future] or [let the Gentiles] declare [to us] the things to come. Show us the things that are to come hereafter [if you pagan Gentiles are able]. (Is. 41:21-23)

We are taught that we should study history that we might learn from history how to make decisions for the present and future. History has proved that the only lesson we really learn from studying history is that we do not learn anything from history. History is a dumb, dull drum of the same old mistakes beaten over and over. History is an auger grinding out the same old mistakes time after time. History is the records of a lot of things, happening in a lot of places to a lot of people, at the same time, all the time, as told by the historians from their particular perspectives.

There is a certain missing core of thought in the human drama as it is presented by secular historians. History is not so much the facts of what happened but is the interpretation of what happened by the particular historian in each instance.

Read world history by an English historian and London is the center of the world. Time itself is determined by Greenwich, England. You might assume that Adam, David, and Jesus Christ were all British.

England's kings reigned by divine right because they believed themselves to be the direct line of David, King of Israel. David's stone foot stool is reputed to be under the British throne. Geologists have proven the stone is from Scotland and not found in Israel. The British consider themselves the Brit-Ish, or men of the covenant. Actually, ברית-איש, BRIT-ISH, means the *covenant of man*, not the *men of the covenant*—a very applicable mistake by the British Israelites.

World history, as reported by the American historian, reflects a Great White Father syndrome, that America is the savior of the world. What we see in British Israelism finds its counterpart in the attitude that America is the Zion of G-d.

Read the history of the world by Russian historians. Their attitude is no different from that of the British or American historian. They are all in some degree like the super race, the Aryans of German pseudo-history. So, history is not what happened but is an interpretation of what happened by a particular historian.

In all historical treatments, whether Russian, English, American, or German, the Jew is treated as a peripheral factor if not indeed a nuisance of history. There could be, though there has not been, an approach to world history whereby the Jew or Israel could be the radial axis rather than a peripheral factor. James Michener, in *The Source*, made such an application to one particular city, Makor, in Israel. If what Michener did with Tel Makor was applied to world history, the Jew would become the radial axis rather than the peripheral factor in the drama of human events. The history of all nations of all recorded time could be stretched out from their primordial beginnings until their disappearances alongside Israel's ancestral story and never touch the fore or hind scope of the history of Israel.

The correlation of world history around the romantic history of Israel will give that core of thought and meaningfulness that will never be attained without it. During the Dark Ages many kings' courts had no one who knew how to read or write except Jewish scribes who kept the records. No other people have kept such a minute account of history as have the Jews, not only of their own history but also of those about them. To the Jew there is a certain sanctity to history that deserves a reverent care. Recorded history, as we know it, generally speaking, is what happened where the Jews were. Where the Jews were not, we have little to go on as far as historic records are concerned.

The history of the world through the historic eyes of the Jew would eliminate much ethno-centric attitudes in the accounts. The Jew, by his perspective, could stand back a few steps farther and be more international in his surveillance of history. To illustrate this, the Jews do not calculate their calendar with Moses or Abraham, but rather with the creation of Adam: *anno homo*.

Not only has the Jew been a witness of history, he has been a part of it. As Mark Twain said, "...he saw them all, and beat them all, and is now what he always was...." Coincidence and chance cannot explain or excuse the repetition of pivotal instances at the intersections of time and events when a Jewish person by word or deed turned the tide of events in the course of history.

History has sought with great effort to ignore the Jew. In most cases his appearance and presence at those particular instances of pivotal importance were totally unplanned and providential. He went, not sent. He came, not called. He served greatly. He was unrewarded and without honor. He said little, passed on, and was forgotten.

The Jew's role in history is like a pencil wasted and ground away on the pages of time. Yet, through that sacrifice to nothingness, the very record itself is created. His indelible image remains immovable.

The Jew's role in history is like a stitch in the seam of a garment. He appears and disappears and reappears with repeated masterful design and direction. Like the stitch, much effort is put into keeping him from being seen. He is unnoted, tucked under, and pressed away. Yet, it is he who holds the entire structure together. Where he fails or is weakened or destroyed, the whole system suffers collapse. Where he is strong and can freely function in his purpose, the entire system prospers. As Gentile nations age, their garments, too, grow old and shapeless. As the vesture of a vagabond, they rag out to threadbare nothingness. They rend in the midst of themselves and give way to looseness. Look closely at these garments and you will note that the stitches are ever so strong.

History robbed the Jew of his kingdom and left him scattered and wandering. Nations have used him, abused him, tucked him under, pressed him away. Yet, his appearing and disappearing is all part of the Master's design.

When he was victorious, history denied him honor as a Jew. Like Benjamin Disraeli, who by sheer providence of the admiral's illness, was temporarily in command of the British fleet. Under his charge, they met the Russian fleet which was enroute to the conquest of Palestine from the Turks. Disraeli led the British in the battle of the Dardanelles and defeated the Russians' first attempt to rule the Land of Israel.

The British smothered Disraeli's Jewishness by knighting him the Lord of Beaconsfield. History neglects to credit him, along with the Rothschilds and Sassoons, for the purchase of the land on which to build the Suez Canal. The Suez was the brain child of a Jew. Jewish money built the passage that has been denied to Israeli ships and cargo for the past quarter century. The Jew again has been raped by the Gentile nations. No mention is ever made that the canal was originally Jewish.

History has raped the Jew, as a Jew, of honor and reputed him as dishonorable. History has exposed his secret parts. The Jew has despised the indignity and shame of this mocking exposure. History has accepted the Jew's mercy, but has denied him justice. History has acted unwisely toward the Jew and has not sought to understand his plight. History has stolen the king's crown and used it for the coronation of thieves. While the true princes of the House of David sat in solitude behind ghetto walls, composing masterful volumes of sacred literature, ignorant, common, illiterate barbarians sat upon thrones as the masters who demanded obeisance and tribute from the regal Jews.

American historians have done no better toward the Jew. Ask any ten people at random in this country these three questions: first, who invented the automobile? Second, who invented the telephone? Lastly, who wrote the original draft of the Constitution and drew the national seal of state of the United States? The stock answers almost always come in that order as Henry Ford, Alexander Graham Bell, and Thomas Jefferson, or occasionally, James Madison.

Henry Ford did not invent the automobile. Bell did not invent the telephone and neither Jefferson nor Madison was the father of the Constitution or drew the National Seal of State.

When little Henry Ford was kicking about in knicker-bottom britches under hazy skies (that was before ecologists called it air pollution), Pappy Ford would say, "Henry! Get that shovel and scoop up that pollution problem your pony created in the neighbor's front yard." Can't you just see little Henry performing that environmental protection task with full disgust? Surely he thought, "It will be good when everyone can drive one of those horseless carriages those Daimler people in Germany are building...Someday I am going to make it so everybody can drive a vehicle that will eliminate this horse pollution problem." Henry Ford did develop the "Bull Run" assembly system that made automobiles cheap enough for everyone to own, but he had nothing to do with the invention of the automobile!

The development of the automobile began with the development of the internal combustion engine. A German Jew named Otto developed the first stage which operated on coal dust. His co-worker, another Jew named Rudolf Diesel, improved the motor by the coal oil injection system.

The Daimler family, relatives of Otto and Diesel, were in the logging business. They installed an Otto-Diesel engine on a logging wagon to help the horses pull the heavy loads from the forest. To their dismay, the engines did not need the horses' help. The first auto-trucks had a wheel and handlebars like a bicycle on the wagon tongue to guide the vehicle.

Gottlieb Daimler and Benz, an associate of Otto and Diesel, merged and began building the auto wagons. Benz's daughter wanted a small engine built for her buggy, so there went Mercedes Benz in her horseless carriage.

Henry Ford did not invent the automobile, nor was he the first to manufacture cars in America. The first automobile manufacturer in this country was the Steinway piano company. (That sounds kosher!)

Henry Ford had a real head for mass production. He sold several Jewish financiers on his ability, and they financed him in the establishment of the Ford Motor Company. Once Ford was strong enough financially, he began to purge the Jews from the corporation. His methods were merciless. Ford took the pseudo docu-

Rudolf Diesel *Nicolaus August Otto*

ments of "The Protocols of the Learned Elders of Zion," which the Russian czar had concocted against the Russian Jews for the pogroms, and published them in his newspaper, "The Dearborn Independent." The lengthy series, entitled "The International Jew," was a rehash of all the bigotry of the Dark Ages against the Jews.

Henry Ford took a Jewish invention, borrowed Jewish money, sacked the Jews not only of their money but had the audacity to take credit for the invention of the automobile.

Alexander Graham Bell invented the telephone just as Henry Ford invented the automobile. Philipp Reis, a German Jew, invented the telephone in 1860. His associate, another Jew named Greenberg, improved the invention and brought it to America for manufacturing and merchandising. A Jewish financier in Cincinnati named Loth sent Greenberg to Bell with his device. When Bell learned that Greenberg was ignorant of American patent laws, he filed a patent under his own name. Loth and Greenberg took the case to the Supreme Court in the Loth-Greenberg vs. Bell appeal. The Supreme Court upheld the Loth-Greenberg claim and made Bell pay a token reparation for stealing the device. For many years following, Bell Telephone Company was anti-Semitic in their employment practices.

American history books are still teaching that Alexander Graham Bell invented the telephone. Why do not the historians write it correctly...a German Jew named Reis invented the telephone; Greenberg improved it, and Alexander Graham Bell stole it!

"America is a Christian nation." "Our Pilgrim fathers came to this country seeking religious freedom for everyone." "Our founding fathers were God-fearing Christian men." These statements are just as true as the Ford and Bell stories. America is not a Christian nation. The word Christian or mention of Jesus Christ does not appear in our founding documents. The Pilgrims who came sought religious freedom for themselves but not for others. Each colony was established as a parochial settlement. Pennsylvania was the Quaker colony, Maryland was Catholic, Massachusetts was Puritan, and so on. Rhode Island was the only colony which granted total freedom of worship and separation of church and state.

In 1636, Roger Williams, a Baptist missionary to the Indians, had been exiled as a heretic from Massachusetts. He went to non-inhabited Rhode Island and applied for colonial charter in 1638. When it was granted, Rhode Island was chartered as a Baptist colony. Roger Williams made a trip to England to clarify the unusual status of his idea of separation of church and state. Finally, in 1663, King Charles II issued a charter for Rhode Island as a United Religious Free Colony with Providence as its capital city.

As providence would have it, during Roger Williams' visit to England in 1640, he chanced to meet a group of Jewish refugees who had come from Spain through Holland in search of religious freedom. They were enroute to South America hoping to find freedom of worship in the vastness of that continent. Roger Williams welcomed them to his proposed United Religious Free colony.

In 1641, their ship arrived at New Amsterdam. Upon their inquiry of transportation to providence, the Duke of York, characteristic of the Dutch, welcomed the Jews to stay in New Amsterdam and to practice Judaism without hindrance from the government.

For the next one hundred years in the New World, the Jews played a vital role in the development of commerce and industry. Since these were Sephardic Jews, most of their business contacts were in the Mediterranean countries and through Venice to Russia. Their major industry was the fur trade with the cold countries of Europe. They had no ties with England and carried on their commerce with the French Rothschild and Sassoon families of the Mediterranean world.

It was in this natural course of events that England was more or less left out of the rapidly growing market. The British crown had no control over trade in the Mediterranean world. When the British began to levy trade restrictions and taxes against these non-imperial transactions, the economies of both the colonies and France with the Mediterranean trade basin were threatened.

Simultaneous with these restrictions in commerce came talk of putting all religious affairs in colonial America under the jurisdiction of the Church of England. The Jews had been expelled from England in the twelfth century and were not permitted to return until Cromwell. The Jews in America saw not only their commerce threatened but also their right to worship and perhaps their very existence. The break with England was inevitable.

A personal friend of George Washington called on him with a proposal for an American revolution against the mighty British Empire. Unlike most revolutionists, this man had an idea, a concept of Talmudic origin: "One nation united under one G-d with freedom and liberty for every citizen," a concept of democracy so free that the republic would be the servant rather than the master of its people. To show his sincerity, the friend offered his entire fortune of 600,000 British sterling to begin the American Revolution.

Who was that man? What have the American historians written about him? Not until two hundred years later did the United States Postal Department issue a commemorative stamp to "Haym Salomon, financial hero of the American Revolution, businessman and broker who was responsible for raising most of the money needed to finance the American Revolution and later save the nation from collapse."

Haym Salomon did far more than put his own fortune into the American Revolution. He made a trip to France and met with his business associates, the Sassoons and Rothschilds. They raised an additional three and one-half million British sterling, or its equivalent, to finance the American cause.

While in France, Salomon got orders from the French government for LaFayette to tender the French arsenal

FINANCIAL HERO
Businessman and broker Haym Salomon was responsible for raising most of the money needed to finance the American Revolution and later to save the new nation from collapse.

to the Revolutionary army of General Washington. He personally delivered those orders to LaFayette.

Haym Salomon also solicited every able-bodied Jewish man to volunteer to fight with Washington's army. Many Jews fought in the American Revolution and soon afterward organized the first American veterans' organization, "The Jewish War Veterans."

The first draft of the Constitution and the Great American Seal were drafted by Haym Salomon. His statement of "one nation under one G-d" was too monotheistic for many trinitarians. It was modified to "one nation under G-d." His concept of freedom for all and justice for all made no allowances for slavery. It took almost another century for that to be reinstated. The conspicuous absence of the word "Christian" or mention of "Jesus Christ" was indeed uniquely different from the Christian countries of Europe of that period.

Salomon's document also included the Great American Seal. It was rejected, so a committee of Franklin, Jefferson and Adams was appointed to come up with a simpler and more acceptable seal of state. After fifteen years of quibbling, Haym Salomon's seal was approved with some modifications. The original seal was lettered in Hebrew. There was a movement at the time to make a total break with England and adopt Hebrew as the national language of the new country. In the revision, the Hebrew was translated to Latin.

The late Rabbi Jacob Friend, a Lithuanian Jew who spent many years in China between the two world wars before moving to Atlanta, Georgia, made some interesting observations about the Kabbalistic symbols in the Great American Seal of Haym Salomon.

If you will take a dollar bill and notice the American Seal on the backside of the note, you will see the dual circles of the pyramid and the eagle.

Rabbi Friend pointed out the significance of the eye in the middle of the triangle over the pyramid. The triangle is the symbol of infinity. The priestly blessing of the Jews is pronounced while the rabbi forms a triangle with his hands.

An aleph א inside the triangle stood for En-Sof, or אין-סוף, PieYN-CoHF, meaning the Incomprehensible One. The letter 'ayin, or ₲aYiN, ע̄, could replace the letter aleph as ע and drastically change the meaning. The name of the letter 'ayin, ע, spelled out, is עין. The word means an eye, and was a circle, as an "O," in old Hebrew. It is made as ʊ in Hebrew script. Both resemble an eye.

A natural spring or fountain in the earth was referred to as Ma'Ayin, מעין, which means "from the place that the eye of the ground is weeping." Thus, where א meant the Incomprehensible One, the ע meant the Fountainhead of all Comprehension. The letter 'Ayin was replaced by the eye on the National Seal.

Above the eye and triangle is the phrase *annuit coeptis*. Rabbi Friend pointed out that the phrase had no coherent meaning in Latin, but was a Latinized transliteration of Ayin-Sof, referring to the Incomprehensible One who became the Fountainhead of all Comprehension.

The empty space between the triangle and pyramid is that distance between the Infinite and the finite of human comprehension. A close look will indicate that the triangle is not directly above the pyramid but is at a yonder distance, appearing out of heaven itself. The aura of the *Shekinah* Glory shines from behind the triangle representing the radiance or aura of the glory of G-d.

The pyramid itself is a key in Kabbalistic application. A pyramid is a quadrant of equilateral triangles. The *Mogen David*, or Star of David, is two such triangles interposing, forming a six-pointed star. The Kabbalists mapped the heavens with two interlocking pyramids like the Star of David. Josephus relates that the pyramids of Egypt were built by the Jews in their forced labor of Egyptian bondage. Until today, the pyramids hold many secrets unknown to modern science.

At the corners of the pyramid are the two small trees representing the Tree of Knowledge and the Tree of Life. The symbols are commonly used in Jewish synagogues today.

Haym Salomon was most astute in his use of Kabbalistic symbolism in this work of art. Notice at the base of the pyramid are the Roman numerals MDCCLXXVI for "1776." Under that in Latin is NOVUS ORDO SECLORUM, meaning the "new secular order." According to Rabbi Friend, this was translated to Latin from the Hebrew phrase: להבסידר החדשה של הבעל העולם. The translation is "to the new order of the master confederacy of the Gentile world." The Hebrew, like Latin, gives a numeric value to each letter in its alphabet. The total numeric value, or the gematria of that Hebrew phrase, is also 1776.

Notice on the opposite side of the seal is the eagle. The eagle is an apocalyptic symbol of a great world empire which shall arise in the last days. The Book of Daniel, chapter seven, and the Book of II Esdras, chapters eleven and twelve, deal with this symbol of that great world empire.

It might be noted here that the Book of Daniel does not appear in the prophetic books of the Jewish canon. It is placed near the end of the Jewish Bible. Daniel was not placed with the prophetic books because it is apocalyptic rather than prophetic in its literary style. The Book of Daniel is the Apocalypse of the Jewish Bible as the Book of Revelation is the Apocalypse of the Christian's New Testament. It is impossible to understand Revelation and its symbolism unless one understands Daniel and his symbolism.

Daniel saw the eagle in connection with the four beasts of Daniel 7. The four Beast Empires which arose out of the "sea" of humanity were symbolic as the Lion, the Bear, the Leopard, and the non-descript amalgamated Beast. In that vision these beasts did not represent the ancient world of Babylon, Media-Persia, Greece and Rome as is the usual interpretation, but four kingdoms of the end times.

What great world empire has arisen in modern history having a lion for its national emblem? What empire has arisen with the bear as its national emblem? What empire used the leopard and Maltese Cross as its national emblem until they were forbidden to do so at the Treaty of Versailles?

The lion is the emblem of Great Britain, the bear of Russia, the leopard was the emblem of the Reich of Wilhelm I and Kaiser Bill. The Third Reich was forbidden to use the leopard.

In Daniel 7:4, "he was beholding the Lion, and as he watched, Eagles' wings grew out of the Lion and plucked [or pulled themselves away] from the Lion." This revolution of the Eagle being plucked away destroyed the imperialistic nature of the Lion and "he was made to stand on his feet as a man and a man's heart was given to it."

Haym Salomon saw the American Revolution as the eagle breaking away from the lion of Great Britain. He used that symbol as the signet of the master confederacy of the United States.

Above the eagle's head on the seal is what was originally a thirteen-pillared cloud. The *Shekinah* Glory dwelt on the Mercy Seat in the Holy of Holies on a cloud of thirteen pillars. This thirteen-pillared cloud was with Israel in the wilderness as a cloud by day and a pillar of fire by night. (Ex. 13:21-22) To the superstitious Gentiles, thirteen is an unlucky number. To the Jews, it is the opposite. Thirteen is the number of perfect unity. There were thirteen tribes of Israel. A Jewish boy has his Bar Mitzvah at age thirteen. Seven times each nineteen years, the Jewish calendar has thirteen months. These seven years with thirteen months keep the lunar calendar in perfect unity with the solar system. There are thirteen rows of stone in the pyramid, thirteen leaves on the olive branch in the eagle's right talon, thirteen arrows in his left, thirteen stripes on the shield on the eagle, and thirteen stars in the cloud representing the thirteen colonies.

Look closely at the five-pointed stars representing the thirteen colonies and you will note that they form the star of David, or the *Mogen David*, meaning the Shield of David. This star was on David's shield, but it did not originate with David. The tradition of the Jewish star goes all the way back to the exodus from Egypt in the Jewish year 2448, about thirty-three centuries ago.

The *matza*, unleavened bread of Passover, was originally baked in triangles. The Jews continued this tradition until the early Dark Ages when the Christians insisted it was symbolic of the Holy Trinity. In reaction to this argument, the Jews simply began baking the *matzo* round. Not until mechanized baking did they begin to make square *matzos*. Many Orthodox Jews still use the round *matzo* at Passover.

The Talmud specifies that the three *matzo* crackers should be laid in a particular order before the father. The first, or bottom *matzo*, should be turned away from him. The second, or middle *matzo*, should be turned toward the father; and the third, or top *matzo*, should also be turned away from the father. The father, in opening the *Seder* service, receives the middle *matzo* that is pointing toward him. He breaks it, giving half to the family and wrapping and hiding the other half as the *Afikoman*.

How could round or square *matzos* be turned toward or away from the father? One looking down on that ancient Passover plate with the three triangular *matzos* in juxtaposition would see a six-pointed star. Another legend tells of David and his men in flight from the armies of King Saul, and they took refuge in the cave behind the waterfall at Ein Gedi. Once David and his men had hidden in the cave, a large spider began to spin a web from the top center of the cave and to each side forming a six-pointed star. When the soldiers of Saul came to the cave and saw the spider's web over the entrance they passed on their way assuming no one had entered the cave. Hence, for this reason David chose the *matzo* star for his coat of arms. The star on David's shield, as on the flag of Israel today, recalls Israel's history all the way back to the Exodus. Every Gentile who ever carried a dollar bill with Haym Salomon's seal has a little reminder of the American prosperity..."I will bless them that bless thee and curse them that curse thee and in thee will all the Gentile nations of the earth be blessed." The Star of David is the national seal of Israel's political economy, while the seven golden candlesticks, or menorah, represent Israel's spiritual or religious economy.

Now, take your dollar bill and turn it upside down. Place your thumb covering the eagle's head, and there the shield becomes the menorah, or seven candlesticks, of Israel's spiritual economy and the official Seal of State for Modern Israel.

Moving the thumb over the shield completely leaves the nine-feathered tail representing the nine flames of the Hanukkah Menorah.

In the right talon of the eagle is the olive branch. Since Noah's flood, it has been the plant symbol for mercy and peace. In Kabbalah the Adam Kadmon was the divine primordial man after whose image Adam was created. In the sphere of his right hand was mercy and might, while the sphere of his left hand was judgment and war, noted in the left talon as the arrows.

In addition to Rabbi Friend's observations on the Kabbalism by Haym Salomon on the National Seal, it might be noted that there are over one hundred twenty Hebrew letters on the texture of the pyramid itself. Whether it is by chance or not, the line patterns of the stones of the pyramids and the texture of the surfaces form certain Hebrew words and letters. The texture of the left side of the second row of stone from the top faintly spells the word ציון, or "TSiYoHN" or "Zion." The third and fourth stone lines spell יהוה, or the *tetragrammaton* for the "Eternal One." In the lower part the letters "Shin," ש, "Yod," י, and "Mem," מ, stand out distinctly.

In the Zohar, the Kabbalistic commentary, the story of creation relates how the Creator uttered creation into being by the Word of his mouth. As the sounds came forth, it was the Torah whose letters were formed by the moving tongues of light. The tongues of white light formed the letters and the tongues of black light produced the sounds. Upon the utterance of Torah, the flames of black and white light brought creation into being.

Rabbi Nahum relates that every word of the Torah was breathed from God. Even if a word is misspelled—and there are misspelled words in the Torah—the misspelling itself has a particular interpretation. Even the smallest letter is of greatest significance and every mark on every letter has a possible interpretation. When the Messiah comes, said Rabbi Nahum, he will give the interpretation of the white spaces between the letters. It was to this that Jesus alluded when he said, "Every jot and tittle or every Yod and Tahg, of the Torah must be fulfilled."

When the pyramid is magnified, one can see how Haym Salomon worked in over one hundred twenty Hebrew characters as white spaces between the lines of the pyramid.

The lines of the stones running vertically and horizontally form other Hebrew letters and words. When the pyramid is inverted, the arrangement is such that what seemed to be meaningless lines in the vertical position form another assortment of Hebrew letters.

No attempt will be made to make an interpretation as to what these Hebrew letters mean. Unless one is versed in the forty-two principles of Kabbalistic hermeneutics, the words themselves or the letter combinations will appear rather meaningless. The objective of pointing out these things is simply to call attention to the "Lion's Paw" in the Jewish origin of the Great Seal of the United States of America.

After twice saving America from financial collapse, Haym Salomon died in his mid-forties, a penniless man. The Third Congress acknowledged the debt to the family and friends of Haym Salomon, but our first national debt has never been paid!

The U. S. A. furnishes military arsenal to her small allies at no charge. This is especially true in the case of the Middle Eastern Arab countries and the Near East. On the other hand, Israel pays hard cash for the military wardrobe bought from the U. S. A. Noteworthy is the fact that from 1947 to 1967, the United States had an arms embargo against and would not sell any offensive weapons to Israel. Yet the United States totally equipped the Jordanian legion. Richard Nixon was the first president to deliver any offensive weapons to the State of Israel, and that for hard cash. The great white father syndrome of Uncle Sam playing Santa Claus to all the nations in the world, except the one nation that made Christmas possible, is quite ironic. Compound this with the fact that Congress affirmed that this country owed the people of Israel a national debt incurred through Haym Salomon who raised from world Jewry three and a half million British sterling to finance the Revolutionary War.

Let us consider this a Federal Reserve note, invested by the Israeli family in 1776. If we make an estimated assumption of the mean average of the British pound being a minimum of $5 exchange, that would mean that the principal value of the loan was $17,500,000. If this sum were considered an investment at four percent simple interest in 1776, the national debt of the United States of America to the nation of Israel in 1976 amounts to forty-five billion dollars. This figure is based on only a mean minimum average. An audit by a CPA would possibly push the figure much higher.

The U. S. government should not ignore this debt. Perhaps a recollection of what happened to the delinquent accounts of Laban to Jacob and the pharaoh's to the brothers of Joseph should remind us that there is, in addition to an Internal Revenue agent, a greater Eternal Revenue agent. G-d keeps good books in the accounts receivable as far as his people are concerned.

Haym Salomon, a Sephardic Jew, financed the American Revolution and later saved the young country from monetary collapse. He drew the National Seal and wrote the original draft to the Constitution. Did your history teacher in high school and college teach you that? Was there any mention of Haym Salomon, Loth and Greenberg, or Otto and Diesel in your textbooks? Were you taught that America is a Christian nation and that our founding fathers were G-d fearing Christian men? Did you think Henry Ford invented the automobile and Bell invented the telephone?

Maybe Uncle Josh Billings had it summed up right when he said: "Man's ignorance ain't cause he ain't ever learned nutten, it's cause he learned too many things that jes' ain't so."

Somewhere, if not everywhere, historians have overtly and deliberately suppressed the Jew. One popular encyclopedia, in naming the people who pioneered atomic energy, did not mention Albert Einstein.

Few people realize that Isaac Newton was a Jew who refused knighthood early in life because it required baptism. He was later knighted without baptism. His religious writings were rejected by the Church of England as being heresies. Sir Manyard Keynes branded Newton as a monotheist of the school of RaMBaM, or Maimonedes. What a joke; Newton was a Kabbalist. RaMBaM was a philosopher. Newton's theological books are rich in both Jewish and Christian thought. It also took a special dispensation from parliament in order for him to be a fellow to teach at Cambridge because he was a Jew who did not believe in the Holy Trinity. He was never even a teacher or master, much less a professor at the university. Why? Because Isaac Newton was a Jew. During his life, very, very few Jews even had the privilege of living in England.

Perhaps it is time to let the Jew be the radial axis rather than a peripheral factor in history. If not, let us stop abridging him of credit and honor as a Jew. This is not to insinuate that every great scientist, artist, musician and philanthropist was Jewish but it might be interesting to know how many were. Proportionate to their number, no people have contributed so much to humanity and gone so unrewarded.

In the same way secular historians have robbed the Jew of credit, honor and due respect, the Christian historians and theologians have robbed Jesus of Nazareth of his Jewishness and made him a Christian. Not only Jesus, but his parents and disciples have been treated as Christians rather than as Jews. There is no statement in the texts of the New Testament that suggests that they, or even Paul the apostle, ever considered themselves to be anything but Orthodox, observant Jews in the most traditional sense of the meaning. They never called themselves Christians, nor were they ever called Christians. The term Christian was coined at Antioch (Acts 11:26), and was only applied to Gentiles who came to the obedience of the faith in Jesus Christ.

The earliest traces of this theological stripping Jesus of his Jewishness are seen at the middle of the second century of the Common Era. That was about a century after the destruction of the Temple at Jerusalem. The destruction of the Temple and Jewish state was necessary for the rift to come between Judaism and Christianity.

The earliest person to advocate the divorce was Clement of Alexandria. His views toward the Jews were expressed in his pseudo "Epistle of Barnabas to the Church at Corinth." Clement made every effort to get that document into the New Testament canon. The church fathers without exception rejected its canonicity. Clement advocated the patterning of the church structure like that of the Roman government and making it a political force in the world. With the coming of Constantine, that idea became a reality. The church had not only a polity like the Roman government, with an imperial head and senate, the church also became Christendom, or Christ's kingdom, in a political sense. With Constantine, the church became the Roman government.

The basic teaching of the "Epistle of Barnabas to the Church at Corinth" was the embryo of replacement theology.

Replacement theology is the concept that the New Testament replaced the Old Testament, Christianity replaced Judaism, the church replaced the synagogue, Sunday replaced the Sabbath, the Christian replaced the Jew as the Chosen People, and the spiritual kingdom of heaven in Rome replaced the earthly kingdom of Israel in Jerusalem.

The Roman Catholic Church may have invented this concept and is truly the mother of all who adhere to it, but Protestantism became even more vicious in the expression and advocacy of these dogmas. Since the Second Vatican Council, the Catholic Church has done more in an earnest attempt to correct the replacement misconception than all other denominations combined.

In spite of some weaknesses in the Vatican II document itself, the spirit of the decree and its effect on the church's attitude have far excelled the letter. It has motivated hundreds of Catholic priests, nuns, bishops, professors, and laymen to genuinely make every effort to bring the church back to its primal relation with the Jewish community. These people and their efforts are to be commended and encouraged. The path they are pioneering is at times a very lonely one. Any Christian, Catholic or Protestant, who chooses to "suffer reproach with the people of G-d" may sometimes find his solitude more severe than did the hermits.

Under the pretense of the back-to-the-Bible theme, Protestantism in general, and evangelical Christianity in particular, are regressing in their reformation all the way back to the middle of the Dark Ages. They have gotten no more than halfway back to the New Testament era. And, in their "zeal for the Lord," they have chosen methods that have resulted in just the opposite effect from that which they claim to have intended. To illustrate this, notice the terminology they use: "Christian crusade," "crusade for Christ," "youth crusade," "revival crusade," "freedom crusade," and so on. One director of a crusade related what a shocking awakening it was for their organization when they set up operations in Arab countries. They had to drop the word "crusade." The word crusade is a bloody, monstrous word to the Arab world. James Michener's *The Source* relates the atrocities executed by the holy crusaders on the Moslems and Jews alike in the name of Christ. "Kill a Jew for Jesus" was the crusaders' slogan.

The New Testament never stated or suggested any such replacement theology. Translators added words to the original text that would indicate so, but such statements are absent in the Greek texts. For instance, Hebrews, chapters nine and ten, plainly develop the concept of replacement theology but an addition of the word "covenant" had to be inserted for the texts to indicate so in the de-Judaizing of Jesus.

What the translators did not accomplish in putting replacement theology into the New Testament, the commentators without a doubt did accomplish in their "expositions" of these key passages. For example, Hebrews 10:9: "Then said he, lo I come to do thy will, O G-d. He taketh away the first that he might establish the second." Commentators from the medieval monks to the modern translators and theologians teach that that passage means that God's will in Jesus was to take away the "old" Jewish system and establish the new Christian system. The Greek word translated "taketh away" is *anaireo*, which means "to slay," or "to kill." That would make the argument even stronger for the replacement theologian except for one consideration: the context is not dealing with the old "covenant" and the new "covenant." The context is discussing *Yom Kippurim*, or the Day of

Atonement. Only on one day a year was the Golden Censer placed behind the Second Veil, or in the Holy of Holies, and that day was *Yom Kippurim*.

Exodus 25 and 37 indicate that the Golden Censer was ordinarily placed in the Holy Place, not the Holy of Holies. It sat between the Menorah and the Table of Shewbread *in front of* the Second Veil. Hebrews 9:4 describes it as being behind the Second Veil in the Holy of Holies, indicating the special occasion. Because of a lack of knowledge of Judaism, however, the commentators argue that this reference contains a mistake, or that a Gentile who did not know the Jewish law wrote Hebrews. Therefore, they insinuate that Paul or Barnabas certainly could not have written the epistle. Since the context of Hebrews 9-10 is first the Tabernacle and second, the Temple, they continue and insert the word covenant so that the latter covenant in Christ replaced the former covenant of Israel. There is no such indication in the text.

Hebrews 9:4 does not contain a mistake! It refers particularly to the censer's special location in the Holy of Holies on *Yom Kippurim*, the one day of the year on which the censer is moved from in front of the veil. (Lev. 16:12) On that one day the high priest offered a bull for himself and two goats for the people. (Heb. 9:13; Lev. 16:1-34) On the Day of Atonement the two goats, *not* the two covenants, were taken. The first lots fell on the goat of the Eternal One; the latter lots fell on *Azazel Yisrael*, the scapegoat for Israel. The high priest "killeth the first goat," not the first covenant, and the second goat, not the new covenant, was taken away and established, or kept alive, as the scapegoat of Israel.

The church needs a reformation but not back to the crusader's period. The church needs a reformation all the way back to Antioch. The Antioch church in Acts *never* sent any missionaries to the Jews. If they had any questions about what Jesus said or meant, they usually wrote two letters to Jerusalem. One was addressed to the Apostles and the other to the Elders. Not the elders of the church but the Elders, or Sanhedrin, of Israel, as reflected in Acts, chapter fifteen.

Before replacement theology could be put into the text and commentaries of the New Testament, the Jewishness of Jesus and the Apostles had to be taken out. To begin carrying out that deletion, theologians began to emphasize Jesus' deity to the point of denying his humanity. Once his distinctive humanity was diminished, they could reshape it into any human figure they desired as long as it was not a Jewish human figure.

The Holy Family and the Apostles never again became quite human. The halo or some other mark of angelness had to be there. DeViolet Bernhardt, a noted art critic, points out that in most of the pictures painted of Jesus, a woman was the model of the body, especially the hands and feet. Make him a woman, but never make him a Jew!

It is not true that Jesus *was* a Jew! Jesus *was not* a Jew at all! To say that Jesus *was* a Jew implies one of two things. First, it suggests that he once was a Jew but that when he began his ministry, he ceased to be a Jew and became a Christian. Or, it suggests that he was a Jew who ceased to be. Jesus was not a Jew! Jesus is a Jew. Ethnically? Yes, he is a Jew! Religiously? Yes, he is a Pharisee in the strictest sense! Nationally? Yes! He is a Sabra Israeli! Jesus is not only human, he is Jewish!

A Christian minister once mockingly said to a rabbi, "Say, Rabbi, could I ask you a question?"

"Surely," replied the rabbi.

"Tell me, what are you Jewish rabbis going to do when your Messiah comes and you discover that he is Jesus Christ?"

"Well, Reverend, you answer my question and I'll answer yours. What are you ministers going to do when Jesus Christ comes back and you discover he is a Jewish rabbi?"

The Jewishness of Jesus, like the Jews in history, has been deprived of its rightful place. Also, like the stitch in the garment, Jesus' Jewishness just appears and disappears with masterful design. Yet, where his Jewishness appears, every effort has been made by the replacement theological tailors to tuck it under and press it away. His Jewishness, like the Jew, has been used and abused, then suppressed to nothingness. Yet, like the Jew, the Jewishness of Jesus has survived, at least in some part. Perhaps it is that surviving part of his Jewishness that holds the whole system intact. Like the Jew, the radial axis of world history, the Jewishness of Jesus is the radial axis of understanding the New Testament. Despite all efforts to ignore it, his Jewishness is still there. Let us note a few overt efforts by the replacement translators to disguise it.

In the Greek text of the Gospels, Jesus was addressed fourteen times as Rabbi. Rabbi was not a title used generally but was used specifically to those who had received a *smechah*, or ordination. No man was called Rabbi without that ordination. To receive that honor, one had to complete the necessary training in a *yeshevah*, or Jewish seminary. There was a level before ordination at which one could be licensed to be a teacher of the Law, but he was not a rabbi. He was a *rabbe*. Only on full ordination could one be called rabbi.

There is a degree above being a rabbi. Once a rabbi is esteemed above his fellow rabbis to the point that the rabbis are looking up to him as a rabbi of rabbis, he is called the *rebbe*. Above the *rebbe* is only one. That is the Chief Rabbi of Israel. He is called the *Rav*. The Sages of Israel, that is, those who stood head and shoulders above all in their generation and their greatness extolled forever, are called the *Rabonim*. Few men were ever called Rabon until after their deaths.

The first thing the replacement monks, translators, and commentators did to disguise Jesus as a Jewish rabbi was to translate the word rabbi into "master." Nine of the fourteen times Jesus was addressed as rabbi, the translators translated the word rabbi as master, or Lord. The meaning is not the same.

Those places and contexts they did not mistranslate, they smothered with erroneous explanations. For example, in the beginning of the book of John (1:37-38), Jesus was addressed as Rabbi. Notice what happened: "And the two disciples [of John the Baptist] heard him [John the Baptist] speak, they followed Jesus. Then Jesus turned and saw them following, and saith unto them, What seek ye? They said unto him, *Rabbi* (which is to say, being interpreted, *Master*). . . ."

Now, notice in the text the parentheses around the words "(which is to say, being interpreted, Master)." What appears in these parentheses are not the words of the Apostle John, but is a monastic note to excuse Jesus having been called Rabbi. After the monks added the words to the text of John, all translators faithfully translated the monks' notes as the very word of G-d.

First, John would not have had to explain what the simple, common, ordinary usual literal meaning of rabbi was to the people to whom he was writing. Every literate person in the civilized world knew what a rabbi was. That was why the monks had to smother it with a non-Jewish explanation.

Second, if John had wanted to use the proper word for "master," and the two disciples had intended to address Jesus as "master," they would have used the word *Adon* or *Adonee*, the Hebrew word for master, or my master. Rabbi is the Hebrew word for rabbi, and never is rabbi interchanged as an allomorph with *Adon* or master.

Jesus was many times called *Adon* or *Adonee* in the New Testament, which the replacement people translated "Lord" rather than "Master." The same word was used in addressing others besides Jesus. It simply meant master or mister, except in probably a more restricted sense than it is used today.

It is also noteworthy that in addition to being addressed Rabbi, Jesus was also addressed as *Raboni* by the blind man in Mark 10:51. But here, the word was translated "Lord" instead of "Raboni," or "exalted Rebbe." This is another overt coincidence of de-Judaizing Jesus.

"At the end of the Sabbath Day that is, *Motzeh Shabbat* or Saturday night, which began the first day of the week, Mary came to the tomb of Jesus and found the stone rolled away." As she spoke to Jesus, thinking he was the gardener, she addressed him as "Adon," master or mister. However, when she realized it was the risen Jesus, she cried out the most reverent name in her vocabulary to address him: "Rabboni!" My exalted Rebbe! Read it in John 20:16: "...she said unto him, Rabboni (which is to say, Master)." Here again, the monks had to eliminate such a nominative of address by inserting the words "(which is to say, Master)." A Rabbonic Jesus could not be melted into the mold to create the golden calf of the Jesus of Gentile Christian theology.

So it goes, both at the opening of the book of John and at its close, the Jewishness of the Rebbe from Nazareth had to be sewed up, tucked under and pressed away. But this suppression of the Jewishness of Jesus did not come for centuries afterward. Those who followed him were never called Christians, but were called *Notzerim*, or the "sect of Nazarenes," (Acts 24:5) which identified them as followers of the Rebbe of Nazareth. This is not an uncommon practice even today among the Jewish people. The Rebbe of *Lubavitch* in White Russia, Schneur

Zalman, was the first Rebbe of the *Chabad Hassidim*. The Chabad Jews are called *Lubavitcher* Jews. The Jews who followed Jesus were *not* called Christians; they were called Nazarenes, or followers of Jesus of Nazareth. The *Notzerim* at that time was not the same as the Gentile Christian.

Another method used by the replacement theologians to eliminate the Jewishness of Jesus was to generalize the Jew out of existence. That is to say, since the death and resurrection of Jesus, the Jew no longer enjoys the particular status he had before the coming of Jesus. Since the death of Jesus, they insist, Israel's distinctive differences no longer exist except in a very-long-ago historic sense. To the replacement theologian, Jesus eradicated the statement in Numbers 23:9: "...that Israel should dwell alone and not be reckoned [thought of] as other [Gentile] nations." They seek to characterize the Jews as being just like everyone else. After all, that is what the New Testament teaches, they say. The Jews are no longer a particular people; instead, all Christian believers are members of the "Israel of G-d." No text of the New Testament makes such a statement or allusion.

It is an entertaining adventure to watch these people who can quote scripture like polly parrots chirping away in a sort of "Polly wants a cracker" intonation: "The Bible says there is no difference between Jew and Greek, chirp, chirp—Romans 3:22; chirp, chirp, Romans 10:12, chirp, chirp—Galatians 2:28; and furthermore! Chirp! Chirp! Chirp! Ephesians 2:14 says 'he Jesus is our peace who hath broken down the middle wall of partition between us...' that is, the wall that separated the Jew from the Gentile in the 'Old' Testament. Chirp, chirp, chirp—Polly wants a cracker! Sqwaaaaak!"

This jest is not really serious enough to be a tragedy, nor funny enough to be humorous. The amusement is that anyone could go to the Holy Scripture with such a narrowminded attitude that he could peep through a keyhole with both eyes at the same time. When they see what they want to see through that keyhole, they jump on their soapboxes and tell the world. One such man said: "Every letter of every word in every line from Genesis to Revelation is talking about Jesus Christ!...If you don't believe that, you are not a Christian!" Such attitudes always reflect more heat than light and more exhaust than horsepower. Only a casual reading of these passages about which it is chirped that there is no difference between Jews and Gentiles will indicate that that is not the meaning whatsoever. In Romans 3:22, the subject is "sin" and not "Jew" or "Gentile." The emphasis is that both the Jew and the Gentile sin. One with, the other without, the Law.

Romans 10:12-13 does not say there is no difference between the Jew and the Gentile, but rather that there is no difference in the G-d of Israel and The G-d of the Gentiles, "...for the same Lord over all is rich unto all that call upon him."

Galatians 3:28 does not say that Jesus destroyed the Jews' distinctive difference and that the Gentiles and Jews are the same. The context teaches that the Jews were not justified by the Law but by faith in the Abrahamic Covenant. Therefore, the Gentiles could not be justified by the Law either, but by faith in Jesus Christ. Therefore, the standing of the Gentile believer was not in his ethnic background, but in the faith by which he was accepted by G-d. To try to force it to teach that there is no recognized distinction between Jew and Gentile would also make it imperative that there is no difference between a male and a female or a slave and a non-slave. If there is no difference in male and female in Christ, why then do churches have segregated toilets marked "ladies" and "gentlemen"? If there is no difference between Jew and Greek, why not unified restrooms? It is all the same verse in Galatians 3:28.

Ephesians 2:14 does not state that the middle wall of partition between the Jew and the Gentile in the Temple was broken down. There was no such thing as a *middle wall* to separate the Jews from the Gentiles in the Temple! The "Middle Wall" between the Jew and Gentile in the Temple was built of the stones of conjectural hyperthesis of Replacement Theology. There were no Gentiles allowed anywhere in the Temple! Hence, no wall was needed! Replacement translators added the words "between us" to make it appear that the distinction between the Jews and the Gentiles had been broken down. Note that the words are in italics or parentheses in the more reliable translations. The context is discussing the "House of G-d...the Temple." (Eph. 2:14-22) The middle "veil," not wall, was broken down, "rent in twain," between the Holy of Holies and the Holy Place (at the death of Jesus, Matt. 27:51), making both the Holiest of

All and the Holy Place one room. The Gentile believer is made a fellow-citizen in the Holies, verse 19, with the Jew, who *already had access* there through the Abrahamic Covenant.

If the death of Jesus was supposed to break down this conjectural wall, or "enmity," between the Jews and Gentiles, Jesus is a vain martyr, not the supreme sacrifice. The death of Jesus not only failed to break down the enmity between the Jews and Gentiles, but it created walls that never before existed. History cries in protest to the replacement interpretation that Jesus' death broke down the wall *between us*.

The sacrifice of Jesus broke down the enmity between G-d and mankind, not between the Jews and the Gentiles. His sacrifice made a way of access for the Gentile so that he could be accepted *with the Jew* in the economy of G-d in the heavenly Tabernacle. The Jew was already there. The cross was not a bridge to bring the Gentiles into Judaism. It was a vertical span to bring the Gentile into that sphere of relationship with G-d that the Jew already had through the Abrahamic Covenant...thus making peace with G-d! We are made fellow citizens with them.

Without the elimination of the distinctiveness of the Jew and the Jewishness of Jesus, the replacement theologians would have had no foundation for their position. There are no scriptural grounds for replacement theology. The only proof the replacement theologians had was to point to the destruction of Judaea and the Temple and say: "See, after Jesus came, there was no need for fleshly Israel or blood sacrifices. Therefore God destroyed the Temple and the Nation of Israel." It is very amusing to note that G-d is a Roman general named Titus.

Now that Israel has had a national restoration, the replacement theologians are really in a dither! They lost more theological ground than the Arabs lost in real estate. This is why many of the major denominations are so pro-Palestinian. In 1952, the World Council of Churches petitioned the U.N. to "force Israel to change its name. The name Israel is confusing to many Christians in the world, especially the Arab Christians." The proof of the pudding was lost in the eating when Israel was nationally reborn.

The tongue-in-cheek excuse of the replacement people

is: "How can we know that the Jews over there are the Jews of the Bible?"

When the Romans wanted to banish the Jews, they knew without doubt who the Jews were. When a crusader wanted to kill a Jew for Jesus, he knew who to kill. The English knew who the Jews were when they banished them from England. Ferdnand and Isabella knew who the Jews were during the Spanish Inquisition. The Czar knew who the Jews were during the pogroms. Hitler knew who the Jews were during the holocaust. The Germans knew who to arrest and tattoo with their concentration camp numbers. Many of those same Jews bearing Hitler's brand returned to Israel and are there today rebuilding the Jewish state. It is audacity to the point of stupidity for anyone to say that we cannot be sure that the Jews in Israel are the Jews of the Bible. Furthermore, the replacement theologians confess their inconsistency by talking about the problem of the Jewish state when the real problem is replacement theology.

The problem of replacement theology has only begun with the establishment of the Jewish state. What will be the repercussions when the Ashes of the Red Heifer are returned to Israel and the Sanhedrin is reestablished? Where will the replacement theologians go when the Tabernacle is recovered and the Temple rebuilt in Jerusalem? What will go with their old adage, "the blood of Jesus replaced the Jewish sacrifices," when the sacrificial system is restored to Israel?

The same prophets who predicted the return of the Jewish state also predicted the subsequent events. Since the Council of Yavneh in C.E. 90, world Jewry have prayed daily for the return of the Land of Israel to the people of Israel; the return of the people of Israel to the Land of Israel; the rebuilding and reuniting of the Holy City, Jerusalem, as the capital of Israel; the return of divine worship in the Holy Temple; and the coming of the Messiah and his establishment of the Kingdom of Peace. In the past half century, three-fifths of that prayer has become history. Every setting of the sun brings the remainder nearer fulfillment.

It was long after the death, burial, and resurrection of Jesus that Paul, in his epistle to the Romans, stated his desire concerning the Gentile Christian attitude toward the Jew and Israel: "For I would not, brethren, that ye

Gentiles should be ignorant of this mystery [concerning Israel]." (Rom. 11:25) Previously, he had asked two questions: "What therefore *is* the advantage all the way around of being Jewish? [Note the present tense *is* after the coming of Jesus.] Or what *is* the prevailing profitability of being of the circumcision [those under the blood seal of the Abrahamic Covenant since the coming of Jesus]?" (Rom. 3:1)

Paul's own answer is directly opposed to the replacement theory! They say the Jew or circumcision has no advantage since Jesus came. Paul says, and that many years *after* the Passion: "Much according to every advantageous direction: First indeed because they are the perpetual unrolling of the Divine Epistle down to the last little rhetoric oracle of G-d." (Rom. 3:2)

One would think that the replacement theologian would read Romans 9-11 and simply admit, "We have been wrong. Israel is still in economic relationship with G-d, and our economy in Jesus is contingent upon G-d's faithfulness to his covenants with Israel." But no! They will not accept Romans 9-11 as such. They back off with a pseudo-sophisticated sneer and talk about "Paul's problem"—not the replacement theologian's problem with Israel, but "Paul's problem with Israel!"

A few years ago the Southern Baptist Broadman Press solved the problem of Romans 9-11 in a very simple way. They published a commentary on the book of Romans in which the table of contents listed each chapter thusly: Romans, chapters 1, 2, 3, 4, 5, 6, 7, 8, 12, 13, 14, 15, 16. That solved both "Paul's problem" and their problem. Just omit chapters 9, 10, and 11.

This omission, or "cutting-out," of Romans 9, 10, and 11 is a good example of performing an epistlectomy instead of a cataractectomy. That is, removing the passage presenting a problem to one's theological view rather than removing the theological cataracts that prevent one from seeing the meaning of the said passages.

In all fairness, this attitude is not the norm among Southern Baptists. A survey taken among Southern Baptist ministers in the early 1950s reflected a very pro-Arab and anti-Israeli sentiment. Another survey in the late 1960s indicated exactly the opposite. Only three percent were pro-Arab on the Middle East question, eleven percent were undecided, and eighty-six percent were pro-Israel.

An interesting story about this transition is related by Rev. L. A. Sartain, over forty years a Southern Baptist pastor:

> Before 1967, when I heard someone preaching about the Jews being the true Israel, I was ready to walk out. Like most everyone else, I believed that the church was the true Israel and those Jews over there were blind, lost impostors. That kind of preaching was associated with Frank Norris fundamentalism, premillennialism, and dispensationalism. I wanted no part of it.
>
> When the 1967 war began in Israel, I watched the television news which reported Tel Aviv was in flames and the Arabs were driving the Jews into the sea.
>
> Not that I was happy to see people being killed; that was tragic! However, I could not help but laugh inside at the thought of what the premillennial brethren were going to do now that Israel was being destroyed. The Arab victory was sort of an endorsement of G-d as to what I had always believed about the church being the True Israel.
>
> Toward the end of the week, the news began to change. Israel had miraculously defeated the Egyptians and the Jordanians and were wiping the Syrians from the Golan Heights.
>
> There I sat—I did not take my eyes off that T.V. around the clock. I said to myself, "Well, the question now is not what are the premillennial and dispensational brethren going to do, but rather what is Brother Sartain going to do." I picked up my Bible and prayed, "Oh Lord, if these Jews over there are really your people, then show me what I am."
>
> From that day forward, my Bible has been a new book to me. It changed my ministry. It is so good to experience the study and preaching of the Bible, letting it say what it says to the Jews as to the Jews and to me as to me. It surely has been an experience I cannot explain.

The riddle of Israel, like the riddle of the Messiah, has its own mystique. A chosen people, yet a suffering people. No other argument is so strong as the very evidence that Israel, the eternal people, the everlasting nation, still remains while all others pass away. "The Eternal One's portion is his people, Jacob is the lot of his inheritance . . . ." "I am the Eternal One, I change not, therefore the Sons of Jacob are not consumed."

ASK THREE QUESTIONS BEFORE YOU READ CHAPTER III

Below is a list from *Lands Of The Bible* by Yohanan Aharoni p. 102-103, cf p 147-152. The first question; why did the nonsemetic Egyptian language records of the cities names lists in the Hametic "Land of Canaan" have over 160 Hebrew names long before the birth of Abraham?

Question Two: From the Garden of Eden to the Tower of Babel there was one speech and one language on earth. According to Rashi what was that language?

Question Three: In the few instances where G-d spoke from Heaven, in what language did he speak?

Egyptologists' Transcription	*Semitic values Hebrew*	*Proto-Sem.*	*Egyptian*	*Examples Hebrew*	*English*
ꜣ Middle Kingdom	ל	l	i-ś-q-ꜣ-n	אשקלון	Ashkelon
	ר	r	. ỉ-ꜣ-ḫ-b-w-m	(א)רחב(ם)	Rehob
Late Kingdom	(vowel sign)		ʿ-ḳ-ꜣ	עכו	Accó
ỉ	א		ỉ-t-r-ʿ	אדרעי	Edrei
y	י	y	ỉ-y-r-n	אילון	Aijalon
ʿ	ע	ʿ	ʿ-y-n	עיון	Ijon
w (vowel or semi-vowel)	ו	w	y-p-w	יפו	Joppa
	י	y	r-w-ś	ליש	Laish
b	ב	b	b-t-ʿ-n-t	בית ענת	Beth-anath
	ב	b	ỉ-b-r	אבל	Abel
p	פ	p	p-ḫ-r	פחל	Peḫel (Pella)
	פ	p	ỉ-p-q-n	אפק(ן)	Aphek
note also	ב	b	k-p-n	גבל	Gebal (Byblos)
f	פ	p	ḏ-f-t	צפת	Zephath
m	מ	m	y-b-r-ʿ-m	יבלעם	Ibleam
n	נ	n	k-n-n-r-t	כנרת	Chinnereth
note also	ל	l	k-p-n	גבל	Gebal (Byblos)
n͡w	נו	no, nu	ỉ-n͡w	אנו	Ono
n͡r	ל	l	ỉ-s-q-n͡r-n	אשקלון	Ashkelon
r	ר	r	r-ḫ-b	רחוב	Rehob
	ל	l	r-t-n	לד(ן)	Lod
note also	נ	n	b-t-s-ỉ-r	בית שאן	Beth-shean
h	ה	h	n-h-r-y-n	נהרין(ם)	Naharain(m)
ḫ	ח	ḫ	b-t-ḫ-w-r-n	בית חרון	Beth-horon
ḫ	ח	ḫ	ỉ-n-ḫ-r-t	אנחרת	Anaharath
ś	ש	ṯ	ʿ-ś-t-r-t	עשתרת	Ashtaroth
	ש	ś	ś-w-k	שכה	Socoh
s (=ś)	ש	ṯ	ʿ-s-t-r-t	עשתרת	Ashtaroṯh
š	ש	š	m-š-i-r	משאל	Mishal
late (Shishak)	ש	ś	š-ỉ-k	שכה	Socoh
q (ḳ)	ק	q	t-m-ś-q	דמשק	Damascus
	ג	g	q-b-ʿ	גבע	Geba
	ע	ǵ(gh)	q-ḏ-t	עזה	Gaza (Ghazzeh)
k	כ	k	ʿ-k-ꜣ	עכו	Acco
	כ	k	t-ʿ-n-k	תענך	Taanach
	ג	g	k-b-ʿ	גבע	Geba
	ג	g	m-k-t	מגדו	Megiddo
g	ג	g	n-g-b	נגב	Negeb
	ע	ǵ(gh)	g-ḏ-t	עזה	Gaza (Ghazzeh)
t	ת	t	ḫ-m-t	חמת	Hammath
	ד	d	m-k-t-r	מגדל	Migdal
	ט	ṭ	t-b-y	טוב	Tob (Ṭūbu, *EA*)
ṯ (tj)	ת	t	k-n-ṯ	גת	Gath
	ז(ס ?)	z(s ?)	ỉ-n͡r-ṯ	—	Ullaza (Ullassa ?) *
d	ד	d	q-d-š	קדש	Kadesh
	ט	ṭ	d-b-ḫ	טבח(ת)	Tibhath (Ṭubiḫi, *EA*)
ḏ	צ	ḏ or ẓ	ḫ-ḏ-r	חצור	Hazor
	צ	ṣ	ḏ-f-t	צפת	Zephath
	ז	z	q-ḏ-r	גזר	Gezer
late (Shishak)	ג	g	ḏ-d-p-t-r	גת (פדל)	Gath-padalla (*EA*)

Chapter III
THE RIDDLE OF THE LANGUAGES

"And a superscription also was written over him in the letters of Greek, and Latin, and Hebrew,...

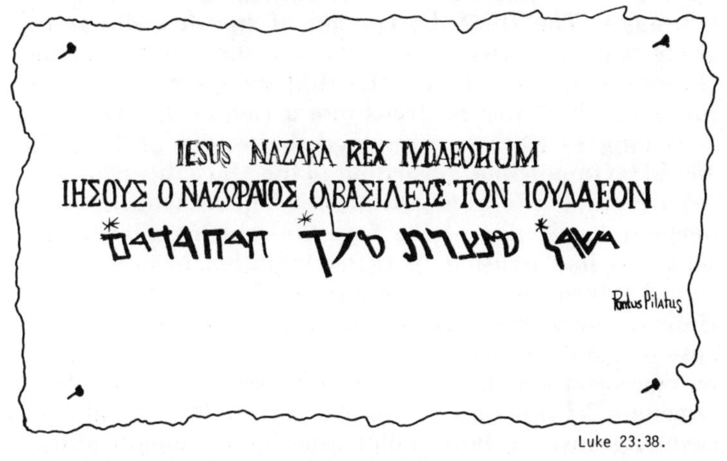

Luke 23:38.

Pontius Pilatus had a linguistic problem. That same problem is the greatest dilemma Christianity and Judaism are faced with today concerning the message of Jesus. The linguistic problem is: *What did Jesus actually say in the language he spoke?* Second to the linguistic question is that of hermeneutics: *What did his words mean to those who heard him?*

Back to the first question, what did Jesus actually say in the language he spoke? We must wade through a lot of gobbledygook to determine what tongue Jesus actually used. The most popular thought today is that Jesus spoke Aramaic. Some insist he spoke Greek, while others seem to think he spoke Shakespearean English. There are a few who believe that Jesus' teachings were in his native Hebrew tongue.

Almost all, if not all, who hold the replacement theological position, insist that Jesus spoke Aramaic. This is not difficult to understand because the Aramaic theory is a product of replacement theologians. All their commentaries and books, which are myriad in number, state that Jesus spoke Aramaic. In order to totally divorce Jesus from Judaism, it was mandatory in the final step to divorce him from the Hebrew language. The Emperor Hadrian knew that in order to destroy the Jew, Judaism must first be destroyed. And the only way to destroy Judaism was to do away with the Hebrew language. The same applies to Jesus.

After the replacement theologians had sacked Jesus of his Jewishness, as Titus had sacked Jerusalem and Judaea, only that one obstacle remained: the Hebrew language. The final destruction of the Jewishness of Jesus was to destroy any evidence that he spoke the Hebrew language. This is the Hadrian decree intended for the assimilation of Jesus into a Gentile figure.

As long as Hebrew remained the tongue of Jesus, it would be impossible, according to the Maccabean adage, "to disguise his circumcision." There would be a perpetual rejection of the foreskin which replacement surgeons had grafted in transplantation to create the Gentile Jesus of replacement theology. Destroy the Hebrew language in Jesus' vocabulary, and his Jewishness would die of its own accord. His circumcision could be disguised and he could be "divorced from the Holy Covenant." Unfortunately, there was no Bar-Kochba to revolt against this latter edict opposing the tongue of the prophets in the teaching of the Prophet from Nazareth. The result was that the Jewishness of Jesus was totally destroyed, except in those musty old books few people choose to read.

What are the evidences set forth in the musty old books about the question of the language which Jesus spoke? If we go back before the edict of the replacement theologians to de-Judaize the language of Jesus, what evidence do we find that he spoke Hebrew?

The first old book we shall observe to give us information about the language spoken by Jesus and his contemporaries is the Old Book itself. What does the Bible have to say about the tongue spoken by the Israelis during the entire Second Temple period?

The replacement theorists speak with ben trovato authority that the Jews lost the Hebrew language through the Babylonian captivity, and that Aramaic then became the language of the Jews. Therefore, on this ben trovato assumption, each time the word "Hebrew" appears in any text, the replacement linguists simply footnote it as "i.e., Aramaic" or "literally Aramaic."

Who can argue or dispute the hundreds or even thousands of books which make these statements? History can dispute it! Linguistics can dispute it! Archaeology can dispute it! The Bible itself harshly disputes it!

The first Biblical evidence against the theory that the Jews lost Hebrew as a spoken language during the Babylonian captivity is the testimony of the post-captivity prophets. If Aramaic was the spoken language of the Jews following the Babylonian captivity, why did the post-captivity prophets Haggai, Zechariah, Ezra, Nehemiah, Malachi, and even Daniel write in Hebrew instead of Aramaic?

Agreed, there are many Aramaic words in these books. But let us not be so general in that conclusion; let us be more specific in our evaluations.

First, it is necessary to define what Aramaic is. There is an Eastern Aramaic called Old Aramaic, or Chaldaic. Then there is Western Aramaic which is called Syriac. The two are about as relative to being the same language as French and English. There are many identical words in each, but they do not always have the same meaning. There is also North Eastern Aramaic, which is spoken by the Armenian people. All of these languages came from the families of Aram (Genesis 10:22), while Hebrew came through Eber, or עבר, 'Ever (Genesis 10:24). His name was actually GaeVehR and his tongue עברית, Ǵ'VehRiYT, 'Ivrit, which is the name of the Hebrew language.

In addition to the above, the compilers of the Babylonian and Jerusalem Talmuds, living in the third to the fifth centuries after the destruction of the Temple, used a literary style that was unique. The text of the scripture was written in bold traditional Hebrew, but the commentary was written with a different letter style so that the reader would not confuse the word of G-d with commentary. Furthermore, in order to distinguish commentary from text, they adapted many Eastern Aramaic words to write the commentary of the Torah.

Onkelos made a Targum, or translation, of the scripture that appears under the Hebrew text itself to use in the rabbinic commentaries. The Aramaic of the Talmud is linguistically in a class of its own and is not Chaldaic or Syriac, Armenian or Ukaretic per se.

All these languages, including Hebrew, Persian, and Arabic, are sister Semitic languages. Many words in each are the same. Many are almost the same. Therefore, in the early chapters of Genesis in Hebrew, there are words that appear in all the Semitic languages. Can we then say that because Moses used a Hebrew word that appears in Aramaic or Arabic that Moses spoke Aramaic or Arabic? Such words do appear in the Torah. Does this not rather strengthen the arguments by Rashi that Hebrew was the original language and that other tongues developed from it? Or shall we be more pseudo-intellectual and say, "Moses spoke Aramaic"?

The replacement theologians who are so positive that Jesus spoke Aramaic have never told us exactly which Aramaic Jesus spoke! Would they dare to say he spoke rabbinic Aramaic? To admit that would only emphasize him as a rabbi, would it not? They do not specify whether it was Old Chaldaic Aramaic or Syriac or Armenian Aramaic. They simply generalize that he spoke Aramaic. That statement is enough to de-Judaize him and that is really the objective of the theory from the beginning.

Let us look back to the specific usage of Aramaic by the post-captivity prophets and Daniel. The Aramaic found in these books is restricted to particular sections, except for words and phrases that are found in both languages and have been borrowed from one or the other. Let us begin with the pre-captivity prophet Jeremiah as a springboard to the study of the use of Aramaic in the later prophets. Jeremiah was the first prophet, and the only one before the captivity, to consciously use Aramaic for a definite purpose in his writing.

In Jeremiah 10:11, the Eternal One had a one-verse message to the pagan gods of the Gentiles. To get that message across, he wrote that single verse in the Chaldaic dialect of Aramaic. All the other verses in the entire book are a simple Hebrew, almost identical to the Hebrew spoken in Israel today.

The Book of Daniel, chapters 2:4b to 7:28, is also in the Old Chaldaic Aramaic. The other sections are in Hebrew. Following the principle of Jeremiah, Daniel expressed his message to the Gentile nations in a Gentile language. The first chapter, which was the account of the capture of Jerusalem, was in Hebrew. The apocalyptic visions at the end of the book concern the nation of Israel and their national restoration in the last days. Hence, the language vehicle of these visions was again Hebrew.

The book of Ezra, 4:18-6:18 and 7:12-26, contains certain letters which were written by the enemy neighbors of Israel to Artaxerxes, and includes a description of the context of that correspondence. In Ezra 4:7b is an explanation in Hebrew as to why the Aramaic appears in the Hebrew scroll: "...the writing of the letter [to Artaxerxes] was in the Syrian tongue, and is *interpreted* [Hebrew is Targum, actually untranslated and here recorded] in the Syrian [Aramaic] tongue." Since the correspondence was originally written in the Syriac Aramaic tongue, why does Ezra repeat "it was translated in the Syriac Aramaic tongue"? What Ezra the scribe is explaining is that since the correspondence was originally written in the Aramaic tongue, the original Aramaic text of that correspondence is here recorded in the Hebrew text, untranslated as it appeared in the original Aramaic document.

In the light of this explanation by Ezra himself, those who seek to prove that Aramaic was the language of the Jews at the time of Jesus, refer to the "Aramaic influence on the post-captivity prophets." They ignore the Hebrew script in the remainder of the book of Ezra. They also ignore the explanation of Ezra and his reason for the use of the Aramaic Targum which he inserted as historic documentation into his Hebrew text.

We must admit that there was a departure from Hebrew during the post-captivity period. Nehemiah, another post-exilic prophet, expressed the problem thusly: "In those days also saw I Jews that had married wives of Ashdod, of Ammon, and of Moab: And their children spake half in the speech of Ashdod, and could not speak in the Jews' language, but according to the language of each people." (Nehemiah 13:23-24) In the minute description of the linguistic departure from the

Hebrew language, Nehemiah stressed the "Jews' language," Hebrew, and denounced the impure tongue of the Ashdodites (Philistinic), Ammonites, and Moabites (archaic Arabic). There is a glaring absence of the pollution of Hebrew by Aramaic in Nehemiah's description.

Except for the words which are generally identical in one of the Aramaic dialects and Hebrew, and the specific portions of Daniel, Ezra, and Jeremiah, the language of the Jews after the Babylonian captivity was the holy mother tongue of Hebrew.

This is not to say that foreign words do not occur in the Hebrew language. Even today, Hebrew uses international words like hello, telephone, radio, television, and so on. Dr. Robert Longacre, a linguist with the International Linguistic Center, points out also that the first twelve chapters of Genesis have a very unique Hebrew style and a predominance of verbs with two-letter roots. Many times in these chapters, the noun root of the subject is the same as the verb root of the predicate. After Genesis 12, the shift to more three-letter verb roots can be observed, and the strong correlation of the noun and verb can be seen; yet, the parallel of the subject and predicate decreases.

The late Dr. Robert Dick Wilson of Princeton University called attention to the fact that after Genesis 37, many Egyptian words are used in the Hebrew texts. Most of these naturally are proper names of people and places. That is no evidence that the Egyptian language was the language of the Hebrews after the Egyptian exile of four hundred years. If the Hebrew tongue could be preserved in the four hundred years of the harsh Egyptian bondage, is it unthinkable that it could not be preserved for a mere seventy years of the Babylonian captivity?

During the period of Antiochus Epiphanes, the Greeks attempted to force the Jews to Hellenize. During this time, there was a definite attempt to destroy the Hebrew language. The Greeks changed many of the names of the towns in Judaea and Galilee to Greek names. There was a vain attempt to force the Greek language upon the people of Israel. The harder Antiochus pushed the Jews to incorporate Hellenistic customs into their culture, however, the more obstinate the Jews became in their resistance. The language of the streets of Jerusalem *never* became Greek, yet those who insist that Jesus spoke Greek deny the history of the Maccabean Revolt.

While the books of the Maccabees retain the Hebrew names, it may be argued that Flavius Josephus used many Greek words to define cities and geographical locations. And Josephus is recognized as a major primary source for historians of that period. Josephus was, we must remember, writing the history of the Jews for the Greek world. He would, therefore, naturally use terms familiar to the Greeks to identify the various places and figures.

One objective of the Maccabean reforms was to purge the Greek and other foreign words from the language of the Jews. It is a matter of record as pointed out by the Hebrew linguist and father of modern Hebrew, Eliezer Ben-Yehuda, that by eighty years before the common era, the Hebrew language had been refined to its state of purity.

Ehud Ben-Yehuda, the son of Eliezer Ben-Yehuda, in the preface of his dictionary of the Hebrew language, explains that development:

> The language of the sacred writings of the Jews, from the earliest documents of the Bible down to modern times, has been Hebrew. Its history extends over a period of three millennia, during which time the language had naturally undergone significant linguistic development.
>
> The *Jewish Encyclopedia* lists two broad phases of this linguistic development: (1) the creative period with its pre-exilic, post-exilic and mishnaic phases, and (2) the reproductive period, beginning with amoraic literature (third century C. E.) and continuing until the present.
>
> Biblical or classical Hebrew, concise, vigorous and poetic, underwent little change during the first commonwealth. Beginning with exilic times, however, Aramaic influence on Hebrew began to be felt: increased number of word-borrowings, greater aramaization of its syntax, and its entrance into tannaitic literature, the chief work of which is the Mishnah. [Two centuries later.]

Eliezer Ben-Yehuda

Ehud Ben-Yehuda

New Hebrew or postbiblical Hebrew emerged as the language of the reproductive period, the second phase of linguistic development. The writers of talmudic, midrashic and liturgical literature adopted mishnaic Hebrew, avoiding the more poetic biblical Hebrew.

The translation of Arabic works on philosophy and science necessitated a remodeling of mishnaic Hebrew, which was insufficient for the treatment of scientific subjects. A philosophic Hebrew, the language of medieval translators, grammarians, poets, and writers, enriched the old language. New vocabulary items were coined; Arabic words and syntax patterns were borrowed. However, neither the Arabic influence on the Hebrew of medieval times nor the Aramaic influence on the Hebrew of biblical times impaired the essential characteristics of the Hebrew language.

The period of enlightenment followed by the rise of national consciousness throughout European Jewry created a modern Hebrew — a synthesis of biblical and mishnaic Hebrew, fusing the rhetoric and grandeur of the one with the clarity and simplicity of the other.

The revival of Hebrew as a living, spoken language and the advocacy of a return to the ancestral homeland inspired dedicated men to coin new terms for new ideas. Biblical, mishnaic and medieval sources were culled by these dedicated men and were used as a scaffolding on which to enlarge the Hebrew vocabulary and serve modern times.

Another collection of musty old books of the period between the Maccabean period and that of the New Testament record is the recovery of over 1,300 documents of the Dead Sea Scrolls. These Qumran documents contain not only the scrolls of scripture, such as the book of Isaiah, but also commentaries on passages and books such as the "Commentary on the Book of Habakkuk." These commentaries were written in the common language of the late Second Temple period. Among the Dead Sea Scrolls were routine descriptions of the details of the Qumran community and their daily lives. Of these 1,300 parchments, *not a single one was found* written in Aramaic. They are all written in Hebrew!

"While there were some Aramaic and some Greek fragments found in the area, they were not written by the people of the Qumran community. There was found a marriage license written in Greek; also found were deeds and documents, unrelated to the community in an older Aramaic form, and bits of unidentifiable scraps of Aramaic from an earlier period. The paleography of the Aramaic is not that of the Qumran writers.

Professor Frank Cross of Harvard University dates these few supernumerary fragments in languages other than Hebrew, at least in a pre-Maccabean period. In fact, as pointed out by Edmund Wilson and Yigael Yadin, the only Aramaic document found between the Book of Daniel in the third century B. C. E. and the "Scroll of Fasting," written in the late second century C. E., is the "Genesis Aprocyphon." This pseudepigraphic document is also dated at least a couple of centuries before the time of Jesus. Five hundred years' absence of any Aramaic evidence is a *nolo contendere* that the Aramaic theory is the simple conjectural hypothesis of replacement theologians to de-Judaize the language of Jesus. There is no archaeological evidence that Jesus or his community spoke anything other than Hebrew! Archaeological evidence indicates that Aramaic was not the language of that period!

Now you may ask, what do the replacement theologians and linguists have to say about that archaeological discovery? What is the reaction to those who say that Jesus spoke Aramaic because that was the common language of that day? If Aramaic was the common language during that time, why are the Dead Sea Scrolls not in Aramaic rather than in Hebrew?

The first reaction the replacement people have to the use of Hebrew in the Dead Sea Scrolls is *absolute silence.* They do not want to discuss it. The second answer they give when confronted with the issue is more hilarious than the silence. Tongue-in-cheek, they label it as "the problem of the Dead Sea Scrolls." They treat it with such sophisticated arrogancy that they would have you think the sons of Zadok at Qumran had the language problem instead of the problem being in their own ben trovato theory.

Under the "Dome of the Crock" at Hebrew University is an exhibit of the actual parchments of the Dead Sea Scrolls written in the Hebrew language. These documents were discovered by an illiterate Arab shepherd boy who was throwing rocks at his goats. One of the rocks ricocheted into a cave and gave a dull thud as it struck a pottery crock containing one of the scrolls.

Thirty years later, that rock is still richocheting and cracking a lot of crocks...with a dull thud.

Providence chose an Arab lad who could not read or write to make obsolete all the books that have been written telling us that the Hebrew language was lost during the Babylonian captivity and that Jesus spoke Aramaic instead of Hebrew.

The goats of the replacement theory are still running over the hills, bleating about the "problems of the Dead Sea Scrolls." The one question that really "gets their nanny" is: Why are the Dead Sea Scrolls of Jesus' generation written in Hebrew instead of in Aramaic? The problem is not with the Qumran documents; the problem is the crackpots who hallow the argument and seek to uncircumcise Jesus by cutting off his native Hebrew language and transplanting a Gentile tongue into him.

Other musty old books that testify that Hebrew was Jesus' language were written during the same generation as the Qumran documents. They are textual records within the New Testament itself. There are at

One hundred thirty-three years of documents which prove the language of Jesus was Hebrew from Les 'Petites Grottes' de Qumrán, M. Baillet, J.T. Milik and R. De Vauxop Oxford 1962. p. 219-220.

The script of the Copper Document and related Herodian and post-Herodian scripts.

Line 1. A typical early Herodian formal script (c. 30—1 B.C.). From a manuscript of the Order of the War (IQM).

1

Line 2. An early Herodian 'Round' semiformal hand (c. 30B.C.—A.D. 20). From an unpublished exemplar of Numbers (4QNum[b]).

2

Line 3. A late Herodian formal bookhand (c. A.D. 20-50). From an unpublished exemplar of Daniel (4QDan[b]).

3

Line 4. A late Herodian formal script (c. A.D. 50). From an unpublished exemplar of Deuteronomy (4QDeut[j]).

4

Line 5. A late Herodian 'Vulgar' semiformal script (c. A.D. 25—68). From an unpublished manuscript of Canticles (4QCant[b]).

5

Line 6. The script of the Uzziah Plaque (c. A.D. 50).

6

Lines 7—8. The Script of the Copper Document from cave III, 3Q15.

7

8

Line 9. A late Herodian formal script (c. A.D. 50—68). From an unpublished manuscript of Psalms from cave IV.

9

Line 10. A post-Herodian biblical hand (c. A.D. 70-100). From fragments of a biblical scroll preserved by members of a camp of Bar Kochba from an unidentified site.

10

Line 11. A semiformal script from a Hebrew contract dated A.D. 133, Mur 24, DFD II, pls. XXV—XXVI.

11

least thirty-one statements of this nature in the twenty-seven books of the New Testament.

The superscription written by Pontius Pilatus was recorded by each of the four Evangelists. Pilatus wrote the criminal charge against Jesus on his execution stake so that all the people who passed that way could see the penalty of one making himself king against Caesar. The triglott was written in Latin so the Roman soldiers could read it. The Greek was so written for pilgrims from Egypt, Macedonia, and others who could read the Greek language. Pilatus had the inscription written in the bold letters of the Hebrew script so that the native populous of Judaea could read it. The emphatic statement that it was written in Hebrew and not in Aramaic cannot be changed.

The same Aramaic theorists who insist that the Qumran people had a problem also tell us that Pilatus' superscription was literally Aramaic instead of Hebrew. What they are telling us is that Matthew, Mark, Luke, John and Pontius Pilatus did not know the difference in the designation of the two languages.

Following the four references to the Hebrew language in the inscription of Pilatus, there are seventeen direct statements in reference to the Hebrew tongue in the New Testament texts. The following list is provided so the interested reader will not be burdened with searching out the references.

The numbered reference will be given with the Hebrew translation in reference to each particular word. The transliteration is supplied for the convenience of those who do not read Hebrew. Many times the monks gave an improper translation of the word. In such cases, a better translation is supplied:

1. *Matthew 1:23* — "...IM-MAN-U-EL which being interpreted is, G-d with us." עמנואל , ǤiMahNoU ?aL, literally, "G-d of our people," or "G-d with us." This is Hebrew, not Aramaic.

2-3. *Mark 15:22, John 19:17* — "...a *skull*, which is called in Hebrew Gol-go-tha." גלגלת , GouL'GohLT, as stated by Mark. This is the Hebrew name of a hill north of Jerusalem. Both Greek and Aramaic is Golgotha, but its origin is Hebraic.

4. *John 1:41* — "...the *Messiah,* which is, being interpreted, the Christ." המשיח, HaMahSHiYKH, or haMashiyah, The Anointed. The Aramaic again had to borrow the word Messiah from Hebrew.

5. *John 5:2* — "...a pool, which is called in the Hebrew Tongue *Bethesda.*" בית-חסד, Beit Hesed, BaeYT-KHshCehD, or House of Grace or Mercy.

6-7. *John 19:13* — "...called the *Pavement,* but in the Hebrew also Gab-ba-tha." גבעת, GIV'ȻaT, Givaht, the Mound or Bema of Pilatus' judgment seat.

8. *Acts 13:8* — "But *Elymas* the sorcerer (for so is his name by interpretation...." Elymas in Hebrew is אלי-מעשר, ?aeLiY-Ma'ȻaSaeR, Eli M'asar, an alms beggar or literally G-d's financial burden bearer. The word "eleemosynary" in English comes through Greek and Latin from this Hebrew word. The tithe is called מעשר, Ma'ȻaSaeR.

9. *Acts 9:36* — "...*Tab-itha* which by interpretation is called Dorcas." Dorx in Greek or Dorcas in Latin, means a gazelle or antelope. In Hebrew it is צבי, TS'VieY, or feminine, צביה, TS'VieYahH, or Tsviah. Tabitha in English is almost a transliteration of the Hebrew word for an antelope.

10-11-12. *John 1:38, 21:16; Mark 10:51* — "Rabbi, (which being interpreted is Master)." this monastic note was discussed in chapter two of this book. Rabbi is Hebrew, not Aramaic.

13. *John 9:7* — "*Si-lo-am* (which being interpreted is Sent)." Hebrew, שלח, SHah LahKH, or Sha-lah, means "let go," "send out," or "liberate." The pool was given that name as is the pool at the end of Hezekiah's Tunnel, which liberated the city from the oppression of the siege.

14-15. *Hebrews 7:2* — "Mel-chiz-ed-ek, King of Salem...First being interpreted King of Righteousness, and after that also King of

Peace." מלכי-צדק, MaL'KieY-TSehDehK or mal*khitse*deq, means King of Righteousness. מלכי-שלום, MAL'KeiY-SHah LaeM is King of Peace in Hebrew.

16. *Revelation 9:11* — "...Whose name in the Hebrew tongue is A-BAD-Don but in the Greek tongue hath the name A-POL-LY-2ON." A-BAD-DON in Hebrew is אב-עבדון, ?ahV'-ǤaV'DohN, meaning the father of bondage. This was contracted to אבדון, PaVieYDohN, or Avdon, in reference to Satan (Abodah Zarah 17b).

17. *Revelation 16:16* — "...A place called in the Hebrew tongue AR-MA-GED-DON." Hebrew הר-מגדון, HaR-M'GiDDoH, Har Megido, is Mount Miggidon, the proper name of that particular mountain in Israel.

There is, in the New Testament, an occurrence of Aramaic words in the Greek texts. Whether they were actually in the original documents as written by the authors, or perhaps were translated into the texts by later translators, is a question that awaits further findings, either linguistically or archaeologically.

For example, in Mark's account of the crucifixion, Jesus cried out with a loud voice the first verse of Psalms 22: *"Eloi, Eloi, lama sa-bach-tha-ni?"* Matthew's account, however, differs somewhat from Mark's: *"Eli, Eli, lama sa-bach-tha-ni?"* In Mark's account, "Eloi, Eloi" is Aramaic; *"lama"* is Hebrew, and *"sabachthani"* is again Aramaic. Hence, Mark's quote has three Aramaic words and one Hebrew word. Matthew, on the other hand, records *Eli, Eli, lama*..., which is all Hebrew and then *sabachthani*, which is Aramaic.

At this point, it is of importance to note that Jerome, who saw and copied Matthew's original Gospel, related in the preface to the Vulgate that: "...In which it is to be remarked that, whenever the Evangelist [Matthew] makes use of the testimonies of the old scripture, he does not follow the authority of the seventy translators [Septuagint, LXX] but of the Hebrew [scripture]."

The "old...Hebrew scripture," as Jerome related, is different from either Matthew or Mark. It differs from Matthew, however, only in the word *sabachthani*. The Hebrew is, as David and Jesus said it: אלי אלי למה עזבתני ,

?aeLiY, LahMahH ⱸa'ZaV'TahNiY, or Eli, Eli, lama 'ahzavtini.

Since Jerome insisted, as a witness of Matthew's own handwritten copy, that Matthew transcribed it as David wrote it, it is evident that the Aramaic was the work of the monks who copied the manuscript and translated it to Aramaic and later to Greek. With this *fortiori* evidence, the question is, how much, if not all, of the Aramaic forms in the New Testament are the work of copiers rather than the work of the Evangelists themselves?

There is little doubt that the Jewish disciples who went to Babylon after the destruction of the Temple by Titus soon made a translation of the New Testament into Aramaic even before it was translated into Greek. The old Aramaic New Testament is quite different from the Greek codex. In fact, it contains a book of III Corinthians absent in the Greek copies. Perhaps the older Greek manuscripts were copied partly from an Aramaic translation that would give occasion to the few Aramaic forms which appear in the Greek texts.

It may be observed in transliteration from Hebrew to Greek that those letters which appear in the Hebrew which did not have a corresponding letter or sound in Greek, were simply omitted in many transliterations by the Greek translators. For example, the עז, ⱸa'Z, or 'ahz, as it would be expressed in Hebrew, was simply translated *sa-vach-thani* in Greek, dropping the ע, or 'ayin, since the Greeks did not have an equivalent sound or letter. Then they simply changed the z̄, ז, or zion, to an s, or sigma.

The Hebrew for "a son" is BeN. The Aramaic is BaR. The Aramaic form of "Bar" occurs seven times in the New Testament. Each of these is used in a proper name: Bar-Rabbas in Hebrew would be Ben-Avi. Bar-Tholomew would become Ben-Talmon. Bar-Jesus becomes Ben-Yeshuah. Bar-Jona becomes Ben-Yona. Bar-Nabas becomes Ben-Navi. Bar-Sabas becomes Ben-Tzovah. Bar-Timaeus becomes Ben-Teman. It is not unlikely that those names could have occurred at that time in the Aramaic form. Neither is it unlikely that at least some of them would have occurred in the Hebrew form. For example, in John 1:42, Jesus, speaking to Peter, said, "Thou art Simon, the son of Jonah: thou shalt be called Cephas, which is by interpretation, a stone." The word "stone" in Greek is *petros*. Hereafter, in all the accounts, Simon was called "Peter" from *petros.* In the reality of their day to day communications, Jesus, speaking in the Hebrew tongue, would have addressed him as Cephas rather than as Peter. The Hebrew word for Cephas is *TSeh-FehT*, צפת.

This particular use of the word "stone" has to do with the chapiter as is used in II Chronicles 3:15 as the stone which joined the columns. A city in the mountains of Galilee, not far from Nazareth and Tiberias, had the same name. It is found in Judges 1:17 as Zephath. It is most probable that when Jesus addressed Peter, or when Peter was referred to in the Hebrew accounts of the Gospel, he addressed him as *Tsephet.* When, however, the Gospels were translated into Greek, his Hebrew name was dropped and the word "Petros" was substituted and it became Peter.

It has been shown, therefore, that almost all the names occurring in the New Testament were Hebrew names, each having a particular meaning in the Hebrew language. During the course of translation, however, many names were apparently given the meaning of the Aramaic, Greek or Latin so that those names we refer to today have been far removed from the nominatives of address used by the people themselves.

Elizabeth, for example, was actually called *Ali Shavah*; Mary was *Miriam*; John was *Yochanan.* Jesus himself was never called *Jesus*, but was always addressed as *Yeshua.* Bar-Kochba is an Aramaic form; he is commonly called by that name in Jewish literature today. However, in the older records, it was Ben—not Bar.

In addition to the four accounts of the Hebrew tongue in the superscription of Pontius Pilatus, the seventeen references of the Hebrew tongue found in the texts and the Eli, Eli, there are three statements concerning the apostle Paul which attest to the fact that the language of Jesus' day was Hebrew instead of Aramaic. In Paul's account of his revelation on the Damascus road, in Acts 26:14, he said, ". . . I heard a voice speaking to me, and saying in the *Hebrew tongue*, 'Saul, Saul. . . .'"

Again, in Acts 21:37 to 22:2, we see Paul addressing the people, not in Greek nor in Aramaic, but in Hebrew:

> And as Paul was to be led into the castle, he said unto the chief captain, May I speak unto thee? Who said, Canst thou speak Greek? Art not thou that Egyptian, which before these days madest an uproar, and leddest out into the wilderness 4,000 men that were murderers? But Paul said,

> I am a man which *am a Jew* of Tarsus, a city in Ci-li-ci-a, a citizen of no mean city: and, I beseech thee, suffer me to speak unto the people. And when he had given him license, Paul stood on the stairs, and beckoned with his hand unto the people. And when there was made a great silence, *he spake unto them in the Hebrew tongue* saying, men, brethren, and fathers, hear ye my defense which I make now unto you. (And when they heard that *he spake in the Hebrew tongue* to them, they kept more silence...).

It is quite amazing to see the influence the monks' interpretations on Hebrew words have had even in Jewish sources. In Mark 5, Jesus was summoned by Jairus, the president of the synagogue in Capernaum, to heal his twelve-year-old daughter who lay sick of a fever. En route to the house of Jairus, the woman who had had an issue of blood for twelve years reached through the crowd and touched the tsitsit, or fringe, on the hem of Jesus' *Talit*, or prayer shawl, and she was healed.

When Jesus arrived at the house of Jairus, he bound the hands of Jairus' daughter with the tsitsit and covered her with his *Talit*, as Elijah had done in the raising of the son of the widow of Nain. In Mark 5:41, Jesus addressed the corpse thusly: *"Talitha cumi."* The monks added a note saying "...(which is, being interpreted, Damsel, I say unto thee, arise)." Talitha cumi does not mean, "Damsel, I say unto thee, arise." Had Jesus addressed her thusly, she being twelve years old, he would have said, "YahL'DahH QoUMiY," or yaldah cumi. Had she been thirteen to seventeen years old, he would have said, "'Almah cumi," which means "teenage girl, arise!" Had she been eighteen or over, and unmarried, he would have said, "Betulah cumi," or "Miss, stand up." The word טליתה , *tahLieYTahH*, means "she which is in the *Talit*," or she which is in the prayer shawl, and קֻמִי , *QouMi*, is Hebrew feminine imperative for "arise!"

During a discussion with Ehud Beh-Yehuda, he pointed out that the word *Talitah* was Aramaic, used in Mishnaic sources, for a young woman or damsel twelve years or younger, and was equivalent to the Hebrew word "YahLDahH." As we checked the origin of the word "Talitah," the oldest source we could find for it to mean "damsel" was the monastic note in Mark 5:41. In old Aramaic, or Chaldaic, the word *tal* means a "covering, as dew covering the ground." It is also the word for the cloth used in making tents. The word tahLieYT, in Hebrew, as well as in Aramaic, means a pup tent. The word was adopted for the Jewish prayer shawl, because the prayer shawl actually was a little tent for the individual in ancient Israel who prayed toward the Big Tent, *Mishkan*, or Tabernacle. Today, its exclusive Hebrew meaning is prayer shawl. It is more apropos to think of Paul, the Rabbi of Tarsus, as working with his kinsmen, Priscilla and Aquila, making Jewish prayer shawls instead of making Bedouin tents in the marble city of Corinth.

The replacement theologians and linguists, in their final attempt to de-Judaize Jesus totally from his religion, his people, and his language, have ignored a very basic principle of hermeneutics. This principle was well stated by the late David Cooper in what he called the "golden rule of interpretation": "When the plain sense of scripture makes common sense, seek no other sense; therefore, take every word in its primary, ordinary, usual literal meaning, unless the facts of the immediate context, studied in the light of related passages and axiomatic and fundamental truths, indicate clearly otherwise."

The Temple had been destroyed. All the apostles were deceased. The first quarter of the first century of the Common Era had just transpired. Many of the aged still remembered the destruction of the Temple and the scattering of the Jewish people. Those who had witnessed these events were the living generation. Polycarp, Pliny, Papias and the Ebionites were contemporary with the passing generation of the Tannaiim and present sages, Yohanan Ben Zakkai, Rabbi Akivah and Bar-Kochba. At this very time, Hadrian issued his decree against the Hebrew language.

All of Armenia, Syria and Babylon spoke Aramaic in one form or another. The decree was not against their language; it was against the Jews' language, Hebrew! *Hadrian did not consider Hebrew and Aramaic synonymous!* His taboo was not against "Hebrew—i.e., meaning Aramaic or literally Aramaic"! He spelled out H-E-B-R-E-W in an absolute, emphatic declaration! This Hebrew-speaking generation was threatened with death if they taught, wrote, or spoke the Hebrew language. Aramaic was permissible.

Simeon Bar-Kochba, who died to preserve the Hebrew language, had an Aramaic prefix on his surname in the word "Bar." Ah! The most intriguing observation is pointed out by Dr. Yigael Yadin that in the Roman records, Bar-Kochba was called Simeon *Ben* Koseba, not *Bar* Kosba! Like the probability that those seven "Bar's," used in New Testament names, were actually "Ben's." Simeon Ben-Qoh Kha ViY, in a more kosher jargon, spoke, wrote, fought, and died for the Hebrew tongue, not the Aramaic.

How can we be certain Bar-Kochba wrote in Hebrew! Go to Hebrew University Museum and read the very letters he wrote and signed in Hebrew. They are preserved there until this day.

Following the period of the New Testament, what are the evidences from the church fathers as to whether Jesus spoke Hebrew or Aramaic? St. Jerome, who lived in the third century of the Common Era, made a pilgrimage to Bethlehem to translate the Old and New Testaments into Latin. As he began his work on the Vulgate translation, he used copies of both Testaments in the Greek language. He discovered glaring differences between the Greek Septuagint (LXX) translation of the Old Testament and references to those texts as quoted in the New Testament. In a dilemma, he went to the Jewish rabbis in Jerusalem and sought their help in solving this problem. The rabbis convinced Jerome that it was impossible to understand the scripture unless he understood the Hebrew language. He followed their counsel and moved to Tiberius where he studied Hebrew for fourteen years before returning to Bethlehem to undertake the Latin Vulgate translation.

That translation has been the most widely used of any translation ever published for over 1,600 years. The Latin Vulgate and the King James translations have been noted by Dr. David Flusser as being the most accurate translations in Bible history on a literal word to word concept.

In *Catal. Script. Eccl.*, Jerome pointed out that he was informed that he could find a *copy of the book of Matthew in the Hebrew tongue* at the library in Caesarea. These are the words of Jerome's account of his search for that Hebrew manuscript:

> Matthew, who is also Levi, who from a publican came to be an apostle, first of all the Evangelists,

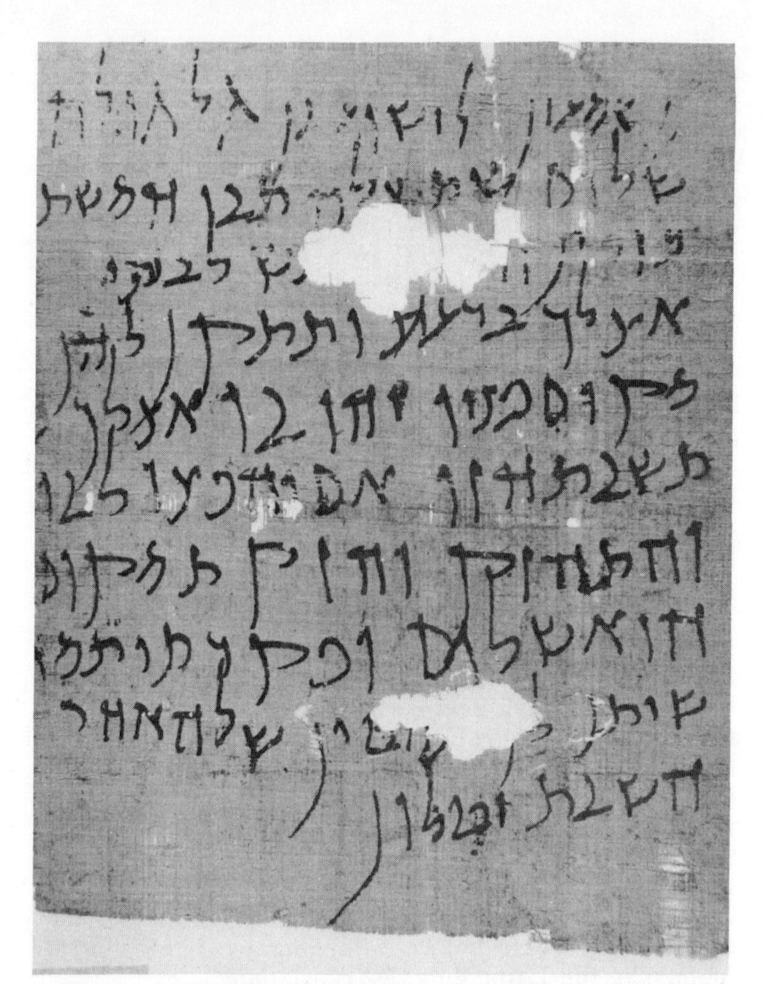

137 A.D. — This Bar Kochba letter in Hebrew shows that the language was not Aramaic. Courtesy of Dr. Magen Broshi, Israel Museum Shrine of the Book.

composed a Gospel of Christ in Judaea *in the Hebrew language and characters* [letters] for the benefit of those of the circumcision who had believed. Who translated it into Greek is not sufficiently ascertained. Furthermore, the *Hebrew* [copy] itself is preserved to this day in the library at Caesarea which the martyr Pamphilus so diligently collected. I also was allowed by the Nazarenes [Notzriim, Jews who followed the tradition of the Rebbe of Nazareth] who used this original volume [original scroll written by Matthew himself] in the Syrian city of Beroea, to copy it. [This was about the middle of the fourth century C. E.] In which it is to be remarked that, wherever the Evangelist [Matthew] makes use of the testimonies of the old scripture, he does not follow the authority of the seventy translators [Septuagint], LXX, but of *the Hebrew*.

To say that the great linguist, Jerome, did not know the difference between Aramaic and Hebrew during the third century after Jesus, requires a great deal of audacity on the part of modern scholarship. Jerome's linguistic community was much nearer, both in time and space, to both those languages, than we are today. In fact, both Hebrew and Aramaic were prominent languages during his life. They were spoken where he lived. He undoubtedly could communicate in either language.

Papias, the first disciple of Polycarp (who was the first disciple of John), related, according to Eusebius in *Historia Ecclesiastica*, III.39: "Matthew indeed gathered those writings of the Word in the Hebrew dialect. [Each] translator interpreted them [the Hebrew words] according to his ability [to translate or interpret]." Other church fathers and commentators, namely, Pliny, Hegesippus, Justin Martyr, Tatian, Irenaeus, Panteus, Origen, Symmachius, and Clement, make reference to the Hebrew language in the original Gospels and other New Testament writings. Not a single church father refers to the language of Jesus or people of his day as being Aramaic! There are references to these Hebrew originals as late as the eighth century of the Common Era. What happened to these Hebrew documents or even copies of these Hebrew documents remains the mystery that could be the key to unlock vast treasures of truths about what Jesus actually said in the language he spoke.

There is a possibility that somewhere in the sealed catacombs or in the archives or libraries of Rome, these documents have been laid away and forgotten. If this dream be true, the pope who would produce such manuscripts would, no doubt, far exceed the magnitude of Pope John XXIII in contribution to a new era in Jewish-Christian relations. Such a discovery would be of equal or greater significance to the Christian world than the finding of the Dead Sea Scrolls was to the Jewish world. Rome possesses the treasure of knowledge of the last two millennia. The Catholic church has more Biblical scholarship than all other Christian groups combined. May G-d grant them the vision to share that knowledge with the world. If every scrap of manuscript and book in the Vatican library were microfilmed and shared with world scholarship, ecumenism could achieve its first great step toward reality. Every Catholic devoted to the cause of better understanding of Christians with Jews and Christians with Christians should endeavor to give occasion to such opportunity.

Linguistically, the texts of the Greek New Testament, especially the Gospels, have posed problems for many years. These problems did not originate with modern scholarship but with the Greek Orthodox Church in the very early centuries. The Greek language in the codex was not readable by the Greek clergy or laity. Therefore, it was necessary to make a readable translation of the old Greek from the codex form. The Greeks had no problem reading Homer, Plato, or Aristotle, but Matthew, Mark, Luke, and John presented a different situation. To explain this difference, linguists casually excused it as being "koine," or marketplace Greek. Problems still remained, however, as was pointed out by Dr. Robert Dick Wilson of Princeton University. In 1921, he issued a paper stating, "The Greek of the Gospel accounts is not 'koine' Greek." Doctor Wilson's argument was simple: here are "koine" documents; analyze these parallel with the Gospel accounts and you will see that they are not linguistically the same.

Later, David L. Cooper did his doctorate thesis at Louisville Seminary on the "Differences in the Koine Greek and the Greek of the Gospels." In Doctor Cooper's observation, he noticed several differences: the overuse of the "kai" (and) and the overuse of the definite article in the Gospel texts as compared to that of the koine Greek. Another glaring contrast was that the codex, in most cases, had an inverted word order on the phrase and clause level. The general structure of the codex was linguistically different from the Greek of any period of history. The appearance of many words in the Greek New Testament could not be found in any other period or source of the Greek language. Neither Doctor Wilson nor Doctor Cooper gave a solution to this dilemma.

Many students who read the New Testament in Greek fail to realize that many of the footnotes indicating changes of word order, omissions of superfluous words, and all the exceptions to the rules in Greek, are trying to tell us there is a problem in the Greek itself. We must realize that the New Testament as we have it in Greek is a product of endless renditions and editions from the codex to a Greek that is readable. This is not true of older classical Greek manuscripts nor of later writings and, most especially, the koine Greek of that period.

Tagmemic linguistics is a specialized structural approach to language study developed by Kenneth L. Pike and Robert Longacre, primarily for use by the Wycliffe Bible Translators. It is a scientific method applying the slot-function approach of modern algebra to universal language analysis. For example, the Tagmemicist asks, "What is the function of this slot in the sentence? What class of words can fulfill that function?" This method can apply to the smallest form of a word that has independent meaning or expression, such as the "'s" which means possessive form of nouns, to the largest form of discourse, such as a volume of the Encyclopedia Britannica.

By application of Tagmemic linguistics, perhaps we may give an answer to the problem of the difference between the koine Greek and the Greek of the New Testament.

Before we discuss the Tagmemic application, let us look at contemporary scholarship which is researching in this area.

Dr. Robert L. Lindsey, a Southern Baptist minister recognized as an outstanding linguist of both classical and Biblical languages, has lived in Israel for nearly forty years. He has done a Hebrew-Greek diglott on the

Gospel of Mark. In the introduction to that book, Doctor Lindsey says:

> Rather to my surprise, the preliminary study of the Greek text of Mark turned up the conclusion that the Greek word order and idiom was more like Hebrew than literary Greek. This gave me the frightening feeling that I was as much in the process of 'Mark's restoring' an original Hebrew work as in that of creating a new one. Like many a Semitic student before me, as I later realized, I wondered if the Gospel might not be a literal translation from some Semitic original. . . .
>
> Having long supposed that Luke, as a non-Jewish companion of Paul, had tended to modify his text to make it more understandable to the Greeks of pagan background, I was even more surprised to note that the Lukan text was almost always easier to translate to idiomatic Hebrew than was Mark. After several more years of study in which this observation has been confirmed again and again, I, today, find my early supposition amusing. But, the point that I was quite unprepared to suppose, that of all the synoptists, Luke should prove to be the best preservation of the earlier text.
>
> An even stranger conclusion, if it is possible, began during these early days of research, to force itself into my consciousness: where Matthew is parallel with Mark and Luke in any given story or sentence, but not all, of the Markian translation difficulties reappeared in Matthew in the same or somewhat modified form. But, where Matthew was not parallel to Mark (whether in the stories only Luke and Matthew share or in those given only by Matthew), his text showed the same ease of translation as that of Luke.

Doctor Lindsey's words well illustrate the dilemma as stated by his transition from the traditional view to the factual observation. The mark of a scholar is not necessarily being able to quote all the authorities, but rather in his ability to evaluate their statements in the light of all the evidence at hand. As Irving Fisher so aptly put it, “To unlearn the taken-for-granted is sometimes harder than to learn the hitherto unexpected.” Or, as Albert Schweitzer said, “Man’s biggest problem is that he just does not think.”

It is a real test of character when one comes to realize that he has held a popular pre-supposition that he must surrender for the sake of truth. Especially is this decision difficult when the new factual finding is in variance with, or sometimes directly in contradiction to, the mores and popular thoughts of the masses.

In response to Doctor Lindsey’s observation, one of the leaders in his denomination very readily agreed that the doctor’s work was genuinely authoritative and undoubtedly correct. “But,” he said, “if we accept Lindsey’s findings, that will mean that thousands of volumes written on the subject will be obsolete. It will also mean that our whole approach in making Jesus meaningful today is wrong. We will have to scrap all we have said and stop all that we are doing and start over. I don’t think we can afford that expense.”

This kind of reaction to truth is only comparable to that of Alexander the Coppersmith, who cried, “Great is Diana of the Ephesians!”

Jewish scholarship—most especially Jewish scholarship—recognizes that the language of Jesus was Hebrew. Professor Martin Buber stated, “Jesus, undoubtedly, when addressing his people, spoke in the Hebrew tongue.”

Dr. David Flusser of Hebrew University, lecturing to the Institute of Judaic-Christian Research in 1968, said:

> We can only be as certain that Jesus and his disciples spoke Hebrew as we can be certain that he was a Jew and lived in Eretz Yisrael. If Jesus was a Jew who lived in this place during that purported time, the question then is, “did he speak his mother tongue?”
>
> Those scholars I have known who seem most fanatically certain that Jesus did not speak Hebrew, but spoke Greek or Aramaic instead, for the most part do not themselves know either Hebrew, Aramaic or Greek, apart from a very limited exposure on a theological seminary level.

At the beginning of the 17th century, the Dutch theologian Julius Scaliger, spent some time in a Syrian monastery. During that time, he conceived the idea, no more than a theory, that Jesus spoke Aramaic instead of Hebrew. Before Scaliger, no one had ever dreamed that the language of Jesus was anything other than his mother tongue, Hebrew.

More surprising still are the Jewish scholars who, either for the sake of a scholarly image or perhaps a lack of investigation, accept Scaliger's theory without question.

The realization of Doctor Lindsey that he was making a restoration of the text instead of a new translation into Hebrew, is made most emphatic by an application of Tagmemic linguistics to a given message.

Since the Tagmemic approach is much "monk work," and the author's objective in this book is to avoid the mire of deep scholarly investigation, he shall omit the principles involved in a Tagmemic analysis. The conclusion of such an application shows us several fascinating things: (See further bibliography reference.)

1. The inverted word-form in the codex, when translated particle for particle, forms beautiful Hebrew phrase constructions.

2. The superfluous word particles found in the codex which are omitted in most editions of the Greek New Testament become very vital in the transliteration or translation back to the Hebrew word-phrase relationship.

3. Dr. David Cooper's observation of all the extra "and's" and "the's" occurring in the Greek New Testament which are not so prevalent in other Greek documents, prove to be very essential when translated back to Hebrew. The extra "and's" or Kai, become Weh (VeH), וְ —oH, וֹ and —ouH, וּ . The definite articles in Greek, Ho, Tow, and Hay, etc., translate to the Hebrew definite article Hah, הָ and — Heh, הֶ . The occurrence of the Hebrew article is not necessary in either Greek or English, but it is most necessary in the Hebrew linguistic structure.

4. When a passage is translated from the Greek codex back to Hebrew, the thought patterns and punctuation

are vastly changed. When that simulated Hebrew text is translated into English, it renders a different product as compared to the Bible translated from Greek directly to English.

5. In order to render a more accurate account of what Jesus actually said in the language he spoke requires more than the work of linguists. It requires the labors of those who are versed in the jargon of rabbinic Judaism, on every level of interpretation, during that period of rabbinic lore. For example, a person may be most highly qualified in English grammar and yet not be qualified to interpret a Shakespearean drama. This is to say that before we can understand fully what the Rabbi of Nazareth meant in the framework of the Jewish tradition, we must await the willingness of rabbinic Jewish scholarship in the traditional sense of the word to help produce that product.

Unfortunately, the attitudes that exist today among those who are qualified to do so are not conducive to such a production, and it shall not be until there is a sincere change in the attitude of Christians toward Judaism and the Jew. This re-Judaization of Jesus will follow a natural course once the Christian can approach the issue without any ulterior motive for the conversion of the Jews and further de-Judaization of Jesus.

Taking last things first, we must begin with a recognition that Jesus spoke Hebrew. The problem that faces most people in this confrontation is that same old problem of preferring to drag the axle instead of getting out of the rut. Since the 17th century, thousands of books have been written saying that Jesus spoke Aramaic. Can we "afford the expense" of admitting that he spoke Hebrew?

"Our honored professors taught us that Jesus spoke Aramaic. We have learned that the word Hebrew, when occurring in the New Testament or related texts, does not mean Hebrew at all, but means instead, the foreign language, Aramaic. Since we have learned these things, we have taught others the same. They believed us; therefore, we make the assumption in the light of all these facts that Jesus spoke Aramaic regardless of the evidence of other findings. Even if we must ignore all the evidence of the post-captivity prophets, the Dead Sea Scrolls, over thirty references in the New Testament, modern scholarship and Tagmemic linguistic analysis, we cannot "afford the expense" of admitting that we have accepted a ben trovato conclusion, and must continue to accept that Jesus spoke Aramaic rather than his mother Hebrew tongue."

Those who desire to perpetuate the ideas of replacement theology cannot admit that Jesus spoke Hebrew. They know it would not stop there. Martin Buber in his classic "I and Thou" described this attitude thusly:

"*Mundus vult decipi:* the world wants to be deceived. The truth is too complex and frightening; the taste for the truth is an acquired taste that few acquire.

Not all deceptions are palatable. Untruths are too easy to come by, too quickly exploded, too cheap and ephemeral to give lasting comfort. *Mundus vult decipi;* but there is a hierarchy of deceptions.

Near the bottom of the ladder is journalism: a steady stream of irresponsible distortions that most people find refreshing although on the morning after, or at least within a week, it will be stale and flat.

On a higher level we find fictions that men eagerly believe, regardless of the evidence, because they gratify some wish.

Near the top of the ladder we encounter curious mixtures of untruth and truth that exert a lasting fascination on the intellectual community.

What cannot, on the face of it, be wholly true, although it is plain that there is some truth in it, evokes more discussion and dispute, divergent exegeses and attempts at emendations than what has been stated very carefully, without exaggeration or onesidedness. The Book of Proverbs is boring compared to the Sermon on the Mount."

Or as Lewis Entzminger said, "Even rat poison is 98% good corn meal."

Chapter IV
THE RIDDLE OF INTERPRETATION

"The Jews insist upon a literal interpretation of the scripture based on thirteen laws, but we know that the spiritual interpretation is far superior."

Jerome

Inseparable from the linguistic question: What did Jesus actually say in the language he spoke? is the hermeneutical question: What did his words literally mean to those who heard him?

Hermeneutics is that science of applying basic laws of interpretation to any given document. One of the greatest differences between Judaism and Christianity is that Judaism has a very sophisticated system of hermeneutics which is universally accepted by all traditional Jews. Christianity differs, not in *another* system from the Jewish one, but in that Christianity has no established system of interpretation whatsoever. Because the Jews have an agreed-upon system of universal principles of hermeneutics, there has not been the schism of denominationalism in Judaism as there has been in Christianity.

Even with the divergence in this century of Jewish institutions into Orthodox, Conservative and Reform movements, they still remain undivided on the question of interpretation. The latter two depart from traditional Judaism only in the matter of authority and observance of the Jewish law. There is no argument between the strictest Orthodox and the most radical Reform as to what Moses said or what he meant. The differences are in the questions of observance, of whether or not, or to what extent those words are binding, on the individual today in each case. The rabbinic principles of hermeneutics are the bond that has maintained the unity of the Jewish people for four thousand years.

Unfortunately, since Clement of Alexandria, Christianity has rejected these rabbinic principles. In their place, the Church has substituted the principles of Greek mythology and philosophical logic. This substitution was done without a premise of any system or laws of interpretation. Therefore, church council after church council, bull after bull, dogma after dogma evolved in trying to explain the literal meaning of spiritual interpretation, prefaced only upon a rejection of the literal interpretation as exercised by the Jews. Eventually, these dogmas were solidified into a theological system that was much more akin to pagan Greek mythology than it was to the historic Jewish faith. These dogmas became so dictatorial that anyone who did not agree with them was considered a heretic, an apostate, or an infidel. The Jews were looked upon by the Church as infidels who totally rejected the evolution of Jesus into a Hellenized image.

In this evolution every effort was exerted to depart, in some degree or totally, from the Jewish meaning of words. The result of this re-definition has become such that the very basic vocabulary of the Christian and the Jew of today are worlds apart. Words such as Bible—the Word of G-d—inspiration, Law, grace, Messiah, Lord, redemption, and salvation have an entirely different meaning to the Jew than they have to the Christian. What authority does the Church have to change the definitions of words of Hebrew and Jewish origin?

Today, perhaps more than at any time in the past eighteen hundred years, more and more Christians are vitally interested in knowing the literality of the meanings of the words of Jesus rather than the disposition of meanings as they have evolved through Christian theology.

Theology is an accommodation of particular truths based on the given meaning of terms into a system of dogmatic expression. It is relatively easy to educate a community in that system and ignore the over-all body of divinity. Therefore, the Christian religion has become divided institutionally, and fragmented within those institutions, over the quibbling about the emphasis or de-emphasis of those doctrines. Theology is an instrument of division and the devil's best substitute for the study and understanding of the Bible.

There is no such thing as Jewish theology in the traditional aspect of Judaism. Since the Jews have a hermeneutical system that gives occasion to an over-all study of the scriptures, the creation of Jewish theology was not only unnecessary but impossible. With the broad hermeneutical approach, the scripture in any given passage or word could never be restricted to one single interpretation. Simon Peter makes that expression in these words: "Knowing this first, that no prophecy of the scripture is of any private interpretation. For the prophecy came not in old time by the will of man: but holy men of G-d spake as they were moved by the Holy Spirit." (II Peter 1:20-21)

One Merkabah rabbi said, while discussing the possibility of meanings of each word of Torah, "Every word has seven meanings."

"Not so," answered his colleague. "Every word of Torah has seventy meanings."

Then answered the third, "Each word of Torah has not seven, nor yet seventy meanings. Each word of Torah has a myriad of interpretations. Each time the words of Torah are read, the *RoUGahKh Ha QahDohSH* [Holy Spirit] gives a new meaning to each word to meet one's need for that day."

Unfortunately, the Christian has been educated to think that there is one—and only one— meaning to each prophetic word. He also thinks that the Holy Spirit is an exclusive Christian revelation and that it is unknown to the Jews.

The word "hermeneutic" comes from a construction meaning "speaking by the Spirit." In Greek mythology, Hermes was the *speaker* for the gods, the one who brought their message to men and interpreted it to them. As in *The Odyssey* of Homer, "We gods had warned him, sent down Hermes Argeiphontes, our most observant courier. . . ."

Pneuma is the Greek word for spirit; hence, hermeneutics is "speaking or interpreting the message of G-d by the spirit." It is not a systemless interpretation by hunch or I think-isms. Neither is it an unknown tongue. The "Spirit of the Holy of Holies," or the "breath of G-d," in the Jewish concept, is never at variance with the Written or Oral Law. Each interpretation, though they be myriad, cannot violate these basic laws of rabbinic hermeneutics. All interpretations by the Spirit are according to, and never violate the laws of, rabbinic hermeneutics. They are as concrete as the laws of physics; they work in harmony, not in opposition, to each other. There is a vast breadth and depth of possibility and expansion of meaning within the operation and manipulation of the laws of the Jewish hermeneutical system.

Jerome's words, "We know that a spiritual interpretation is far superior," and his mention of the thirteen rabbinic laws, indicate that he knew *of* the hermeneutical system of the Jews, but was ignorant of their entirety and their meanings.

The first reason for the Christian's departure from the rabbinic system was the simple *rejection* of that system only because it was Jewish. The void created by this rejection of rabbinic hermeneutics and any hermeneutics and literal interpretation of the Jewish system demanded a *substitute* to accommodate the *spiritual interpretation* in place of the *literal*. Immediately, church councils had to be called in order to define the *new spiritualized* meanings of words. The words and phrases took new meanings *unrelated* to their Jewish origins. The result was that the sermons, homilies, and expositions became mere accumulations of personal hunches and gee-whiz-isms which, amazingly enough, solidified into a hocus-pocus, gobbledygook commonly known as dogmatic theology. This theology was based on an inconsistent application of paganistic Greek logic which stirred the Church even further from its Jewish heritage.

The rabbinic laws of interpretation are divided into four levels. The first level is the *Seven Laws of Rabbi Hillel*. The second is the *Thirteen Laws of Rabbi Ishmael*. The third is the *Thirty-two Laws of Rabbi Eliezer Ben Gallil*. The fourth and highest level is the *Forty-two Laws of Kabbalah*. These levels, or laws, did not originate with these four rabbis. This simply means that it was they who redacted them from the Oral Law given to Moses on Mount Sinai.

Tradition tells us that Rabbi Hillel was only seventeen years old when he wrote the seven laws during a Sanhedrin trial in Jerusalem. He lived to be one hundred thirty-seven years old and died during the time Jesus was a teenager in Yeshiva near Nazareth. This redaction, therefore, was before 100 B.C.E.

These four levels of rabbinic interpretation are called the פרד"ס, *PaR'DehC, Pardes*, or Paradise, discussed in the first chapter of this book. The uncontracted word פרדס, *PaR'DiC*, or Paradise, means orchard or Gan Eden, the Garden of Eden. Upon these laws "the Eternal One, the Creator, brought all the living creatures unto Adam to see what he would call them: and whatsoever Adam called every living creature, that was the name thereof." (Gen. 2:19-20) Therefore, the tradition of the principles of hermeneutics is not exclusively Jewish, but instead is universal.

Some of these principles appear in other schools of logic and methods of interpretation in non-systematic form. Others occasionally become utilized unconsciously. The Jews, however, have preserved the entire system in perfect form from the Oral Law at Mount Sinai. Why should the Church reject that perfect form for an imperfect and incomplete one, or for no system at all?

The main reason the replacement theologians rejected the rabbinic hermeneutical system was simply because it was Jewish. Another reason is that if theological seminaries taught all these levels of hermeneutics, they would create in the students the ability to think for themselves. Seminaries that develop in their students an ability to think in the parameter of rabbinic logic would create a clergy that is more interested in asking pertinent questions than they are in giving dogmatic answers. This approach would soon diminish the petty theological concepts that the particular denominational schools wish to propagate and try to educate their laymen to believe. The acceptance of dogmatic theology not only does not require the individual to think for himself, it does not permit him to think at all.

What and how the clergy *thinks* is directly reflected in attitudes of the laity, "like priest, like people." It is the clergy who are educated to make snide remarks about the Jews that have educated Christianity to have the same attitude. When a thinking clergy, oriented in rabbinic hermeneutics, is produced, they will produce a thinking laity which will have a more appreciative relationship with their Jewish neighbors. Many thinking Christians today have disassociated themselves from their churches simply because they are tired of hearing the same parochial bigotry and nothingness of dark age theology. To reinstate the Jewish concepts into Christian thinking will mean making a sacrifice of the golden calf of Christian theology. That sacrifice will bring a new era to Christianity. No organized force could ever bring about this total reformation. It will only be brought about by uncontestable revitalizing of Israel's sacrificial economy in the coming decade.

A proper explanation of the four levels of rabbinic hermeneutics and the articulation and explanation of each law with its illustrated application, is a beautiful study. That, however, is a book unto itself. Here we shall engage ourselves only in a broad explanation of the levels as they apply to the Gospels.

The name of the four levels, פרד"ס, *PaR'DehC,* Pardes, comes from the application of one of the laws of the Kabbalah. This is the law of Notarikon, or an acronym. A common illustration of the Notarikon used by the early Christians was IXΘΥΣ. The word IXOUΣ was produced by taking the first letter of each word in the Greek phrase *Iησοῦς Xριστος Θεοῦ Yιοῦ Σωτηρ,* which means "Jesus Christ, G-d's Son [and] Savior." When this Notarikon is assembled, it spells the Greek word "fish," IXOUΣ.

The name of the classification of the Seven Laws of Hillel is the "simple," or פשט, *PaSHahT,* or Peshat, level of interpretation. The word Peshat represents the *P,* פ, in *PaR'DehC.* This simple level is the interpretation for the "simple people," the common, ordinary man. The word Peshat means simple. The common man wanted to know, "What does the Torah ask of me? What must I do to fulfill the words of Torah in my life?" There were agricultural laws for the farmers and herdsmen. Holy Seasons, Sabbaths, and feasts were included to be observed by everyone. There were laws for women concerning marriage, the Jewish home life, and the proper preparations of kosher foods. The Torah contained criminal and civil decisions for everyone's day to day routine. There were laws in the Torah which applied only to the priests and the offering of sacrifices. Then there were laws of general application to the Israeli public concerning ritual cleansing, hygiene, and laws of ritual purity.

The simple level was a grammatic interpretation of the law on a simple, codified level. By applying the Seven Laws of Hillel to the words of Torah, the Five Books of Moses were made meaningful to the average person.

This level gave a simple guide to the actions and conduct of ordinary or common people.

This application of the Seven Laws of Hillel produced the commentary called the Mishnah. The word *Mishnah* means "from the second." The first is the Torah; second to the Torah is the Mishnah.

The Mishnah has six volumes. The first is *Zeraim*, or seeds, and concerns agricultural laws. The second volume, *Mo'ed*, deals with the Sabbath and Holy Days. The third volume is *Nashim*; it gave the laws concerning women, marriage, the Jewish home, and the preparation of kosher foods. The fourth volume, *Nezikin*, or Sanhedrin, deals with civil and criminal laws. The fifth volume, *Kodashim*, has to do with holy things, sacrifices, and the priesthood. Volume six is *Taharot*, concerning ritual purification.

Each of these major volumes was divided into tractates, called *Mesichtoth*. Each *Mesichtoth* was subdivided into smaller *Mishnayot*.

The second level of hermeneutical interpretation is the Thirteen Laws of Rabbi Ishmael. It is called the רמז, *RehMehZ*, Remez, meaning the "hint" level of interpretation. It represents the ר, *R*, in *PaR'DehC*. While the first level of Hillel was simple, grammatic exposition for the simple people, Ishmael's laws were on the allegorical level, and were written for the elite aristocracy. This level was higher in its aim, more noble in its content, and generally more applicable to the professional strata of the community. It was for the doctors, lawyers, teachers, philosophers, and those of noble class. It was for those who wanted to know more than the minimum required to fulfill Torah.

The Remez, or hint level of interpretation, did not replace the simple or Mishnaic level of interpretation, but rather gave grace and seasoning to its presentation.

The application of the thirteen allegorical laws of Rabbi Ishmael to the Torah produced the Gemara, which means "from the teaching." The generation that wrote the Gemara were called the Amoraim, from *Moreh*, meaning "teachers." The Amoraim in Jerusalem compiled the Mishnah and Gemara into one massive library and called it Talmud Yerushalmi, or Jerusalem Talmud. Far away in Babylon, other Amoraim led by Rav Ashi, Ravina, and their peers, compiled the Talmud Bably, or Babylonian Talmud.

During this period, there was little migration of the Jews. It is doubtful whether any of those in Babylon or in Jerusalem corresponded with each other. Yet, their products were in agreement *because they were applying the same laws of interpretation.* They did not have to be together in person to agree on the meanings because they were together in the principles of hermeneutics. *Only when the Christians rejected these principles did Judaism and Christianity begin to rift in their relationships.* It must be observed, too, that it was the Christians who departed, not the Jews.

The Seven Laws of Hillel produced the Mishnah, and the Thirteen Laws of Rabbi Ishmael produced the Gemara. The Mishnah and Gemara comprise the Talmud. למוּד, TaL'MoUD, comes from the intensive form of the word למד, LohMehD, which means to "study." One can spend a lifetime studying and never master the Talmud. However, many great and noble men have devoted only a few weeks' intense study to this lore, and have become completely mastered by the Talmud.

Many Christians who read this literature are shocked at how much of the New Testament is clearly stated in the Talmud. It surprises the Christian even more when he realizes that the Talmud is not quoting the New Testament, but rather that the New Testament is quoting the Talmud. A simple perusal of the Jewish Prayer Book will illustrate this.

The third level of interpretation is the דרש, *Drosh,* representing the ד, *D,* of the word *PahR'DehC.* To D'RohSH in Hebrew means "to thresh." If one were to take a head of wheat, rub it briskly in his hands, shell out every grain of wheat, and then blow away the chaff, he would have *droshed* the wheat. This D'RohSH level is produced by the application of the Thirty-two Laws of Rabbi Eliezer Ben Gallil. This is the exegetical level of interpretation, producing a commentary known as the *Midrash.*

Where the Mishnah is the simple level to the simple people and the Gemara is that to the aristocratic and noble, the Midrash is לְמֶלֶךְ, *LaMehLehhK,* or "to the King." This is regal, the *rexis,* the kingly or majestic level of interpretation.

As the first level is the simple *grammatical,* and the second level is the elite *allegorical,* the third level, the

Drosh, is *parabolic* in its literary approach. Many times the prophets delivered the message of G-d to the kings in the form of parables as Nathan did to David (II Sam. 12:1-5), and as Jotham did to Abimelech (Judges 9:6-21). The *PahSHahT*, or Mishnaic level, is the simple truth in the codification and denotation of plain words. The *RehMehZ*, or Gemaric level, is the figurative connotation or the emblematic truth that the simple words symbolize by means of suggestion.

The Drosh, or Midrashic, level is even higher on the literary scale than is the Gemaric. It is parabolic. The parabolic bases its symbolism on the entire narrative rather than on the word-phrase level. In the sphere of the Midrashic interpretation, the suggestive possibility takes in even more territory.

The Thirty-two Laws of Rabbi Eliezer Ben Gallil, when applied, on that regal level of the parabolic, to the Torah, produced the rabbinic commentary called the Midrash, מדרש, *MiD'RahSH*, meaning "from the Drosh," or "threshing." This commentary contains parable after parable. Amazing also is how many stories of kings and kingdoms are used in the parables of the Midrash. Since it is the regal level of interpretation, one might expect to find much to do with the kings and kingdoms.

The fourth level of rabbinic hermeneutics is the סוֹד, *CoHd*, or Sood, meaning the secret level. It represents the *C*, ס, in the *PahR'Deh*C. Very few, even of the most learned Jewish scholars, proceed into this level. Those who receive this level are called Kabbalists. The word קבל, *QaBahL*, means to "receive." They who receive that secret of the *Sood* level are called Kabbalists for their reception of the secret level of interpretation.

The Sood level is ever so much higher than the regal, the noble, and the simple that at first, it appears to have no relationship at all to them. This is the divine level, the other-worldness sphere of interpretation. It is the Torah as G-d sees it—the heavenly interpretation.

Though this is the highest level, it was the first level given to Moses on Mount Sinai. Each level regresses from there to the simplest. All Jewish commentaries proceed from the highest to the lowest. The Talmud itself was simplified to the *Halacha*, which means "the walk," or conduct. Later, Rabbi Joseph Caro, the greatest of the Kabbalists, wrote the *Shulchan-Aruch*, which means "a prepared table." He wrote this to make the Halacha even simpler so that any Jew who desired to learn could do so.

The Kabbalists, by applying the Forty-two Laws of Kabbalah to the Torah, produced the commentary called the *Zohar*. זהר, Zohar, in Hebrew, means "the Radiance" or "the Aura." The Kabbalists define the Zohar thusly: As the dawn approaches, the horns of light radiate (Zohar) over the horizon like the winged, feathered fingers of the sun, pushing away the darkness of the night. Yet, when the sun appears, the Aura (Zohar) of the *Radiance* vanishes. So it is with the Torah. When one is looking directly at the words, the Zohar cannot be seen. Only one who stands in the twilight can see the Radiance (Zohar) of the Torah. The Zohar was not only the first level given to Moses, it was the first of all four levels to be redacted by Rabbi Shimon Ben Yohai in Pe'quin at the beginning of the second century C.E. This was about the same time as the writing of the Apocalypse of John. Both the book of Zohar and the book of Revelation are Kabbalistic in nature. Both were written by Jews in Roman exile.

The Kabbalist is the Jewish mystic. He is concerned with the divine, the other-worldness. In him is vested the Spirit of Prophecy. He is the one who sees the material world through the miraculous, rather than seeing the miraculous world through material. Even here, he is subject to more hermeneutical laws than to any other level. He is the dreamer, but his dreams are governed by principles far stronger than the former three. In this he differs from the secular or Christian mystic. He is totally subject to the words of Torah and the forty-two principles of interpretation. He has gone into the garden, the Pardes, or Paradise, and has gone up to its highest plateau.

Genesis is the book of Beginnings. The other four books, Exodus, Leviticus, Numbers, and Deuteronomy, are the Torah given exclusively to Israel. In the strictest sense, the words of the Torah to Israel are the four latter books of the Pentateuch. There are four books of the Jewish law, and four levels of interpretation. They are intercollated but are not parallel or chronological.

How many books are there in the Christian New Testament which relate the life of Jesus? There are four, no fewer, and no more. Four books of the law to Israel, four levels of interpretation, and four accounts of the life of Jesus. Did you ever wonder why there are four, no fewer and no more?

There are four writers of the four Gospels. One was a simple man, a slave. One was an aristocrat, a physician. One was a regal son of the priestly tribe, a tax collector in the king's court. The last was a dreamer, a mystic, who stretched his fishing nets under the skies of Galilee, not far from Safed or Safat—a city known as the city of the Kabbalist.

The first, the *simple* man, was John Mark. He wrote a brief, concise account of the life of Jesus for those who were on his own level—the servants, the merchants, and the farmers and herdsmen. Mark wrote for those who wanted the *simple* facts. His account was on the level of those who *simply* wanted to know, "What must I do to fulfill the words of Torah?"

Christian commentators who are far removed from any knowledge of the Mishnah called Mark's account "the action Gospel," "the businessman's Gospel," or "the Gospel of essentials." These designations may be observed by even the casual reader. (The reader who wishes to pursue a study of Mishnah can get Danby's English translation.) The Christian who studies Mishnah will at first be impressed by how blunt and Mark-ish it is. After considerable study, he will begin to discover, however, just how Mishnaic Mark is. Remember that the Mishnah in the oral tradition had been handed down since Moses.

The Mishnah is a codification of the Torah. Therefore, its literary style is that of a codification, brief and non-exhaustive. It is not concerned with the chronological order of the six hundred thirteen commandments. The Mishnaic rabbis would take a word or a thought and twist it with every verbal synonym of thought they could think of.

For an example of Mark's Mishnaic word style and phrase structure, note his description of the woman with an issue of blood in Mark 5:25-26.

a. And a certain woman,
b. which had an issue of blood
c. twelve years
d. and had suffered many things
e. of many physicians
f. and had spent all that she had,
g. and was nothing bettered,
h. but rather grew worse...

One familiar with Mishnaic jargon will recognize immediately the Mishnaic codification of the woman's condition by Mark's description. He did not write in this style about the woman because he was a chiropractor putting down the medical doctors and the A.M.A. He deliberately wrote in a Mishnaic style. That same Mishnaic structure can be observed in his description of the demoniac of Gadara in verses 1-5 of the same chapter. The Mishnaic rabbis used this style to reach the common people who demanded such descriptive definitions on the simple level.

Mark's codification of the life of Jesus, like that of the Mishnah, is brief and non-exhaustive. The book of Mark is a dossier on the life of Jesus. Mark is not concerned with the chronological order of the events as is Luke. Mark is the realist and makes no emphasis on the "Son of G-d" as does John. The reference in Mark 1:1 to "the Son of G-d" is monkish, not Mark-ish. It is absent in the older Greek texts. Who is interested in the birth and background of a servant? Mark, for that reason, omits the first thirty years of Jesus' life. This is characteristic of a Mishnaic presentation.

Mark is a simple, common man. He writes on the level of simple, common people. He chose the literary style that he knew best—his own! He presents the life of Jesus, the Servant of the Eternal One, the Suffering Servant who ministered to the poor, the naked, the helpless, and the hungry, as it related to those simple, common folk. Mark writes as Mark is. His message is to those on his own strata of society. His account lacks the philosophical jargon of Luke as well as the words of regal poise of Matthew. Nor does he get carried away with the Radiance of Zohar as does John.

Mark is Mishnaic. Each account that he relates is a brief codification of the life of Jesus, developed in agreement with the grammatic Hillel's principles. He is fenced into the basic framework of those seven laws. In each story there are phrases which tabulate into the six sections, or the Tractates, of the Mishnah.

While Matthew in chapter thirteen gives seven parables of the kingdom of heaven, Mark, in chapter four, mentions only two of them, and makes no reference to the kingdom of heaven. The two that Mark records are the parable of the sower and the parable of the mustard seed. Why only these two? Because they are relative to the first volume of the Mishnah, *Zeraim* (seeds).

Mark makes much reference to the Sabbath Day and the festivals of Israel. Although his references are brief, they are frequent; and in their details, they relate directly to the second volume of Mishnah, *Mo'ed*.

With great length and detail, Mark, in chapter five, describes the healing of the woman with an issue of blood. This relates to the third volume of Mishnah, *Nashim*.

Mark explains that when the woman with an issue of blood touched the *Tsitsit* on Jesus' prayer shawl, Jesus was ritually defiled. Jesus' reaction as Mark records it in 5:30 was: "And Jesus, immediately knowing in himself that virtue had gone out of him, turned him [self] about in the press [of people] and said, 'Who touched my clothes *[Talit]*?'"

None of the other writers recounts this story. Why does Mark make such an issue of it? The ritual defilement of blood had to do with the sixth volume of Mishnah, *Taharot*.

According to *Taharot*, Jesus is now defiled by blood; he cannot go with Jairus to heal his daughter because he is now ritually unclean until evening. At evening, however, he will be able to wash himself and his clothes and become ritually clean again.

The dilemma of this moment is critical. There stands the woman who has just been made whole. In imparting his virtue to her, Jesus has himself become ritually defiled. By imputing to her his purity, he has assumed her impurity.

Why is this important for Mark, the Mishnaic, to mention? In the fifth volume of *Kodeshim* is the tractate on the Ashes of the Red Heifer. In that Mishnaic prescription, a ritually clean man is to be chosen to sprinkle the Sanhedrin with the water of the Ashes of the Red Heifer. In that process, the Sanhedrin is ritually cleansed for their coming year's service. But, during the ceremony, the ritually clean man who sprinkles the Sanhedrin in their purification, takes their uncleanness onto himself.

Here is the woman made clean. For the first time in twelve years, she does not have to cry, "Unclean, unclean!" as she walks the streets of Kafar Nahum. Her eyes are filled with joy, peace, liberation and gratitude until they meet the eyes of Jairus. She realizes only now that she has snatched away the only hope of his little twelve-year-old daughter's life.

Tearful, defeated, disappointed, and alarmed, Jairus has realized that the hand that has just touched Jesus' Talit has smothered hope for his daughter's life. He knows that Jesus' defilement by blood would now prohibit the Rabbi from going to his house. How can Jesus fulfill the commandment, "to save a life," and not violate the law of restriction in the "separation of one who is ritually defiled"?

Jairus, the president of the synagogue, wonders what decision Jesus will make. Jesus is seemingly spared from making that decision as friends from the house of Jairus are solemnly approaching in a mournful hundred-meter cadence, and saying, "Trouble not the Rabbi—your daughter is dead."

Jesus, Mark relates, does go on to the house of Jairus. He takes his Talit and binds the daughter's hands with the Tsitsit and covers her with the shawl. In the imperative, he cries, "Talita Cumi!" The girl arises from beneath Jesus' Talit. The *twelve-year-old* child has been brought back to life by the same garment that had only a few moments before cleansed the woman who had had an issue of blood for *twelve years.*

Why did Mark make such a long story of this? He did so because in the Nashim and Taharot, it is written: "If a woman with an issue of blood touch a piece of common bread, the bread is defiled by her uncleanliness. But, if she touch a piece of Hallach [priest bread], the Hallach is not defiled because the holiness of the Hallach is greater than her defilement. If she touch the priest's garment, the priest is unclean, but the garment is not defiled because the Holiness of the priest's garment is greater than her defilement."

Since Jesus is ritually defiled, but his Talit is not, he uses his Talit to raise the daughter of Jairus. Everything that Mark says in this long story has to do with the Mishnaic tradition. Mark is the Mishnah on the life of Jesus. The words he chose to describe the intricate relationship of Jesus to the Mishnah were different from the descriptive words used by the other writers in their accounts of the story of Jesus. Mark's words and style are more akin to the Mishnah itself than they are to the words and style of the other Gospel writers.

Luke is a physician and an aristocrat. He writes to a philosopher, Theophilus. He addresses him in Luke 1:3 as the *"Most Excellent."* The nominative of address is modified by the Greek word from which we get the words *"most aristocratic."*

Luke's account of the life of Jesus is delivered in the flowery rhetoric of a noble. Listen to Doctor Luke, M.D., in his opening words of chapter one: "Forasmuch as many have taken in hand to set forth in order a declaration of those things which are most surely believed among us.

"Even as they delivered them unto us, which from the beginning were eyewitnesses, and ministers of the word.

"It seemed good to me also, having had perfect understanding of all things from the very first, to write unto thee in order, most excellent The-oph-i-lus, that thou mightest know the certainty of those things, wherein thou hast been instructed."

Doctor Luke is very meticulous in his professional description of the impregnations of both Elizabeth and Mary. Throughout the books of Luke and Acts, he uses a doctor's vocabulary to describe any situation that concerns anatomy. For example, he uses technical words that Mark, Matthew, or John never used. He speaks of the gestation periods of Mary and Elizabeth with exact detail as to the particular months of their pregnancies in the sequence of the events of the story. Luke gives a medical case report and writes the most chronological account of the life of Jesus of any of the other three writers. The book of Luke is a *Case History* on the life of Jesus.

Luke is the noble. He is the student of the Gemara. As a Gemarist, he describes Jesus through his own eyes and experiences, addressing his writings to the people of his level. Luke presents the life of Jesus in a higher framework than the simple Mishnaic vocabulary of Mark.

Luke deals in the allegorical, the noble, the aristocratic. As we have observed, if a man were a slave, who would be interested in his pedigree or genealogy? No one! Therefore, Mark gives no genealogy of Jesus. Luke, however, is presenting the nobility of his day with the nobility of Jesus. It is necessary for a noble to give his family tree. Luke did not forget to relate the pedigree of Jesus in chapter 3:23-38, all the way back to Adam.

Luke presents Jesus as the "Son of Man." In Luke's Hebrew tongue, the "Son of Man" is "Ben Adam." In presenting Jesus as Ben Adam, Luke retraced his genealogy 3,757 years back to the creation of Adam.

Like the Gemara, Luke's account is basically allegorical. Every word is a Remez, or hint, to another higher parallel. His account in the "Magnificat," in chapter 1:46-56, is most suggestive of that prayer of Hannah in I Samuel 2:1-10, but he does not mention the source. In Zechariah's prophecy, as recorded in Luke 1:67-79, is one cliche after another from the *Tanach* (Old Testament). No writer of the four Gospels is more intricate in his descriptions of the Jewish law on the level of Gemara than is Luke. Unlike Matthew, who would cite the particular passage and say "that it might be fulfilled which was spoken by... ," Luke, in an assumption that his readers on the Gemaric level would take the *hint*, only *suggests* those sources in his choice of the holy jargon. He draws no pictures except by suggestion. He writes on the hint level of the Gemara. Only a suggestion is expedient. A full reference of source would be redundant and would betray the Gemaric style in Luke's letters.

Luke does not quote book, chapter, and verse as Matthew does. Because of this, Christian commentators who are unfamiliar with the rabbinic method of the Gemara, conclude that Luke was a Gentile. In reality, however, Luke uses more Hebraisms and rabbinic jargon in Gemaric expression than any other author in the New Testament. His book is interwoven in a sophisticated manner with the thirteen allegorical principles of Rabbi Ishmael.

Noteworthy is the observation that John Mark was a witness of the Acts of the Apostles through the first fifteen chapters, and Luke, the author of the book of Acts, was a witness throughout the remainder of the book. In the first half of the book, Luke describes the narrative in the third person, "he," "they," "them." In Acts 15:36-41 and 16:10, we note the shift of the pronoun from third person "they" during Luke's absence, to the first person plural, "we" and "us" after Luke became the companion of Paul. Where Silas (Silvanus) is with Paul, Luke uses the first person plural pronouns "we" and "us." But where Silas is not with Paul, Luke uses again the third person pronouns, "he," "they," and "them."

Does this possibly suggest that Silas or Silvanus, and

Luke, Lucas or Lucius, are indeed one and the same person? Perhaps his name was Lukeis Ben Sela, or Bar Sela, and the name was corrupted to Silas or Silvanus with the consequent loss of the synonymous identity of Silas and Luke through translation and the disassociation of the Jewish and Christian communities in the ensuing centuries.

"Lucas," of Philemon 24; and "Lucius," of Acts 13:1 and Romans 16:21; and "Luke," of Colossians 4:14 and II Timothy 4:11; and "Silas," or "Silvanus," of Acts 15:22-41, 16:25-39, 18:5, II Corinthians 1:19, I and II Thessalonians 1:1, and I Peter 5:12, are names that never appear together in the registers or salutations. One or the other of the names always appears, but never any two of the names together. Luke, Lucas or Lucius, the *beloved physician*, plays sort of an incognito part as the noble prophet-apostle Silas or Silvanus—the *aristocratic scribe*. The nature of this irony is a "Clark Kent-Superman" syndrome which was of no intent on the part of the New Testament writers. If the name Lukeis Ben Sela or Bar Sela is substituted each time the name Silas or Silvanus or Lucius appears, the narrative would take on much more dimension, since Luke, as "Luke," only appears twice (as quoted above) in the New Testament. For one who wrote two books in the New Testament and was a companion to Paul, Peter, and Timothy in the entire drama, it is hardly honorable mention to be named only twice.

Silvanus, or Luke, according to I Peter 5:12, served as a scribe for the aged Peter in Babylon where the epistle was written. He may have been the penman for Paul also in some of his epistles. After the destruction of the Temple, in the "sister" galut or diaspora, I Peter 5:12-13, Mark was with Luke in Babylon, the very city where, shortly afterwards, the Babylonian Talmud would be redacted.

Mark and Luke together make a Talmud or an intense study on the life of Jesus. Matthew is not so near to either Mark nor Luke as the Talmudic pair are to each other. Matthew stands distinctly apart in his literary style and presentation. Acts is an Aggadah to this pair. An Aggadah is a story related to a text. Acts, a continuation of Luke, is the Aggadah to Mark and Luke.

In the rabbinic arrangement of the Gospels, following Mark-Luke and Acts of the Apostles would occur the

Midrash of the Gospels, Matthew. In this arrangement, the parabolic Midrash would itself interpret, at least in part, by parabolic definition, the foregoing books.

Matthew, or in Hebrew, *Mattai Ben Khalfi*, is of the tribe of Levi. As a Levite, his position in the nation is above that of the other Israelis, with only the Cohens, or priests, ranking higher in the religious strata. As a tax collector, he is seen daily in the royal courts. Therefore, he is probably not so highly esteemed by the common people personally, but his religious standing and political prestige are paramount. His entire life had been *la melechut*, or "to the Kingdom." Those with whom he deals are not only the elite, they are the "people in power" in his day.

Matthew the Midrashist, being who he is and what he is, sees Jesus through regal eyes. What he sees, he writes; and since his readers are of the kingdom strata, he structures his material to appeal to their level. Matthew, and Matthew alone, uses the term מלכות-השמים, *Melechut ha Shamyim*,or the "kingdom of heaven," which is only a Midrashic jargon. The other writers use מלכות-שדי , *Melechut Shaddi*, or the "kingdom of G-d."

Biblical critics have raised much issue over what they called the "contradictions between the genealogy of Jesus as given by Matthew and that given by Luke." When one understands the rabbinic level upon which Matthew was writing, there is not a single contradiction. Luke traces the pedigree of Jesus through his mother, Miriam, *all the way back* to Adam. This is a true retro-grade genealogy.

Matthew, on the other hand, opens his book with the ancestral line beginning with Abraham, through David to Jechoniah. According to Jeremiah 22:30, the line of Jechoniah was cut off from the regal house of David. No heir of Jechoniah would ever prosper on the throne of David. Nevertheless, Matthew proceeds to follow the line of Jechoniah to Jacob, the father of Joseph, the *husband of Mary*. If Jesus is not the son of Joseph, why does Matthew record this genealogy? If he is the son of Joseph, a descendant of Jechoniah, that alone disqualifies him as the Messianic king of Israel.

Those who make such an issue about the so-called "contradiction" and try to compare the genealogies of Matthew and Luke seem to miss the very evident statement. Matthew gives the *generations of Joseph*, while Luke gives the *genealogy of Miriam*. If they agreed perfectly, Jesus would be a son of incest because Miriam and Joseph would have been brother and sister.

The beautiful contrast between Matthew and Luke is that while Luke is giving the genealogy of Jesus through Miriam, Matthew is *not* giving a genealogy but is giving instead a *chronology* of the regal Son of David. Matthew emphasizes not the pedigree but the time element of the birth of Jesus. In a chronology, it is not necessary to be accurate in pedigree, but it is necessary to be accurate in chronological time sequence. In Matthew 1:17, he states that very purpose of his chronological table of generations: "So all the generations from Abraham to David are fourteen generations; and from David until the carrying-away into Babylon, are fourteen generations; and from the carrying-away into Babylon, then unto the Messiah are fourteen generations." Those who are on the regal level of the Midrash are vitally interested in the chronological time in which this son of David was born. On the other hand, those who are on the noble, or aristocratic, level of the Gemara, are vitally interested in the genealogical pedigree of the ancestry through the mother.

Matthew was a tax collector, the internal revenue man in Herod's court. The Midrash is the most lengthy commentary of the four levels. Matthew, the Midrashist, likewise uses the long form. Every minute detail has to be accounted for. Therefore, it takes twenty-eight chapters for Matthew to tell of the life of Jesus. Mark, by contrast, the working man, does not use the "long form," but chooses a "W-2" with only sixteen chapters. None of the evangelists sought to lose his own personality and distinctive method of presentation in his own particular level.

Matthew, the Midrashist, uses the literary style of the third level of interpretation, the parabolic. He, as no other, emphasizes the parables of Jesus. The higher one ascends into the four levels of the Pardes, the more complex one finds the laws of interpretation; and the more one probes into the book of Matthew, the more complex he finds the teaching of the Rabbi of Nazareth. On the parabolic level, we see Matthew developing that teaching through the application of the thirty-two laws of Rabbi Eliezer Ben Gallil.

A parable can be given as much to conceal a truth as it can to reveal one. Matthew records both uses of the parable. As they always do with all other scriptures, the average Christian commentary usually spiritualizes the parable also. In so doing, they leave much to be desired in their interpretations. Only when the thirty-two laws of Eliezer Ben Gallil are applied to the parable does it become fully meaningful. Those symbolisms used in the parable must be understood in the Midrashic sense of the symbol; otherwise, they become humble-mumble nonsense.

A parable also must be distinguished from an illustrative story. The latter is usually a true account which is prefaced by "There was a certain. . . ." The parable, on the other hand, is not a true story but is a suggestive supposition in the form of a narrative and is preceded by the statement that it is a parable or by the suppositional clause: "Such and such is like unto. . . ." Luke used more illustrative stories, while Matthew employed the use of the parable. The accounts of the Kingdom of Heaven, in Matthew 13, are obviously parables. The account of the rich man and Lazarus in Luke is an example of the illustrative story: "There was a certain rich man. . . ." Matthew contains no such illustrative stories. His style was always parabolic.

If one makes this distinction between the parable and the simple illustration story, he can note a considerable contrast between the illustrative parallels of Luke and the parabolic similies of Matthew. The same nature can be seen in the distinctive differences in the Gemaric stories and the Midrashic parables as employed by Luke and Matthew. Mark records only three parables, and John records absolutely none. Matthew alone, with regal Midrashic candor, records the use of twenty parables in his Midrash on the life of Jesus.

The meanings of the parables Jesus uses have never been interpreted to their full Midrashic tenor. They shall never be until the Jewish Midrashic scholars get them into a simulated Hebrew text and interpret them in the axiomatic principles expressed in the thirty-two laws of Eliezer Ben Gallil.

Matthew, the regal agent of the king's courts, has been recognized by the Christian commentators as the "kingdom Gospel," "the Gospel of the King," "the King and the Kingdom," and other such royal titles. Even without a knowledge of the Midrash, the most casual reader can note this majestic emphasis in the book of

Matthew. Yet, before the twentieth century, only Andrew Jukes noted the distinctive contrast between the Gospels. Ironically, most Christian commentators wrestle in an attempt to make a harmony of the Gospels. The very opposite is their true nature. Making a harmony of the Gospels would be as difficult, or indeed impossible, as making a harmony of the Mishnah, Gemara, Midrash and Zohar. The very evidence that each level exists on its own strata of hermeneutical interpretation excuses the necessity for making them harmonize. A harmony of the Gospels was never intended by the writers.

Each level of the Pardes and each level of the Gospels demands its own choice of emphasis. Each has its own order of presentation. Each has its own writer to express, in the vocabulary of his strata of life, the proper choice of words in describing any given event. The more the effort was made to create a harmony, the more the contrast stood out.

"Harmony was not the objective," Andrew Jukes pointed out in 1853 in his book, *The Characteristic Differences in the Four Gospels.* As the four levels of the rabbinic commentary were to develop contrast and to multiply the meanings of the words of Torah, so the accounts of the four Gospels were given to show multiplicity of meaning to the readers of each level.

In the arrangement and compilation of the four levels of rabbinic commentary, the Mishnah and Gemara appear together in the Talmud. The Midrash, much more voluminous than the combination of the former two, is distinctly separate in its own volumes. While the Mishnah and Gemara are studied as a unit in the Talmud, the study of the Midrash is a separate school in itself.

The Gospels, if arranged in rabbinic order, would begin with a unit of Mark-Luke and then be followed by the book of Acts as an Aggadah on the unit of the two books. The literary structure of the book of Acts is one dramatic *act* after another. The very style is more like a script for a theater production with the Eastern Mediterranean as a stage. The end of the book of Acts is not an end at all. It is most anti-climactic. It even suggests that the end of the original scroll may have been torn off. The abrupt unending end of Acts seems to demand that more be said. This is the nature of the Aggadah. It expects something to precede and to follow it. Such is the nature of the Aggadah—such is the nature of the book of Acts! Following the book of Mark-Luke and the Aggadah of Acts, Matthew would be the Midrash, or Regal study of the life of Jesus.

The fourth and paramount commentary in the Pardes is the Zohar, or "Radiance." It is much further removed from the Midrash than the Midrash is from the Talmud. So far, in fact, is the Kabbalah from the Midrash and the Talmud that it is not another "ball park"; it is an entirely different game altogether.

John, the mystical Kabbalist, in writing the Zohar on the life of Jesus, is likewise far removed from Mark, Luke and Matthew. As a matter of fact, those who seek to make a harmony of the Gospels usually omit John altogether and appropriately so, for John does not fit in any fashion with the other three.

The Kabbalists are the mystical workers of miracles in Judaism. John centers his entire book around seven miracles in the life of Jesus. The key to his book is chapter 20:30-31: "Many other signs [miracles] truly did Jesus in the presence of his disciples, which are not written in this book: But these are written that ye might believe that Jesus is the Christ, the Son of G-d; and that believing ye might have life through his name."

"Signs or miracles," "Son of G-d," "the Messiah," "believing the miraculous," "life in the world to come," are all the subjects and the vernacular of the Kabbalist.

John, in Revelation 13:14-15, describes the creation of a *Golem.* When a Kabbalist receives the secret of the Holy Name or the Tetragrammaton, he tests his ability to pronounce properly by the creation of the *Golem.* In this procedure, an image of a man is made of clay. The word אמת , *Truth, ?ahMehT,* is written on the clay forehead of the image. The Kabbalist then chants the seventy-two intonations of the Holy Name over the clay image. If the sounds are correct, the image comes alive. The soul-less beast is then destroyed by rubbing away or covering the א , aleph, in אמת , from his forehead. This leaves the letters מ , Mem, and ת , Tav, which spell מת, MehT, meaning "death." The image of the beast of the *Golem* goes back to clay. In Revelation 13:18, he states that the number of the name of the image of the *Golem* shall be 666. This is a direct statement of one of the principles of the forty-two laws of the Kabbalah. This principle is called Gematria.

John is not interested in the meticulous details as is Mark. He makes no allegorical similes as does Luke. John does not use one single parable as does Matthew. He is not so interested in the words as he is in the Aura, the Radiance, the Zohar, of Jesus.

John speaks of the "Light" (as winged, feathered fingers of the Incomprehensible *En Sof*) shining out of the darkness. He makes much in his writings of the Sons of Darkness and the Sons of Light. He uses the vernacular of the mystical Sons of Zadok at Qumran. John stands in the twilight of the upper and lower worlds in his Apocalypse. No! John is no simple Midrashic, no allegorical Gemarist, nor even a parabolic regalist. His plane is the divine, the other worldness, the life into the Ages of Ages. John is the man of dreams and visions. He is the Daniel of the New Testament.

Concerning the creation and the Torah, for example, the Kabbalists teach that: "In the beginning there was the Torah. The Torah was in the beginning with G-d. G-d was the Torah; the Torah was G-d. By the Torah were all things created; without Torah, nothing was created which was created. By the Torah, the ages were framed up and are unrolling as a scroll according to the Rhetoric oracle of Torah. By the Torah came the Light [En Sof]. By the Light of En Sof came Adam [Man—literally Adam Kadmon—after whose image earthly Adam was formed]."

As a preface to his Zohar on the life of Jesus, John opened his account with the quote from this oral tradition of the Kabbalist. Then, in 1:14, he said: "And the Torah became flesh, *dwelling* among us, *tabernacling*, and we beheld his *Glory*. . . ." *Dwelling* is שקוּן, *SHah KoUN*, *Tabernacling* is משכן, *MiSH'hKahN*, which is G-d's dwelling place; *Glory*, in Hebrew שכנה, *MiSH'hKieY NahH*, is the radiance of divine presence. All of these are words in the vocabulary of the Kabbalist. Each of these words came from the same root, שכן, *SHah hKahN*, meaning "he dwelt." John 1:1-14 is directly from that Zohar concept. There is nothing original about that text.

John is the mystic of the Gospel writers. In his presentation of the Zohar of Jesus, there is no effort to make it synonymous with Mark, Luke, and Matthew. Since the Church divorced itself from an understanding of Jesus in the framework of rabbinic commentary, they had to substitute another theory to attempt to explain the four Gospels. This theory is expressed in at least half a dozen views in what is called the "synoptic problem." According to these theories, each of the Gospels is a copy of a former Gospel or "Q" source or sources. The theorists say Luke copied Mark, and Matthew copied Luke, Mark, and one or more other "Q" sources. Among the synoptic theories, there are any number of combinations of ideas as to precisely who copied whom and exactly who cued the "Q".

This is not to say that synoptic approach to the subject of textual analysis and criticism is worthless. On the contrary, a comparative analysis of each text is not only profitable but is expedient. The extravagance of the typical synoptic approach is its negative attitude toward the Hebraic originality of the language of the Gospels and its divorcement from the principles of rabbinic hermeneutics.

If the linguistic principles of the synoptic approach were applied within the framework of the simulated Hebrew original and quadrate to the four levels of rabbinic interpretation, the "synoptic problems" would become "synoptic solutions." This, however, cannot be achieved by subjecting the rabbinic principles to the synoptic mechanics. Only when the synoptic mechanics are subjected to the rabbinic principles can this be done. The former is laws, while the latter is methodology. The spirit of the "synoptic problem" is the epitome of replacement theological theory. This cannot co-exist with the rabbinic approach.

Having departed from the Jewish concept of rabbinic interpretation, the replacement monks, translators, commentators, and modern scholarship have sought out many inventions, most of which are Rube Goldberg contraptions of say-nothing-isms to explain Jesus and the New Testament apart from Judaism. The mechanics go on and on. One translation comes after another, one commentary supersedes another, saying the same thing, only with new cliches. Each and every one is a little farther away from Judaism than the former. Each is a little, or sometimes very much more, anti-Semitic than the preceding. New idealism, higher criticism and modernism have come and gone. One rabbi aptly summarized them thusly: "Higher criticism is higher anti-Semitism."

In the other camp, neo-orthodoxy, the evangelicals, the fundamentalists and the charismatics, are passing their way. Some are pro-Israel. A few are even mildly pro-Judaic, but almost all are esteeming some method to convert the Jew to Christianity. Yet, even among these is a prominent number who are anti-Judaic, anti-Jewish, and anti-Israel. Unfortunately, in both camps, the scum of anti-Semitism seems always to float to the top, for in both are found a total rejection of the rabbinic hermeneutical authority.

The 1967 Middle Eastern crisis did not kill Jewish-Christian dialogue—it only presented the habeas corpus!

There can be no dialogue or profitable reason for Jews and Christians to attempt to understand each other until the problems of language and interpretation are solved. This burden was created by the Christians, not by the Jews. The responsibility of change is the responsibility of the Christians; yet, only the Jews can supply the information for this transition.

Some people, both Jews and Christians, are vitally interested in "what did Jesus actually say in the language he spoke?" and "what did his words literally mean to those who heard him?" Others say, as one clergyman put it, "All of that would be nice to know, but what I am really interested in is *what can Jesus do for me and my church today.*"

A rabbinic interpretation of Jesus will swell his every word with the pregnancy of his message. It will brood a myriad of meanings. It will enrich and endow each disciple with an unction of his own service to the Master. A crown of majesty, wisdom and understanding awaits those who seek to understand that primal experience of the Jewishness of Jesus and his message to those who heard and continue to hear the echo of his words.

Chapter V
THE RIDDLE OF THE SEQUENCE AND HARMONY OF THE EVENTS

When they begin to study all four Gospels together, many Christians find in them a confusing jumble of events with no apparent organization, either historical, chronological, or didactic. A comparison of corresponding accounts of the same events reveals differences even more perplexing. The problem grows progressively more frustrating as one attempts to establish a chronology by comparing and harmonizing the various accounts or to determine an appropriate sequence of events.

There is an approach to the study of the life and ministry of Jesus which provides a dramatic chronology and an explicit order of events in his life.

The Torah was given to Moses on Mount Sinai on two separate occasions and in two different manners. The first tables were written by the very finger of G-d in perfect chronological order as they exist in heaven. These tables were broken by Moses when he descended from the mountain and found Israel worshipping the golden calf. The second tables were like, yet different from, the first. Moses wrote the second tables as dictated by G-d, but they were not in chronological order as the first and heavenly Torah.

The four Gospels, likewise, do not seek to relate in perfect chronological order the life of Jesus. Luke's intention, "to set forth in order a declaration of those things which are most surely believed among us. . . ," was the most orderly account of the four, yet not in perfect order of occurrence regarding the day to day life and ministry of Jesus.

Moreover, the ancient codex of the Gospels is not divided into chapters and verses as our modern translations are. This division into chapters and verses was made by a monk who was riding horseback on a pilgrimage from Milan to Rome. Evidently, where his horse was tired and walking slowly, the monk made the verses very lengthy. When his horse began to trot, the verses became short and choppy. Each time the horse swished his tail, a new chapter was begun. This is the only rhyme and reason for the chapters, verses, and punctuation as they presently occur in the New Testament. There are many places where a chapter division occurs in the middle of a discourse. This, of course, adds complexity to the continuity of the narrative.

If the Gospel accounts were to be translated from the codex back to Hebrew, there would be no need for chapter and verse divisions. If, in that translation, the cantation of the Hebrew melody is maintained as it is in the classical Hebrew of the Jewish canon, the punctuation would be automatic. In that Hebraic approach, all the narratives and their contexts solidify into exactly three hundred sixty-five *PehRehQieYM*, or sections. Such a division breaks down beautifully into one for daily reading each day of the year.

Today, the Jews in synagogue read through the Torah, which is divided into similar sections, once each year. With the reading of the Torah each week, there are selections from the prophets and other writings which are called Haftorah. The Haftorah readings are cross-referenced by subject and are intercollated with each section of the Torah. A pious Jew reads once each year, according to this schedule, the entire *TaNahK*, which Christians call the "Old Testament."

During the days of the Second Temple the reading schedule was much longer. The reading of the Torah was sequenced with the zodiac, the festivals, the new moons, and the Sabbatical years. Each forty-nine years, the Torah was read fourteen times. There were two readings of the Torah each Sabbatical year, or every seven years. It took three and one half years on this schedule to read once through the Torah.

With the Temple in service, the reading of the Torah in the synagogues was much slower because each sacrifice required by the Sabbath reading of the Torah was made during the week following the particular reading of the Sabbath day. The Temple was the dramatic stage upon which the precepts of the sacrificial laws of Torah were enacted. If the reading of the Law of the Leper was the order of the sequence of that day, the offerings of the Law of the Leper were executed accordingly.

The Temple choir and orchestra sang and played the passages relative to each offering and feast. The non-Jewish world has never produced a symphonic drama to compare with the daily routine of the Torah and the Temple worship in Jerusalem during that time. This was the religious atmosphere of Jerusalem during the life and times of Jesus.

Concerning this worship, Jesus said to the Samaritan woman, "...we know what we worship, for salvation is of the Jews." (John 4:22) He did not say, "Salvation is of the Christians." Jesus is an orthodox, observant Jew of the school of the Pharisees. Concerning his attitude toward the Torah, he says in Matthew 5:17-18: "Stop thinking I am come to destroy the Torah and the prophets! I am not come to destroy but to [personally] fill them up! Amen! I say unto you, till heaven [and] earth die, not one jot nor one tittle shall in no wise pass from the Torah till they all be fulfilled." What did Jesus mean by the "jot" and the "tittle" of the Torah? The jot is Yod, י, the smallest letter of the alphabet. The tittle is Tah GiYn, which is a decorative crown set upon the top of certain letters. They are called the *SHAT-NAYZ-GAYTS* letters, because, contracted, they form the word שעטנז״גצ. Jesus is telling us that the smallest letter and the smallest mark on every letter must be literally fulfilled.

SHaǤat'NaeZ...GaeTS

*Mt. 5:19: The "Jot" is the YoHD, the smallest Hebrew letter. The "Tittle" is the little crown which adorns only seven letters of the Hebrew alphabet. They are called the Tagin or the SHaGat'NaeZ...*GaeTS letters.

Jesus says he came to fulfill personally the laws of Torah. He did not mean, as replacement theologians teach, that he came "to do away with them." That would mean he came to destroy the Law completely. He explicitly said this was not his purpose (Matt. 5:17) and imperatively stated "stop thinking I am. . . ." What did he mean, then, that he would fulfill the Torah?

Three and one half years Jesus ministered in Israel. Three and a half years it took to read the Torah in the Temple and synagogues in the land. What is the relationship of this parallel?

Jesus was born on Rosh Hashanah. Twenty-nine years later he turned thirty and began his public ministry.

The ten days between Rosh Hashanah and Yom Kippurim are called the days of Repentance. Mark-Luke, Matthew and John each give considerable space to these ten days in the initiation of the ministry of Jesus: "In those days came John the Baptist preaching repentance . . ."! Why is John preaching repentance in those days? He is preaching it because those are the ten days of repentance between Rosh Hashanah, the first day of the month of Tishri, and the tenth day of that month, which is Yom Kippurim. Every priest in the Temple is preaching repentance. Every psalm and lilt that the Temple choir chants concerns repentance. Every rabbi in every synagogue in Israel and the lands abroad is preaching repentance. Why should not the prophet John also preach repentance? Had he been preaching anything else, he would have been a false prophet!

John hesitates to take Jesus into the *MiQvahH*, or Jewish baptistry, and insists that Jesus baptize him. Jesus replies, "Do it right now! [It was the last day of Repentance before the tenth day of Yom Kippur.] It is a must for us to fulfill all righteousness [required by the Torah]."

Jesus makes his baptism by John an imperative matter at this particular time of the ten days of Repentance, according to the Torah reading at this season. This he does to fulfill, in a dramatic personification of the Torah, his own life and conduct.

The next day is the tenth day of the month of Tishri. It is also the tenth and final day of the ten Days of Repentance. Tishri 10 is the most solemn day of the ten; it is Yom Kippurim, the Day of Atonements. On this Day of Atonement, the two goats are brought before the High

Priest, and lots are cast on the goats. The first goat is the Goat of the Eternal One; it is sacrificed as a sin offering. The second goat is the scapegoat; in living, it bears away Israel's sins.

"The next day," after the baptism of Jesus, John addresses Jesus with a nominative of Yom Kippurim: "Behold the Lamb of G-d, [as the one sacrificed] that taketh away [as the scapegoat] the sins of the [Gentile] world." Note that John does not say, "...that taketh away the sins of Israel."

The prophet John sees Jesus as one who would wrap up in himself the essence of Yom Kippurim and extend its provisional benefits to the human community outside Israel. Israel has an inseparable relationship with the Torah and the Eternal One. The Gentile is outside that economy, separated, afar off. To give the benefit of Yom Kippurim to the Gentile, Jesus has to wrap himself in it completely. On that particular day, Tishri 10, John's reference to Jesus as the "Lamb of G-d which taketh away the sins of the world," has pertinence it would not have any other day of the year. The chronological sequence of the Jewish calendar with the Torah reading at that particular day, and the significance of the remarks of each writer about "those days of repentance," strikes a vibrant chord in the beginning of the symphonic overture of Jesus' drama in fulfilling the Torah in his ministry. Jesus' baptism is Scene I in the drama.

From the fifteenth to the twenty-second day of the first month of Israel's civil calendar, or the seventh month of their Levitical calendar, is the exalted Feast of Sukkot, or Tabernacles. The people of Israel must dwell in booths or brush arbors during these eight days. It reminds them that when their fathers came out of Egypt, they dwelt in brush arbor huts for forty years in the wilderness. This feast begins five days after Yom Kippurim.

Mark, Luke, and Matthew each record that "immediately after" the narrative of the ten Days of Repentance and Yom Kippurim, Jesus, too, is dwelling in a wilderness. He personifies the Torah experience not for the prescribed eight days, but for forty days and nights, precisely one day for each year Israel spent dwelling in booths.

During those forty days, the Torah readings are the completion of the fifth book of Moses, or Deuteronomy. Since this book is a review by Moses of the experiences of

Israel in the wilderness, there are only the routine daily sacrifices to be made in the Temple. The reading of this book is much more rapid than the reading of those books requiring the special sacrifices. Today it is approximately two and a half weeks from Yom Kippurim until the completion of the Torah readings in Deuteronomy. During the Second Temple schedules, it was about nine weeks.

During these forty days in the wilderness, every passage that Jesus and Satan quote in their dialogue comes from the book of Deuteronomy, or the Haftorahs which relate to it. Satan is quoting the Haftorahs, and Jesus is replying with quotations from the Deuteronomy section of the Torah, which are being read in the Temple and synagogues at this particular season. The narrative of the Temptation is Scene II in the drama of Jesus' personification of the Torah readings.

In a study on the temptation of Jesus, Kenneth R. Cooper noted several further parallels between the experience of Jesus in the Judaean wilderness and the experience of Israel in the Wilderness of Sin:

> Israel had been initiated into the wilderness journey through its baptism unto Moses in the Red Sea (cp. I Cor. 10:1-4), while the baptism of John served as Jesus' initiation. The "Angel of His Presence," by means of the pillar of cloud, led Israel into the wilderness. After his baptism, Jesus was led by the Spirit of G-d into the wilderness. G-d intended the experiences of both Israel and Jesus to serve as testing for their respective characters.
>
> Each of the temptations of Jesus corresponded to certain incidents in the career of Israel during this forty years' trek. For example, the first temptation focused on a basic need for food. Knowing that Jesus would be hungry after forty days of fasting, Satan attempted to provoke in Jesus a dissatisfaction in the provision of G-d. Satan suggested that Jesus use his powers to achieve his own ends in defiance of G-d's objectives. According to Numbers 11:4-9, Israel grumbled about the provision of G-d for their material needs. They had had enough of the manna, demanding a second course of

meat. Israel pursued their defiance until G-d gave them meat—so much meat that they got sick on it. Jesus refused to succumb to the temptation, responding with a direct statement of his reliance upon the Word of G-d.

In the second temptation, Satan tried to get Jesus to demand of G-d a sign—an outward demonstration of his presence and protection in the life of the Galilean rabbi. "Go ahead and throw yourself down," he chided. "He'll send his angels to save you, and the miraculous demonstration will convince everyone of your Messiahship. Don't do it G-d's way—it will never convince them of anything." Satan's suggestion was aimed at stirring up dissatisfaction with the program of G-d; it was his method of carrying out his own will. Israel, too, expressed dissatisfaction with G-d's methods. Hardly had they left Egypt than they began complaining, "Wherefore is this that thou hast brought us up out of Egypt, to kill us and our children and our cattle with thirst...? And he called the name of the place Massah and Meribah, because of the chiding of the children of Israel, and because they tested the Lord, saying, Is the Lord among us, or not?" (Exodus 17:1-7) Again Israel yielded, but Jesus stood firm.

Finally, Satan tempted Jesus to disregard G-d himself. When Satan showed Jesus all the kingdoms of the world, he offered them all on the condition that Jesus substitute Satan for G-d as an object of worship. G-d himself, according to Satan, is not such a good guy because he demands homage and service and a rough life before Jesus can obtain the kingdoms of the world. Satan played the role of "big daddy" with the big give-away spirit at no cost to the Rabbi.

While Moses was in the mountain, receiving G-d's law, Israel was expressing the same kind of dissatisfaction with G-d. They demanded that Aaron make them an easy-going, less-demanding G-d out of the trinkets of gold they brought to him. Aaron made the idol; and when he stood back to survey his handiwork, he "...built an altar before it; and Aaron made proclamation, and said, Tomorrow is a feast to the Lord." (Exodus 32:1-6) Israel had rejected the Master of the Universe and had substituted a more lenient, materialistic god—a god who appealed to the weakness of the flesh—just as Satan tempted Jesus to do. However, Jesus again refused to yield to the persuasive tongue of the adversary.

In every case, Israel surrendered to the temptation and experienced the judgment of G-d. Jesus, on the other hand, refused to give in; instead, he demonstrated the means of overcoming temptation through the Word of G-d (Psalm 119:105); and each of his answers offers a theological commentary on Israel's wilderness experience. Furthermore, it was to the Hebrews, perhaps in direct reference to their experience, that Paul wrote, "...we have not an high priest who cannot be touched with the feeling of our infirmities, but was in all points tempted like as we [Israel were], yet without sin." (Heb. 4:15).

The Jewish prayer book reminds the pious each day of this wilderness provocation of the ancients.

Simchat Torah is a joyous festival. It celebrates the completion and the renewing of the reading of Torah. This is a homecoming season, a time of family reunions. There is dancing, singing, and feasting on this day of rejoicing in the Torah. The synagogue is the center of this festivity.

"Jesus went home to Nazareth, where he had been brought up: and, as his custom was, he went into the synagogue on the Sabbath day, and stood up [on the *bema*] to read [the Haftorah]... ." The passage he read was from Isaiah 61: "The Spirit of the Lord is upon me, because he hath anointed me to preach the gospel to the poor; he hath sent me to heal the broken-hearted, to preach deliverance to the captives, and recovering of sight to the blind, to set at liberty them that are bruised, to preach the acceptable year of the Lord.

"And he closed the book [rolled up the scroll]; and he gave *it* again to the minister [*Khazin*], and sat down. And the eyes of all them that were in the synagogue were fastened on him.

"And he began to say unto them, 'This day is this scripture fulfilled in your ears.'" (Luke 4:16-22)

On Simchat Torah when the book of Deuteronomy is finished, the reading of the beginning of the book of Genesis is started immediately so that there will be no break between the finishing of the Torah and its new beginning.

The Haftorah passage, "The Spirit of the Eternal One," from Isaiah 61 is a cognate passage to the opening reading of *B'RaeASHaeYT*, Genesis 1:1-2, "And the Spirit of the Eternal One brooded over the faces of the waters." This reading would follow the completion of Deuteronomy. The Haftorahs of this season include the lives of Elijah and Elisha which Jesus refers to on the context of Luke 4:16-30. This is Scene III in the drama of Jesus and the Torah.

The chronological order of the ministry of Jesus is not subject to the order of any of the Gospel accounts. The order and sequence of events in the ministry of Jesus in the three hundred sixty-five sections must be totally subjected to the chronological reading of the Torah over a three and one half year period. Many of the statements found in the narratives of the Gospels correspond more closely to a Haftorah, a Talmudic, a Midrashic, or a passage from the Zohar on the Torah than they do to the Word of Torah itself.

The more effort the replacement theologians made to establish a chronology of the life of Jesus on a harmony of the Gospels, the more disorderly the time structure became.

During the season of the Torah reading at the synagogues concerning offerings for the cleansing of a leper, the actual offerings are being made at the Temple. There is no necessity for the leper to be cleansed to give occasion for the offering. That offering is made according to the prescription of the schedule of the Torah reading. All the lepers who are cleansed go at that appointed time to make their required offerings. The leper is subject to the schedule of Torah. The Torah is not subject to the schedule of the cleansed lepers.

Jesus heals a leper. His action is sequenced with the Torah reading and pertinent sacrifices, and not with the time sequence in which the Gospel writers place it in their accounts. Look at the contrast in the time sequence as recorded by the writers.

Mark, the Mishnaic, records the healing of the leper in the very first chapter, verses 40-45. This places it immediately after the calling of the Twelve and the healing of Peter's mother-in-law.

Luke, the Gemarist, records the healing of Peter's mother-in-law before the calling of Simon Peter, and then relates the story of the healing of the leper in Luke 5:12-16.

Matthew, the Midrashic, does not record the healing of the leper until chapter 8:2-4. This is several months after the call of the Twelve and the events related by the two Talmudists.

In this narrative of the healing of the leper, Mark, Luke, and Matthew all agree on one time factor. "And Jesus says unto him [the leper], 'Get out! Hurry! Don't tell anyone [that I have healed you]! But go thy way quickly [the way of the Torah], Show thyself to the priests [according to Torah requirements] and offer the gift [the sacrifice of two doves, one slain over running water and the other dipped in the blood of the first and set free] that Moses commanded, for a testimony unto them [or a witness to the words of Moses in the Torah, not a witness unto the priests].'"

This healing of the leper actually occurs at the time of the reading of the Torah concerning the Law, or the cleansing of the lepers, and at the time those sacrifices are being offered for the cleansing of the leper. The urgency of the time element is lost in translation. This is another act in the drama of three hundred sixty-five scenes in the life of Jesus. His life drama is symphonically in harmony with each stanza of the reading of the Torah in the Temple, in every synagogue, and in every Jewish home.

Jesus strictly observed the law of the Sabbath, as is required by Jewish tradition. If, however, the Sabbath reading of the Torah gave occasion to a parallel to one of the three hundred sixty-five acts in his dramatization of that passage, he would perform according to the required precept of the script of Torah. In his controversy, or *pil-pul*, with those who objected to his performance of such on the Sabbath day, Jesus' answers were related to the eighth, ninth, and tenth laws of Rabbi Ishmael. In other words, Jesus did not break the tradition of Israel; he did not violate the Torah; he stayed completely within the framework of rabbinic tradition and teaching.

The Feast of Sukkot has come again in the unrolling of the Torah. No feast in the drama of Israel's redemptive calendar speaks with so much emphasis on the "salvation of the Gentiles" as does this Feast of Tabernacles. This feast, as no other, reaches out eschatologically and soteriologically in a universal scope.

The sacrifices of the Eighth Day, the shaking of the branches of the appointed trees with the *EhT-RoG*, or citron, toward the four corners of the earth, and the chanting of the Temple choir, symphonizes the salvation of the Gentiles: "In that day there shall be a fountain opened to the House of David and the inhabitants of Jerusalem...And it shall come to pass that everyone that is left of all the [Gentile] nations which came against Jerusalem, shall even go up from year to year to worship the King the Eternal One of hosts, and keep the Feast of Tabernacles [Sukkot]...The Eternal One will smite the Gentile [nations] that come not up to keep the feast of Tabernacles...." (Zech. 13:1; 14:16)

"Ho, everyone that thirsteth, come to the waters...." (Isaiah 55:1)

"Therefore with joy shall ye draw waters out of the wells of Yeshuah [salvation]." (Isaiah 12:3)

Rabbi Yeshuah of Nazareth is the *actor*. The veranda of the Temple is the *stage*. The Torah, ever so slowly unwinding from the right spindle to the left in its three and a half year cycle, is the *script*. The Haftorahs of the Psalms, prophets, and wisdom literature are unrolled in cross-reference to each word of the Torah and chanted as the *symphony*, both in *commentary* and *cantation*. In the atmosphere of that crisp autumn day, the echo of the Haftorah reading still resounds in the Temple portals, when John records in 7:37-38: "In the last day, the Great Day of the Feast, Jesus stood [on the Temple porch] and cried [chanting in the traditional cantations]: 'If any man [ye Gentiles] thirst, let him come unto me and drink. He [the choir had just sung] hath said, out of his belly shall flow rivers of living water.'"

The Feast of Hanukkah was instituted after the

Babylonian captivity. *KHa'NoUKiYahH*, Hanukkah, in Hebrew, means "dedication." The Festival of Hanukkah, or Chanukah, means the feast of the re-dedication of the Second Temple.

Before the capture of Jerusalem by Nebuchadnezzar, Jeremiah the prophet had instructed that the Holy Oil for the Menorah be preserved. The priests hid the fire in the cistern. One of the priests took the vial of oil prepared for the next day's Temple service, and carried it with him into Babylon.

When the people of Israel returned from the Babylonian captivity in the Jewish year 3408, they spent many years re-establishing the political State of Israel. They rebuilt the walls, the city, and finally, through much struggle, they rebuilt the Temple. It was not until 3622 in the Jewish calendar, or two hundred fourteen years after their return, that the Temple was re-consecrated. This was one hundred thirty-five years before the birth of Jesus of Nazareth.

When the priests went to the cistern, they found that the fire of the altar was no longer there. Instead there was a thick, black liquid. Nevertheless, they prepared the wood and placed a sacrifice on the altar. The priests took the black, syrup-like liquid and poured it over the sacrifice and wood.

The sky was very heavily overcast with dark clouds. Suddenly, a horn of sunlight pierced through the clouds upon the Temple area. No sooner had the sun's aura touched the altar than the thick, black liquid broke into flames. The Holy Fire had been miraculously preserved for two hundred eighty-four years.

One of the priests brought forth the vial of holy olive oil. Two hundred eighty-four years before, it had been consecrated to be the following day's fuel supply for the seven lamps of the Menorah. However, Nebuchadnezzar's destruction of the Temple in the year 3338 had aborted its use.

The one day's supply of oil was put into the lamps. The Temple Menorah had only seven lamps. Each lamp, however, had seven wicks. There were, therefore, forty-nine flames on the Menorah. The miracle of *Kha'NoUKiYahH, ha nuki-yah*, or the miracle of the Dedication, was that the oil which measured one day's supply actually burned for eight days.

In the commemoration of this miracle of the fire and the oil, the day of that event is celebrated by a specially designed Menorah, or candelabrum, which has four stands, or lamp holders, on each side of the main shaft. The regular Temple Menorah has only three branches on each side of the center shaft, making a total of seven candlesticks, or lampstands. The Hanukkah Menorah has eight branches plus the center shaft which serves as the source of fire for the other lamps.

The eight lamps, or candles, represent the eight days the Temple Menorah burned on the one day's supply of oil. The center shaft is always lit. On the first night of Hanukkah, one of the eight lamps is lit from the center lamp. On the second night, two of the eight are lit, and so on, until the eighth day of the feast when all nine are aflame.

During the days of the Second Temple, there was an elaborate celebration of Hanukkah. Nine enormous brazen lamps were placed across the crown-beam of the Temple. Each open reservoir contained several barrels of oil. Seven notches were equally recessed into the brim of each of these bowl-like pools. Large rope wicks, each a hand's span in diameter, made from the discarded linen vestments of the priests, were soaked in the oil and were draped through seven notches in each of the mammoth pools of oil.

Each night of the eight days of the Feast of Dedication, an additional urn on the Temple was ignited from the center flame. On the eighth night, the tongues of fire leaped like an angry inferno. So brilliant were these Hanukkah lights that all the mountains about Jerusalem could be seen from the pinnacle of the Temple. It was said that one could stand on the crest of the Mount of Olives, almost a mile away, and read the tiny scroll of Purim from the lights on the Temple crown.

In the cycle of the Torah, from the Feast of Sukkot through the Feast of Hanukkah, is the reading of the law of the jealous husband. Many pages of commentary are involved in this section. If a man accuses his wife of infidelity and she pleads innocence, she is put through a very grueling ordeal. To prove her innocence or guilt, the elders bring her to the priests. She is prosecuted as though her guilt is established. After much excruciating pain and embarrassment, she is roughly dragged into the Temple area for the final test.

The dust from the Temple floor is swept and mixed with water, and she is forced to drink it. If her stomach bloats, she is considered guilty and is stoned. If her stomach does not bloat, she is freed and her husband can never put her away by divorce.

This is the situation in John, chapter 8, another scene in the dramatic development of Jesus' filling up the Torah. The accused woman is brought before Jesus in the Temple area. There are many ramifications of the actions of Jesus in this situation, relative to the entire "law of a jealous husband." The emphatic drama of the moment is that he kneels and writes twice in the very dust of the Temple floor that will later be swept up for this woman to drink.

What he is writing the first time he kneels down, no one knows. Perhaps it is a list of the names of each man present. As he arises from writing in the dust, he says to the crowd: "He that is among you that is not guilty of *this very* sin [adultery], let him cast the first stone at her."

Then Jesus kneels again and begins to write [very much] in the dust a second time. Whatever he is writing initiates a royal rapid exodus of every man there.

Perhaps he is writing beside the names of all those men present a sizable list of the names of the women with whom they had committed adultery.

All the Pharisees leave, the older men preceding the younger (their lists are probably longer)! The priests see what Jesus is writing; they too quickly find business elsewhere! Simon Peter sees his name and the list of ladies' names, and he leaves also. There follow James, John and the other disciples. Yes, they left too!

"And Jesus is left *alone*. The woman is standing in the middle of the Temple area. As Jesus stands up [he looks about] and sees none [not even his disciples] but the woman alone." With a smile, if not indeed a grin on his face, or maybe even a satirical chuckle, he says, "Woman, where are those thine accusers?" (John 8:1-11)

The story of the woman taken in adultery and the law of the jealous husband intricately parallel Jesus' drama of fulfilling the Torah reading at that season of Hanukkah.

That night, under the first flames of the inferno of the Temple Hanukkah lamps, Jesus cries out in the Hebrew chants: "I [am the] light [of] the [Gentile] world." (John 8:2)

As the Eight Days of Hanukkah proceed in John, chapter 9, the lights of the Temple Menorah, Hanukkah, are burning ever more brilliantly each night. In John 9:5, Jesus repeats, "I am the light of the [Gentile] world." John, in chapter 10:22, penned into the texts the key to this entire dramatic discourse: "And it was at Jerusalem, the *Feast of Dedication*, and it was winter."

During the period of the movement of higher criticism in Europe, the Jewish community was strongly challenged by some in the Reform movement who questioned the historical validity of the Jewish tradition. They claimed that the Talit, the Phalacteries, Purim, and Hanukkah were ghetto inventions created during the Dark Ages. They demanded that the Orthodox prove, *from non-Jewish sources*, any mention of these traditions before the eighth century, C.E.

A Lithuanian rabbi accepted the challenge. The non-Jewish source that he used to prove the antiquity of these Jewish traditions was the Christian New Testament. The Christian Bible could not have been influenced by Jewish scholars in the ghetto during the Dark Ages. The rabbi pointed out that the New Testament was the most ancient written authority apart from rabbinic sources on the historicity of traditional Judaism.

Concerning Hanukkah, he made emphatic reference to John 10:22. "This one verse," said he, "not only shows that the tradition of Hanukkah was celebrated in the Second Temple period, but it shows also that Jesus of Nazareth was there to observe it. And furthermore, the New Testament even tells the season of the year Hanukkah was observed. John 10:22 plainly states that Hanukkah was observed during the winter even as Jews today observe."

In this context of Hanukkah, Jesus spoke: "I and the Father...my sheep...my voice...I lay down my life...I take it up again...I and my father are one."

No one versed in the Midrash could help but recognize that these words are relative to the *Aguddah, Akkiydah*, or binding of Isaac, in Genesis 22.

Gaverial Cohen, professor at the Hebrew University in Jerusalem, pointed out thirty-two parallels and contrasts between the Midrash on the binding of Isacc and the story of the offering of Jesus. Yet, how distant the Midrashic interpretation is from that of the replacement theologians.

For example, "I and my Father are one," is interpreted by the replacement theologians as "one" in number. Altizer, the philosophical theologian, carried that to its final conclusion and said that Jesus replaced the Jewish G-d of the Old Testament. Jesus was G-d; therefore, since Jesus died, *"G-d is dead."*

Jesus did not say "I and my Father are one in number." The Hebrew word אחד, *?ehKHahD*, means one in number. The word Jesus used is found in Genesis 22:6: "And Abraham took the wood of the burnt offering, and laid it upon Isaac his son; and he took the fire in his hand, and the knife; and they went up both of them *together*." The word "together" יחדו, is *YaKH'DahV*; it means one in purpose. Isaac and his father, "went up the two of them as one," in unity of purpose concerning the sacrifice. They did not go up as one in number.

Jesus spoke of his sacrifice, his Akkiydah, or binding, as "this commandment [to lay down my life as Isaac] have I received of my Father. . .in this sacrifice, the two of us are one [YaKh'DahV] in unity of will and purpose." (John 10:18-30)

The Midrash is the commentary on the Torah from the Oral Tradition. The Oral Tradition is Torah as much as the Written Law is. The life of Jesus takes on a totally new dimension when one understands that each of the three hundred sixty-five sections of his three and one half year ministry have a timely relationship to the sequence of the reading of the Torah with each level of Rabbinic commentary.

Very few have missed this traditional dimension in the Passion story. Christian commentators have not failed to observe the unavoidable statements about Passover in relation to the death of the Lamb. However, the full realization of the intricate details have, for the greater part, been overlooked or generalized to meaninglessness. For example, the Last Supper has been confused with the Passover meal. To understand the full difference, we must understand the sequence of the Jewish calendar with the reading of the Torah.

The tenth day of the month of Nisan, or Aviv in this case, was the first day of the "preparation" for Passover. This was four days before the "Passover" proper. At the end of the ninth day of Aviv, sunset marked the beginning of the new day, the tenth of Aviv. That night, the Jews had a feast called the Feast of the First Night.

On the eleventh of Aviv was the Feast of the Second Night. The Feast of the Third Night was on the twelfth of Aviv. The thirteenth of Aviv was different. It was called the Last Supper; it was the last meal at which leavened bread could be served.

John opened the thirteenth chapter with these words: "Now *before* the Feast of the Passover. . . ." All the events in John, chapters 13, 14, 15, 16, and 17, take place in the room at the table of the Last Supper, not the Passover! At the table of the Last Supper, Jesus explained his purpose in being the savior of the Gentile world. There is no reference to any article of Passover in John's account. He completely omits the Passover, the meal of unleavened bread, and resumes the narrative at the arrest in the garden in chapter 18.

In 13:26, "the morsel of torn yeast or leavened bread was sopped and given to Judas." This bread would not have been permitted at the Passover meal, yet it was required at the feast of the Last Supper.

Mark-Luke and Matthew, on the other hand, give explicit details of the Passover, the four cups, the broken matzo of *Afikoman*, the Khad Gadya (the hymn at the end of Passover), and all else that pertains to the Passover feast. However, they do not mention the Last Supper on the previous evening, even as John does not mention the Passover.

Those who try to establish a harmony of the Gospels make the Last Supper, which is on the evening of the thirteenth, synonymous with the Passover, which is on the evening of the fourteenth. By so doing, they create problems. They speak of the problems of genealogy, the problems of chronology, the textual problems, and the synoptic problems. Is it not strange that they never discuss the solutions?

In the unrolling of the Torah scroll, relative to space and time, the evening of the fourteenth of Aviv was Passover. The fifteenth was the Feast of Matzo when all leaven put out of the Jewish homes was burned and buried. The sixteenth was the Feast of Roshat or Feast of First Fruits. This Feast of Fruits was also called the Feast of Oil.

The Bethlehem Scroll, obtained by Professor Yadin after the 1967 war in Israel, gives explicit details about this Third Day of Passover, called the Feast of Oil. The Bethlehem Scroll specifically states that the Feast of Oil was to be observed on the first day of the week. It was the "morrow after the Sabbath," the First Day of the counting of the Omer.

The four accounts in the Gospels symphonize this sequence perfectly. The *"four days of the preparation"* are the tenth, eleventh, twelfth, and thirteenth of Aviv. The thirteenth is the Last Supper. At sundown on the fourteenth is the Passover meal. The Passover ended about midnight and Jesus was arrested in the garden in the early hours of that same morning. He stood trial, was condemned and placed on the cross at the time of the morning sacrifice in the Temple. He died at the time of the evening oblation about three o'clock.

Before sundown that fourteenth of Aviv, he was put in the tomb of Joseph of Arimathaea. He was now "put away" and "buried" before the Day of Matzo began. John calls this Day of Matzo, the fifteenth day of Aviv, the "high Sabbath." (John 19:31) The Sabbath of Matzo and also the Sabbath of the seventh day of the week makes it a "high Sabbath." "At the end of the Sabbath day, as it begins to twilight toward the first day of the week," is what we regard as Saturday night. The women come and find the empty tomb. There also lays the empty linen cocoon cast of his mummy-like form. This now the beginning of the sixteenth day of the month, the Feast of First Fruits, or the Feast of Oil. It is the morrow after the Sabbath of the seventh day of the week, the first day of Omer. On that day, the first day of the week, the Talmudist, in the Mishnaic of Mark 16:12-13, and the Gemarist, Luke 24:13-35, tell of the appearance of Jesus to the two on the road to Emmaus. In Luke's description, 24:21, "and besides all this, today [the first day of the week, the day of First Fruits or the Feast of Oil] is the third day since these things were done [the Crucifixion]."

If this "first day of the week is the third day" since the Crucifixion, the second day was (Saturday) the seventh day of the preceding week. Friday, therefore, is the first day of that event. See further chart page 7:29.

Theologians in the Protestant world have expended much effort to prove that Jesus was crucified on Wednesday or Thursday. They do this in an attempt to qualify the simile of the three days and three nights of Jonah in the whale. Such an expectation of seventy-two hours is not required in the text. A lack of knowledge of the Hebrew idiom "day and night is day one" gave occasion to this discrepancy of calculation.

The fearful response of one evangelical professor to this Jewish reckoning of the Passion Week was: "If we accept this Jewish interpretation, that will mean we are admitting that the Roman Catholics have been correct all the time...where would this finally lead us?" The answer is that it will lead us all, Protestant and Catholic, back to the Judeo-Christian concept. It would not be anti-Catholic nor anti-Protestant; it would be ante-argument.

Any ecumenical movement short of a return all the way back to the primal source, will only be a neo-denominationalism. Any new attempt to re-interpret Jesus apart from his very own religion of Judaism and language of Hebrew will be another step farther away from what Jesus actually said and literally meant.

Jesus came to dwell among us. As the Tabernacle of G-d, he reflected G-d's Shekinah Glory to the Gentile world. The Light of Torah illuminated the universe in creation. In order to be a light to the Gentiles, Jesus had to wrap up in his own life the unrolling of the Torah. "I came not to destroy the law but to fill it up" was his Father's business and the final sacrificial dedication of his life.

For three and a half years, his life was in symphonic accord with the reading of the Torah and the sacrifices of the Temple. All that Israel has in the Torah is personified in Jesus, wrapped up, delivered up, and extended out to the pagan Gentile world.

The pagan Gentile world was alienated from G-d by the giving of the Torah to Israel. The Gentiles are called strangers to the covenants, aliens to the Commonwealth of Israel, children of wrath and foreigners to a relationship with G-d. Jesus personified the Torah. He bore the curse of the law against the Gentile world. The Good News of the Gospels is that the righteousness of the Torah is imparted to the Gentile through faith in Jesus.

The dramatic chronology, the order, and the sequence of his life cannot be synchronized apart from the schedule of the three-and-one-half-year reading of the Torah. All the rabbinic commentaries are pertinent to each of the three hundred sixty-five sections, or chapters, of his life.

Without the aggressive and authoritative efforts of traditional Jewish scholarship, this interpretation and understanding can never be produced. Unfortunately, if all the knowledge of all the Christian scholarship on Judaism were combined, it would not be a droplet in the ocean of these resources.

Great problems arise in this consideration. First is the distrust of the Jewish scholars in the motive and results of such an interpretation of Jesus for the Christian. The second problem is the skeptical attitude of the Christian world in trusting their image of Jesus to a scrutiny through rabbinic literature and laws of interpretation.

In short, there exists a needless fear on the part of some Jewish scholars that such an investigation might prove that Jesus is what they have concluded he is not. On the other hand, the Christian might fear that such a subjection of Jesus to the Jewish tradition might prove that he is not what they have concluded he is. The Jews probably fear the results of that latter conclusion more than they do the former conclusion.

Another problem would be the possibility that a totally new image of Jesus might be discovered by such an examination. It would be ironic that if that rabbinic image of Jesus proved to be "acceptable" to the Jews but "rejected" by the Christians. This could turn the table so drastically that it would be the Jews sending out missionaries to the Christians and asking, "Why don't you Christians believe in Jesus?" Carried far enough, this could unwind history and the Jews might initiate their own pogroms, crusades, and execute their own inquisition against the infidel Christians. As one Rabbi said: "I have no problem accepting a Jesus that I don't have to accept."

Dismissing such humor, the greatest fear that both the Jew and the Christian have in such an understanding is the fear of fear itself.

Chapter VI
RIDDLE OF THE PLURAL COVENANTS

"There is perhaps no part of divinity attended with so much intricacy, and wherein orthodox divines do so much differ as stating the precise agreement and difference between the two dispensations of Moses and Christ."

Jonathan Edwards

Scholars have written volumes developing the history of the covenants, the meaning of the covenants, the relationships between the covenants, the terms of the covenants, the recipients of the covenants, and the limitations of the covenants. The covenants have been sifted, analyzed, broken down and built up—examined and explicated—but when the question referred to by Jonathan Edwards comes up, no answer seems to come forth, and the world of scholarship either falls into puzzling silence or breaks forth into a confused babble resulting in no constructive progress toward discovery of an answer. The question appears simple enough; but upon closer examination, it reveals aspects of complexity that defy explanation, simply because the investigator limits his investigation of the problem to the boundaries of Christianity. If he is to uncover an adequate answer to his inquiries into the Biblical covenants, he must delve deeper into the history of the covenants and examine his subject from the Jewish point of view.

In the history of Judaism, the student finds no controversy at all regarding the covenants, no debate whatever, no subject so plainly expressed, nor issue so clearly defined, as that of the covenants. Judaism deals directly with the origins of the covenants and their entire history is entwined with their development and intimately concerned with their determination.

Before discussing the development of the covenants, it is necessary to define clearly what a covenant is. All that a covenant means is wrapped up in the Hebrew primal root word, ברית, *B'RieYT*, or *Berit*. It means simply a contract, a will, a league, a testament, or a bond. It differs distinctly and significantly from a vow. A vow may involve the participation of one party or more. Unlike a covenant, a vow may be broken by certain conditions of revocation. At Yom Kippur, for example, all vows of the past year are revoked with the *QoHL NeiYD'RaY*, or *Kol Nidre*.

The covenant differs further from the vow in that the covenant always involves more than one person and is perpetually binding by oath. It cannot be revoked, altered, or annulled, nor can a present covenant displace a former one. A latter covenant can enhance, extend, or complement the former, but it can never abrogate it. If the terms of a latter covenant should abrogate or interfere with a former covenant, the terms of the earlier take precedence over the latter.

In a covenant relationship, the individuals involved sacrifice the distinctiveness of their own individual identities, much like the members of a modern corporation. This covenant entity, as used in the Jewish scripture, primarily relates to covenants between G-d and man. In some two hundred thirty occurrences of the word, *B'RieYT*, in the Jewish Bible, over two hundred refer to the G-d-man relationship.

In ancient times, everyone took all the covenants very seriously. A person initiated his covenant with a blood sacrifice, followed by a sworn oath pledging himself fully to his agreement. Such a covenant was so binding that men engraved its terms upon stone or cuneiform tablets. Some have been found which were cast in brass plates. To break a covenant sealed in blood was considered not only a sin but a crime worthy of death.

A covenant had certain definite, distinctive characteristics—its terms always expressed explicitly. It was either restrictive or nonrestrictive, conditional or unconditional. In either case, it could not be both; that is, it could not be restrictive in some parts and nonrestrictive in others. Its terms could not be changed, spiritualized or applied to any conditions other than those plainly stated.

In Judaism there were seven major covenants made between G-d and man. In all of these covenants, the Eternal One was the party of the first part. Four of these covenants were restricted to Israel, except under particular specified instances. The other three major covenants were universal and applicable to mankind as a whole.

The Covenant of Gan Eden

The first covenant was that of Gan Eden, or the Garden of Eden. Its terms are found in Genesis 1:28-30. This covenant gave Adam the scepter of rulership over the entire earth, and restricted both man and animal by dietary laws to a vegetarian diet. Under this covenant, Adam had title to the whole earth, which means that all real estate and chattel belonged to him. The restriction related to a single tree, called the Tree of Knowledge of Good and Evil, which stood in the middle of the garden. Except for this tree, the earth and all therein were Adam's.

According to the Jewish tradition, the very same day that Adam and Eve were created, Eve committed robbery. She took fruit from the Tree of Knowledge of Good and Evil and thereby brought death and exile to the human family. The fruit from that tree was the only thing on earth that she could have stolen. Everything else belonged to her and Adam.

In the eschatological hope of Judaism, the life in the world to come and the primary function of the Messiah will be to restore the whole creation to the conditions under the Edenic covenant. The Kabbalists teach:

> Somewhere there is an Adam within each of us, in need of restoration—in exile from the Garden. The aim of the Kabbalah is to restore that divine man in the medium of the mortal man. We are the laboratory, we are the workers in that sphere and space. All this is to say that there is an intimate relationship between mortal man and his spiritual counterpart. The mystery of that relationship is to be found in the ten spheres of the Adam Kadmon [the primal divine man after whose image Adam was created]. If one can learn to connect the thread dangling free from the ten spheres

> with the fiber of his being—if one can discover the secret opening in the base of the skull—one may begin the work of the restoration.

In Judaism, and therefore, naturally in the Old Testament, there is no concept of heaven as there is in Christian eschatology. Nowhere is there a promise to Adam, to Noah, to Abraham, to Moses, or to any of the prophets of a "piece of pie in the sky in the sweet by and by." Jewish eschatology is totally lacking a heavenly inheritance.

Several years ago, Evangelist Billy Graham was speaking in Jerusalem. Dr. Robert Lindsey, the Hebrew linguist, was translating for him. "You can know," said the evangelist, "that when you die, you will go to Heaven." With those words, the translation stopped. Doctor Lindsey knew that if he translated literally what Evangelist Graham had said, it would mean in Hebrew, or in Jewish thought, that when you die, your body is going to float around in the sky like an astronaut's. Likewise, he knew that if he used the phrase "life in the world to come," he would not be translating what Billy Graham meant because the inheritance of the Jew in the world to come is restricted to a real estate plot in the Middle East. It concerns restoration of the land to the people in the world to come as well as restoration of the land to its former state of productive abundance. Although the Jews do not believe that they will be the only people in the world to come, they do believe that every man who responds by faith to G-d in whatever covenant relationship the Eternal One has revealed to him will have a part in the life in the world to come, or the Messianic Age.

Isaiah the prophet describes this life in the world to come and the return of the world to the condition of the Garden of Eden thusly: "And there shall come forth a rod out of the stem of Jesse, and a Branch shall grow out of his roots...and righteousness shall be the girdle of his loins, and faithfulness the girdle of his reins. The wolf also shall dwell with the lamb, and the leopard shall lie down with the kid; and the calf and the young lion and the fatling together; and a little child shall lead them. And the cow and the bear shall feed; their young ones shall lie down together; and the lion shall eat straw like the ox. And the suckling child shall play on the hole of the asp, and the weaned child shall put his hand on the cockatrice' den." (Isaiah 11:1, 5-8) As Isaiah states, when the Messiah comes, even the carnivorous animals, such as the lion, the wolf and the bear, shall return to their original states of being vegetarians.

The third chapter of Genesis records not only the robbery of the fruit of the Tree of Knowledge of Good and Evil but also the drastic consequences of that theft. When Eve jerked the fruit from that tree and Adam partook of it with her, they brought a curse upon the land, upon the serpent, and upon themselves. The ground was to bring forth thorns and thistles, the serpent was to crawl on his belly, and Adam and Eve were to live a life of strenuous toil. Moreover, Adam and Eve discovered that they were naked.

When G-d challenged their misconduct, Adam, as human nature is even today, passed the buck to Eve. Half blaming G-d, he said, *"That woman you gave me, she. . . ."* When the Creator challenged the woman, her reply was, "The devil made me do it." The effects of the violation of this covenant have continued to the present: man continues to pass the buck of responsibility to someone else.

The Covenant with Adam

In Genesis 3:14-19, the second covenant was made between G-d and man: the Adamic Covenant. The first promise contained in the Adamic Covenant was that the seed of the woman would restore the earth to the Edenic conditions. Meanwhile, however, many consequences would be suffered by the human family. The grief of womanhood would be multiplied: "In sorrow thou shall bring forth children...cursed is the ground for thy sake...thorns and thistles shall it bring forth to thee... in the sweat of thy face shalt thou eat bread, till thou return unto the ground; for out of it was thou taken: from dust thou art and to dust thou shalt return."

This is the Adamic Covenant under which the human family has continued to live for 5,743 years as of the Christian year 1983. Under the Adamic Covenant, however, the punishment levied upon man proved to be ineffective as a corrective factor. According to the Jewish tradition, 1,657 years passed from the Adamic Covenant to the covenant of Noah. Between these two covenants, mankind lived in a very highly advanced civilization. In spite of such advancement, man's moral nature and G-d-consciousness suffered such a great decadence that civilization was finally obliterated by the judgment of the flood of Noah.

The Covenant with Noah

After the Flood, the earth no longer appeared to be the same planet it had been before. Much of the animal life that had existed in those years was destroyed. Much of the plant kingdom also ceased to exist. The earth was unable to produce with the fertility and abundance that it had before. The geophysical features were so totally changed that the family of Noah found an entirely different world when they came out of the Ark.

Genesis 8:20 to 9:17 contains the setting and conditions of the Noahic Covenant. With this covenant, man's relationship to the earth and the animal world was changed. For the first time, G-d made provision for man to eat flesh. According to Jewish interpretation, the Noahic Covenant is broken down into what is called the Seven Laws of Noah. As the Adamic Covenant did not replace the Edenic, but rather complemented it with greater provisions, so the Noahic Covenant neither replaced nor annulled the Edenic and the Adamic covenants.

Basically, the Seven Laws of Noah prohibit idolatry, fornication and murder. Under their provisions, human government was ordained of G-d; and capital punishment, through human government, was so ordained. Dietary changes were also stipulated in the Seven Laws of Noah. While all flesh was now permissible for food, G-d made a very clear distinction between the clean and the unclean animals. Noah had been instructed to take the unclean animals by pairs into the Ark. The clean animals, however, were taken into the Ark by sevens.

Under the Seven Laws of Noah, cannabalism was forbidden. Even eating flesh from an animal before it was properly slain was also forbidden. This was to prohibit man from cutting off a muscle or limb of an animal and eating it, leaving the animal to live maimed.

The eating of blood was also prohibited. Under the Noahic Covenant, an animal had to be properly killed to be used for food. Any animal that was torn of beast, died of itself, or was found dead, could not be eaten.

The Noahic Covenant, like the Adamic, is universal in scope, and is applicable to all men. It is not specifically to Israel.

The Covenant with Abraham

Under the Noahic Covenant of human government, the decadence of humanity in turning to idolatry was much more rapid than it had been in the 1,656 years from Adam to the Flood. Three hundred sixty-one years after the Noahic Covenant, therefore, the Creator appeared to Abraham in the twelfth chapter of Genesis and established the fourth covenant, called the Abrahamic Covenant. This covenant was restricted to a particular descendancy of Abraham through Isaac and Jacob. This covenant separated Israel from the other nations. The specifics of the Abrahamic Covenant, as given to Abraham and confirmed to Isaac and Jacob, can be found in Genesis 12:1-3; 13:14-18; 15:1-21; 17:4-8; 22:15-24; 26:1-5; and 28:10-15. This covenant, too, has seven facets, or sections.

First, it had to do with a real estate arrangement, "a land that I will show thee." Second, "I will make of thee a great nation." Third, "I will bless thee." Fourth, "I will make thy name great." Fifth, "Thou shalt be a blessing;" sixth, "I will bless them that bless thee and curse them that curse thee;" and seventh, "In thee shall all the [Gentile] families of the earth be blessed." The seventh section, and only this section, contains specific, particular provision for the Gentiles. The first six provisions of the Abrahamic Covenant were exclusively to Israel.

The Abrahamic Covenant has certain other definite characteristics. It is a covenant of faith. "And Abraham believed G-d and it was counted to him for righteousness." A Jew's relationship to G-d is a vital relationship of faith based on the Abrahamic Covenant. When a Jew approaches G-d in prayer, he makes his petitions premised on that covenant. The Jew never approaches G-d in the name of Moses because his standing before G-d is not premised upon the Mosaic Covenant. However, when the Jew prays, he opens his prayer with these words: "G-d, G-d of our Fathers, G-d of Abraham, of Isaac and of Jacob . . . ."

The Abrahamic Covenant is a restricted covenant. It alienates all other nations from the economy of Israel. It is an unconditional covenant, containing the repetition of the oath of G-d, who swore by his own name, saying "I will...I will...I will...I will...." This unconditional covenant is contingent upon G-d's faithfulness to Israel, not in Israel's faithfulness to G-d. Despite Israel's failure, the Holy One reassured the prophets, "Yet for my Holy Name's sake, and the sake of the covenant that I made with thy fathers, Abraham, Isaac, and Jacob, I will perform."

The Abrahamic Covenant, like all other covenants between the Eternal One and mankind, is an everlasting covenant; it can never be terminated, can never be altered, or changed or revised. The only demand made upon the Jew by this covenant is his commitment of faith in that covenant relationship established with Abraham, Isaac and Jacob.

The Covenant with Moses

Four hundred thirty years after the giving of the Abrahamic Covenant, Israel requested that G-d reveal to them his requirements of them so that they could exercise the faith and express the standing they had through the Abrahamic Covenant. Therefore, in the Jewish year 2448, G-d gave Israel the Torah on Mount Sinai. This law of G-d is also called the Law of Moses, because Moses himself was personified and wrapped up in the words of that Torah. The Law, or Torah, given to Moses on Mount Sinai, has never been considered by the Jews as the premise of their relationship with G-d. Their relationship with G-d is entirely premised on the Abrahamic Covenant.

The five books of Torah, the Pentateuch, are Genesis, Exodus, Leviticus, Numbers, and Deuteronomy. Moses wrote all five books of the Torah; even the passages that refer to him, he wrote in the third person, for every word of it was dictated to him by G-d.

The way of the Torah teaches the Jew where he came from, where he is, and where he is going. It instructs him in every minute detail of his daily life and relationship to G-d. In this Torah are six hundred thirteen commandments. Of these, two hundred forty-eight are positive commandments, instructing Israel what they must do, while three hundred sixty-five are negative commandments, telling Israel what they should not do.

The Mosaic Covenant strongly emphasizes the distinction of the Jew as separate from all the other nations. While the Gentiles could eat all flesh, the Mosaic Covenant restricted the dietary practice of the Jew to only certain forms of flesh. What was clean to the Gentile was unclean to the Jew. He was instructed not to worship as or with the pagans, and was commanded not to dress or conform to the Gentile standards of conduct.

Time and space took on a special dimension of holiness for the Jew. The observance of the Sabbath day was uniquely designated to Israel alone. According to rabbinic interpretation, a Gentile who observes the Sabbath is worthy of death, because he is stealing a commandment that was given exclusively to Israel. All six hundred thirteen commandments of the Jewish law were explicitly given to Israel alone. The Jew did not obtain salvation or a standing with G-d as a result of keeping the commandments of Torah, for his standing with G-d was already established by faith on the basis of the Abrahamic Covenant. The observance of the six hundred thirteen commandments was the exercise of that faith and standing he already had with G-d. He did not keep the law in order to be a Jew; he kept the law because he was a Jew.

The giving of the Abrahamic Covenant separated Israel from the Gentile nations. The giving of the Mosaic Covenant intensified this separation between Israel and the Gentile nations. Every section of the commandments given to Moses began with the restrictive phrase: "And the Eternal One spake unto Moses, saying, 'Speak unto the children of Israel and command them. . . ."

The Edenic, Adamic, and Noahic covenants were universal and applied to all mankind. The Abrahamic Covenant and the Mosaic are exclusively to Israel.

Under the Abrahamic and Mosaic covenants, Israel was never commanded to convert the Gentiles to their faith or religious practices. On the contrary, they were commanded explicitly not to convert the Gentiles to Judaism. If a Gentile sincerely sought to follow this faith and practice, it was the responsibility of the rabbis to discourage such a decision unless it was proved totally sincere, intelligently made, and clearly understood on the part of the convert.

The covenant of Moses given at Mount Sinai included both the Written Law and the Oral Law. They are inseparable, and the Oral is as binding as is the Written.

This Mosaic Covenant was totally a conditional covenant. The people of Israel, in requesting this covenant, said, "We will do it and we will hear it." They did not say, "We will hear it then we will do it." In this request, Israel committed themselves to obey unconditionally the words of Torah. By acknowledging *obedience to the law* before they heard its terms, they implied that they did not sit in judgment as to whether or not they thought a law was good or bad, whether it was reasonable or unreasonable, whether it was logical or illogical. "We will do and we will hear."

This covenant of Moses at Mount Sinai was the total embodiment of a conditional covenant. "This do and thou shalt live. . . ." "Honor thy father and thy mother—that thy days may be long in the land."

Such statements as these appear connected with almost all the commandments. In Moses' closing address in Deuteronomy 28:58-62, we find the epitome of the essence in the Mosaic Covenant as a conditional covenant:

> If thou wilt not observe to do all the words of this law that are written in this book that thou mayest fear this glorious and fearful name, THE LORD THY G-D; Then the Lord will make thy plagues wonderful, and the plagues of thy seed, even great plagues, and of long continuance, and sore sicknesses, and of long continuance. Moreover he will bring upon thee all the diseases of Egypt, which thou wast afraid of; and they shall cleave unto thee. Also every sickness, and every plague, which is not written in the book of this law, them will the Lord bring upon thee, until thou be destroyed. And ye shall be left few in number, whereas ye were as the stars of heaven for multitude; because thou wouldest not obey the voice of the Lord thy G-d.

A failure on the part of Israel to fulfill the words of Torah did not affect or threaten their standing before G-d in the Abrahamic Covenant, for the former took precedence over the latter, and the latter could not jeopardize or abrogate the former.

The Torah was given to Israel in the wilderness as a premise for their conduct when they would come into the land of Israel. All those commandments related in the acknowledgment by the people were not initiated in the wilderness, and indeed could not be obeyed until they had come into the land. Therefore, throughout the Torah appears the phrase: "When thou comest into the land which the Lord thy G-d givest thee, then shalt thou observe. . . ."

Actually, in the wilderness Israel was under such a special economy that they did not so much as practice circumcision. In Joshua 5:2-9 is the account of Joshua circumcising at Gilgal the male children who were born in the wilderness.

The covenant of Moses was the testament of Moses. Like any other will or testament, it could not be effective until the death of the testator. "For your sakes," said Moses, "I cannot enter into this land." The necessity of the death of Moses was imperative before Israel could inaugurate the fulfilling of the Torah, "when thou comest into the land, which the Lord thy G-d givest thee."

The terms of that conditional covenant focused on obedience, while the penalties for Israel in failing to obey the words of Torah were an expulsion from the land and a scattering among the Gentile nations. By so doing, Israel's relationship to the Abrahamic Covenant was not affected. Their privilege under the conditional covenant of Moses demanded such a diaspora in penalty for failure to keep the covenant. The Diaspora, however, did not terminate the Mosaic Covenant either. The Jew in the Diaspora was still obligated to fulfill ninety commandments. In fact, the Jew today is obligated to fulfill all the words of the Torah except those whose fulfillment are contingent upon the function of Temple worship in the land.

The New Covenant for Israel

The Abrahamic Covenant had made provision for a blessing in the land. The Mosaic Covenant at Mount Sinai made no condition or promise for a regathering of Israel from the dispersion to which it had been sentenced by the Divine judge. Therefore, if the Torah were to have such a provision for a regathering of dispersed Israel so as not to abrogate the Abrahamic Covenant, a new covenant would be required in the Torah.

There is a new testament in the Torah. That new testament, or new covenant, was made with Israel at Mount Moab immediately before the death of Moses. Moses recorded the words of that covenant in the twenty-ninth and thirtieth chapters of Deuteronomy. This new covenant is restricted to Israel and concerns the regathering of Israel from the nations in the last days. "These are the words of the covenant, which the Eternal One commanded Moses to make with the children of Israel in the land of Moab, *beside* the covenant which he made with them in Horeb [Sinai]." (Deut. 29:1)

With the giving of this covenant at Mount Moab, providing for the regathering of Israel in the last days, the clause of the Abrahamic Covenant stating, "I will give thee a land," is reaffirmed. At the same time, the new covenant at Mount Moab in no way infringes upon the lengthy penalty of Israel scattered among the nations as demanded by the Sinaitic Covenant for their disobedience.

Jeremiah the prophet gave a great deal of attention to the regathering of Israel in the last days. In Jeremiah 31:8-11 are these words:

> Behold, I will bring them from the north country, and gather them from the coasts of the earth, and with them the blind and the lame, the woman with child and her that travaileth with child together: a great company shall return thither. They shall come with weeping, and with supplication will I lead them: I will cause them to walk by the rivers of waters in a straight way, wherein they shall not stumble: for I am a father to Israel, and Ephraim is my firstborn. Hear the Word of the Eternal One. O ye [Gentile] nations, and declare it in the isles afar off, and say, He that scattered Israel will gather him, and keep him, as a shepherd doth his flock. For the Eternal One hath redeemed Jacob, and ransomed him from the hand of him that was stronger than he. Therefore shall they come and sing in the height of Zion. . . ."

Not only did Jeremiah predict the return of Israel from the Diaspora in fulfillment of the new covenant, or new testament, that G-d made with Israel on Mount Moab, but he also predicted the revival of Hebrew as the spoken language of modern Israel: "This saith the Eternal One of hosts, the G-d of Israel; As yet they shall use this speech in the land of Judah and in the cities thereof, when I shall bring again their captivity...." (Jeremiah 31:23)

In the context of the *New Covenant*, or *New Testament*, of Mount Moab, Jeremiah's commentary in chapter thirty-one very specifically identifies the Moabic Covenant: "Behold the days come, saith the Eternal One, that I will make a *New Covenant* with the house of Israel and the house of Judah. Not according to the covenant [at Mount Sinai] that I made with their fathers in the day that I took them by the hand to bring them out of the land of Egypt. Which covenant they break...."

This *New Covenant* of Jeremiah 31:31 is the *New Covenant* of Moab, found in Deuteronomy 29-30. It is an unconditional covenant. This *New Covenant* is a restricted one. It applies only to Israel (the northern kingdom) and Judah (the southern kingdom). This *New Covenant* which promises to restore dispersed Israel to their land is one covenant for both Israel and Judah. As in the vision of the "two sticks" in Ezekiel 37, Israel and Judah would return united and be called Israel.

This *New Covenant* with the house of Israel and the house of Judah does not include the Gentiles. It is not the "New Testament in my blood shed for the sins of many [the Gentiles]," spoken of by Jesus at the Passover. The *New Covenant*, or *New Testament*, of Mount Moab and Jeremiah 31:31, is exclusively for Israel. It has no relationship directly or indirectly to the collection of the twenty-seven books of the Christian scriptures called the New Testament. The Christian scripture, called the New Testament, was so named by the church fathers, not by the Apostles. Neither the Christian scripture, called the New Testament, nor the death of Jesus, has any prophetic significance in the *New Testament* of Israel at Moab or Jeremiah 31:31! They are entirely different. The New Testament to Israel has no dimension to the Gentile Christian, and the New Testament to the Gentile Christian has no dimension to Israel.

There are, however, two direct references in the Christian's New Testament to Israel's *New Testament of*

Moab and Jeremiah 31:31. One occurs in Romans 11 and the other in Hebrews 8. Both of these are in the context of the future restoration of National Israel. There is no instance in the Christian scripture where these or any other covenants are "spiritualized" and applied to the church. That again was monk work.

That *New Covenant*, or *New Testament*, in the sacrifice of Jesus has dynamic dimension for the Gentile world. Jesus does not need for the Christian theologian to steal from Israel in order to validate his sacrificial work. The meaningfulness of Jesus' accomplishment is sufficient to stand on its own merit and purpose.

The promise of the *New Covenant* of Moab and Jeremiah 31 is not only unconditional but it is eternal and nonretractable. In verses 35-40, that dimension of infinity or eternality is stated: "Thus saith the Eternal One, which giveth the sun for a light by day, and the ordinances of the moon and of the stars for a light by night, which divideth the sea when the waves thereof roar; The Eternal One of Hosts is his name: If these ordinances depart from before me, saith the Eternal One, then the seed of Israel also shall cease from being a nation before me forever. Thus saith the Eternal One; if heaven above can be measured and the foundations of the earth searched out beneath, [then] will also I cast off all the seed of Israel for all that they have done, saith the Eternal One."

The Covenant with David

The Davidic Covenant was the seventh covenant of the Jewish scriptures and the final covenant made with ancient Israel. Messianic expectation in the Abrahamic, the Mosaic and the Moabic covenants was vaguely suggested but was not a dominant issue. The Davidic Covenant, however, is the stimulus of the Messianic hope of Israel.

Israel had no king from the Jewish year 2488, the year of their entrance into *Eretz Israel*, until the anointing of Saul, three hundred twenty-six years later. Saul reigned forty years. David reigned at Hebron for seven years before his kingdom was fully established in the Jewish year 2854. This was about nine hundred years before the Common Era. David, too, reigned for forty years. Only after his kingdom was established and the Davidic

Covenant was ratified did Messianic speculation become a prominent theme in Israel's eschatological expectation.

Nathan, the prophet, in II Samuel 7:4-17, spoke the words of the Davidic Covenant. Developing their messages from that covenant, many of the prophets spoke in detail of the kingdom of the Messiah, the days of the Messiah and the Messianic Age.

According to the Messianic expectation of Israel, the Messiah will come from the line of David's descendants. The tribe of Judah had been designated as the regal tribe by the patriarch Jacob in the prophetic blessings of his sons in Genesis 49:8-12:

> Judah, thou art he whom thy brethren shall praise: thy hand shall be on the neck of thine enemies; thy father's children shall bow down before thee. Judah is a lion's whelp: from the prey, my son, thou art gone up: he stooped down, he crouched as a lion, and as an old lion; who shall rouse him up?
>
> The scepter [regal staff] shall not depart from Judah, nor a law-giver from between his feet, until Shiloh [the peace giver] come; and unto him shall the gathering of the [Gentile] people be. Binding his foal unto the vine, and his ass's colt unto the choice vine; he washed his garments in wine and his clothes in the blood of grapes. His eyes shall be red with wine, and his teeth white with milk.

This prophecy by Jacob that Judah would be the regal house of Israel was made in the Jewish year 2255. It lay dormant without any particular fulfillment until Nathan expressed the Davidic Covenant at the beginning of the reign of David six hundred years later. Thereafter, Messianic speculation and expectation grew rapidly. The division of Israel into two kingdoms, the moral decadence of those kingdoms, the Babylonian captivity, and the struggle in the reestablishment of Judah made the hope of the Promised One of David even more urgent. The coming of the Romans and the oppression of the Edomite dynasty of the Herods sharpened the Messianic consciousness to a keen edge.

What did the Jews of Jesus' day expect the Messiah, the regal son of David, to be and to do? How, if at all, did their Messianic expectation differ from the traditional view of Judaism today concerning the person and work of the Messiah? First, the Messiah would be human. He would be a descendant of David, and he would be from the City of David, Bethlehem of Judaea. He would make his appearance in a regal form. He would be a triumphant king! He would arise as did David out of the ranks of the common people. The Messiah would appear at a particular time and in a particular situation. His appearance would come at a time of great distress and trouble. He would reveal himself at a dark time when the nation of Israel would be on the brink of destruction. The Messiah, the Son of David, would appear and redeem the nation from gross oppression forced upon them by alien powers. He would destroy all those oppressors. He would purge the land of Israel from apostate rule and religious hypocrisy. He would bring again the Shekinah Glory to the Temple. The law of Torah would once more rule the land. He would avenge the people of Israel and destroy the Gentile nations which had sought the destruction of the people and nation of Israel. He would establish an unprecedented era of peace on earth. The nations would learn war no more. Peace and justice and righteousness would reign upon the earth. In the days of the Messiah, the dead would be raised. Israel would receive its full inheritance from the Nile River in Egypt in the south to the Euphrates River in the north. The earth would be filled with the knowledge of the Eternal One as the waters cover the seas. The Messiah would restore the whole earth and all mankind to its perfect state under the Edenic Covenant. That Messiah would never die, but he would live forever and ever, ages without end. Of his kingdom, there would be no end. He would reign forever and ever.

These are the expectations of the Davidic Covenant with all its developments through the prophets. This is what the Jews of Jesus' time expected the Messiah to do and to be. This is what traditional Judaism today expects in the person and work of the Messiah. The Jews have never, they can never, they will never accept anyone as Messiah who does not meet these expectations and performances.

These seven covenants are the covenants of the Jewish scripture. They express the promises of G-d to Israel and the expectations Israel has of his G-d. The Edenic, the Adamic and the Noahic covenants are universal and are to the Gentiles. Israel is involved in these covenants only in a restricted sense. The Abrahamic, the Sinaic, the Moabic, and the Davidic are primarily to the separate people of Israel. The Gentile nations or individuals are involved only in a restricted measure to these covenants of Israel.

At this point, a vital question arises demanding an answer: What did Jesus mean when he said, "This cup is the New Testament [or New Covenant] in my blood shed for the sins of many"? To which of the seven covenants was he making reference? Or, was he making reference to any of the former covenants? Was the New Testament spoken of by Jesus an entirely separate economy from any of the former? If it was a separate economy from the seven covenants of Israel's scripture, what is its relationship to them?

Replacement theologians paint one big sign on the Jewish Bible and call it the "Old Testament." This implies, naturally, that it is antiquated, abrogated, obsolete, done away with, and destroyed. Now the "Old Testament" is *replaced* by the "New Testament." They have treated the "Old Testament" like a junk car in a wrecking yard. These theologians use the Jewish scripture only to rip off a part here and there, modify it to their own designs, and use it to make functional their theology of the "New Testament."

In ripping off or stealing parts from the Jewish canon, these replacement mechanics even switched the name-plates of the vehicles. They took the words "Israel" and "Jews," repainted them with the enamel of spiritual interpretation, and attempted to pass them off as "True Israel" and "True Jews" as designations of the Church and the Christians.

The theologians took sadistic pleasure in calling the ancient people of Jacob "old," "fleshly," "earthly," or "natural Israel." They considered the Jews of the *Old Testament* heritage as no more purposeful than the other debris scattered in their theological wrecking yard.

Replacement theologians not only junked-out the people of the covenants of Israel, they also reduced the holy, immutable, eternal covenants of oath to mere vows which could be revoked by *Kol Nidre*. Any benefits found in those covenants were ripped off and applied to the Church. Christianity and Christian theology became the new vehicle of divine revelation, a vehicle made from selected parts from the Jewish *Old Testament.*

The tools used in making this modification were the terms of Greek logic and mythology as well as the content of Greek philosophy. Pagan words and pagan definitions totally alien to Jewish thoughts were substituted for rabbinic concepts. Foreign terms such as *incarnation, theophany,* and *trinity* were introduced into the new system. These pagan mythological cliches became the dogmatic expression and credo of the new vehicle.

Every field of systematic theology was affected by this replacement concept. The concept of the Jewish G-d of the *Old Testament* was treated as a legalistic G-d of wrath and judgment. He was contrasted to the new G-d of the Christian *New Testament,* who is a G-d of love in Jesus. The Law of Torah became a bitter, vulgar and obsolete thing, while the sweet Christian love could create holy wars, crusades, the Inquisition, and pogroms. That sort of "Christian love" strikes one's taste buds like a mouth full of cold, slick oatmeal.

The anthropology of replacement theology wiped out all suggestion of the Jews as a chosen or separate people. In this new order, Jesus did away with Israel as separate from the Gentile nations. The Jews became not only like all other peoples, they were relegated to a subhuman class. Much of Goebbels' propaganda against the Jews during the holocaust consisted of direct quotes from Christian literature and liturgy. The Chosen People are the Christians, not the Jews.

To illustrate how humbug the logic of Christian anthropology became, the Jew who converted to Christianity had to deny his Jewishness. At his baptism, he vowed to renounce Judaism and all its "heresies." After his baptism he was told that he was no longer a Jew, but was now a Christian. In many cases he was forced to change his name from a Jewish to a Christian one.

After these renunciations of his Jewishness, he began to study the catechism which taught that the pagan Gentiles who become Christians became true spiritual Jews. The logic of Christian anthropology is more a double *in*version rather than a simple *con*version. The Jew who became a Christian became a Gentile, while the Gentile who became a Christian became a Jew. Such metamorphosis is nowhere to be found in nature (or in the scriptures).

The soteriology of replacement theology deals with replacement doctrines of salvation. In this concept Jesus came to be the Savior of Israel. Israel, accordingly, rejected the Savior and crucified him. In this crisis, the "god" of Christian love quickly put the pieces of this tragedy into a new plan, producing the crisis theory of the Gospel of salvation made available to everyone.

The church soon became the object of this salvation through dogmas, sacraments, or other institutional demands. As time passed, parochialism developed in the various denominations. Most of the Good News propagated by the missionaries today is to convert other Christians to their own denomination's "salvation," while they admittedly declare "millions have never heard the Gospel."

In all the various Christian salvation messages, there are only two classes of people in this world and in the world to come. There are the saved and the lost. The saved are those who accept a given particular message. Those who do not obey the various particular interpretations of the Gospel are the lost. More than anyone else, the Jew is treated as lost, blind, stubborn and damned. The "god" of Christian love has put all of his eggs in one basket now—the Christian church.

In 1973, over one hundred forty denominations decided to drop all doctrinal differences and join hands in the "Key '73" project. One single objective was in focus. "Let us reach the whole world with the Gospel message in the next decade." The Key '73 program spelled out its own failure. The problem was that the one hundred forty denominations could not agree on what the Gospel really is. If Christianity cannot define and agree on the "Gospel of Jesus Christ which is the power of G-d unto salvation," how could they ever agree on anything?

Soteriology is the most emphatic and important section of Christian theology. This is especially true in evangelical Christianity. Yet, in this very field, that same Christian theology finds its greatest weakness.

Ecclesiology is the study of community or church. Since salvation is only in the Gospel of Jesus Christ, according to replacement theologians, the only true community of G-d would be the Church. Parochialism found its strongest expression in ecclesiology. It erased the distinction between soteriology, or salvation, and ecclesiology, or the church. Parochialism made the church and salvation synonymous. "Our church is the one and only true religion"; "Our church is the pillar and ground of the truth"; "Our church is the body and bride of Christ; other Christians may be in heaven, but they will only be friends of the bridegroom—we are the true church"; "G-d raised up our church to call all the true believers out of the apostate churches in our city." These quotations and other statements, such as "the plain truth," "facts you need to know about G-d's will for your life," "our denominational distinctives," are common to the vast majority of Christian organizations throughout the world. At the same time, they all deny the community of Israel, the Jewish people. Israel has no place in the economy of G-d, according to strict replacement theology.

If the Christian believes that the Church is the only true community of G-d, and that his particular denomination enjoys a special favor in that economy, he finds himself experiencing a great difficulty in recognizing the legitimacy of other Christians being on equal standing without a compromise of his own denominational distinctives. It would be totally foreign for him to accept the idea that Israel had a community relationship with G-d completely separate and apart from his own.

When, however, the Christian makes the discovery that Israel has a place in the economy of G-d, it will revolutionize his attitude toward, and his relationship with, Jewish people, with his neighbor Christians, with the study of the Bible, with himself, and with G-d. Ecclesiology made no allocation for a plural community either in this world or in the world to come.

The fifth and last field of systematic theology deals with the last days and things in the world to come. This field is called eschatology. The replacement theologian considered the "earthly kingdom of carnal, fleshly Israel" to have been replaced with the spiritual kingdom of heaven, the Church. The definitions of the kingdom are as diversified in the writings of Christian theologians as are the definitions of salvation, the Gospel, and the Church.

In the hard core replacement position, the Church is the kingdom of G-d. The Church rules as Christ's political kingdom upon the earth. There is no need for a national

Israel; the Church is the *corpus deo politico*. In this interpretation, there is no line of distinction between ecclesiology and eschatology. The Church, the Christian kingdom of G-d, is here and now. This was the message of the crusades, the Spanish Inquisition, and the creeds of postmillennialism. The Church failed to conquer the world in righteousness as the postmillennialists had prophesied. They had predicted: "Through the preaching of the Gospel, the world is getting better and better."

The postmillennial prophets preached that World War I would be the war that would end all wars and that within fifty years, there would be a church on every city block throughout the whole earth. Prisons would be emptied and the kingdom of G-d would reign upon the earth. This would be the millennial age in which the Jew and Israel would find no part.

After two world wars and the worldwide moral decadence, the replacement postmillennialists had to find an escape hatch from their embarrassment of world conditions and the failure of their prophecies. The escape hatch for the postmillennialists was simply to become amillennialist. This group reverts to a strong replacement position. They believe that the prophecies made to Israel are *all* fulfilled in the Church. Since this is true, there is no need for a millennial reign and no place for the future economy of Israel.

Dispensational premillennialism is a school of interpretation that cut hard across the grain of replacement theology. It specified an exact literal interpretation in scripture concerning the Church, Israel, and the kingdom. It recognized the historic economy of Israel as the Chosen People and the future eschatological economy of Israel as valid in the economy of G-d.

The strange thinking about dispensationalists, however, is that they followed the traditional replacement theologian's attitude toward the Jew individually, Judaism as a religion, and Israel in any present economy. Dispensationalists traditionally do not recognize that the Jewish people today have a vital relationship with G-d through faith in the Abrahamic Covenant. To this there are exceptions. Occasionally a dispensationalist will hint, tongue in cheek, that the Jews today are in somewhat of a mystical exclusive economy. For example, the Scofield Reference Bible, the textbook of dispensationalism, in the

Book of Habakkuk, chapter two, footnote two, reads: "His ancient Israel is cast out of the land and judicially blinded, but in covenanted mercy, the individual Jew may resort to the simple faith of Abraham and be saved."

Another interesting observation by way of exception to traditional dispensationalism is found in the Statement of Faith of the Dallas Theological Seminary, page 11:

> We believe that it has always been true that "without faith it is impossible to please" G-d (Heb. 11:6), and that the principle of faith was prevalent in the lives of all the Old Testament saints. However, we believe that it was historically impossible that they should have had as the conscious object of their faith the incarnate, crucified Son, the Lamb of G-d (John 1:29), and that it is evident that they did not comprehend as we do that the sacrifices depicted the person and work of Christ. We believe also that they did not understand the redemptive significance of the prophecies or types concerning the sufferings of Christ (I Peter 1:10-12); therefore, we believe that their faith toward G-d was manifested in other ways as is shown by the long record in Hebrews 11:1-40. We believe further that their faith thus manifested was counted unto them for righteousness (cf. Romans 4:3 with Genesis 15:6, Romans 4:5-8, Hebrews 11:7).

Such a statement on the part of any Christian group is most encouraging. Until the Christians take this attitude toward the Jews, there will never be a basis for Jewish-Christian relations or dialogue. The greatest inconsistency with this position is that these dispensational groups laid a very strong emphasis on Jewish evangelism. If the Jew has a vital relationship with G-d through faith in the Abrahamic Covenant, what then is the objective of trying to convert the Jew to Christianity? Dispensationalists generally believe that Israel will not come into G-d's favor until they first accept Jesus as their savior.

The Plymouth brethren were the forerunners of dispensationalism. They took a leading role in giving occasion to and enhancing the establishment of the Jewish state. They expected, with the establishment of the state of Israel, the Jews would immediately become converted. When this did not happen, the Plymouth brethren movement became very sarcastic in their attitudes toward the present Jewish state as having any place in the prophetic economy and prophetic expectation of Israel.

It must not be ignored that Plymouth brethren, such as the Rt. Rev. William Heschler, Lord Balfour, Ord Wingate, and many others, made great contributions to the reestablishment of the Jewish state.

Claude Douvenoy, in his book, *The Prince and the Prophet*, relates that Heschler was an Episcopal minister who advocated the reestablishment of the Jewish state in the late 1880s. His lifelong dream of being the bishop of Jerusalem almost became a reality. He was en route to the Holy Land when the Church of England reassigned him to be bishop of Vienna. The traditional theologians in the Church felt that his pro-Jewish attitude would create problems with the Church of England in the Ottoman Empire.

In the providence of this occasion, Heschler met Theodor Herzl. They spent the rest of their lives establishing the World Zionist Organization. It was Heschler who arranged meetings for Herzl with the heads of state of Russia, Turkey, Germany, England, France, and the Baltic states. Heschler named Herzl "the prince who would regather Israel," While Herzl called

William Heschler

Theodor Herzl

Heschler "the prophet of the coming Jewish state." The Zionist organization today seems hesitant to recognize that the prophet behind Theodor Herzl's life work was not a Jew but an Episcopalian minister.

During World War I, the British arsenal had been converted from black to smokeless powder. A necessary chemical, acetone, was used in making nitroglycerine for this ammunition. The German U-boat blockage of England cut off the vital source of acetone. With less than a month's supply of ammunition left for the troops, the British Parliament appealed to the British Scientific Academy for a substitute for acetone.

Two days later, Chaim Weizmann fulfilled the request and saved the British cause. For this great contribution, Lord Balfour presented the Balfour Declaration on November 3, 1917, which promised a national homeland for the Jewish people in the land of Israel. Balfour, like Heschler, believed in a literal fulfillment of the restoration of Israel to the Jewish people. He was a modern Cyrus, giving occasion to the reestablishment of the Jewish state.

Ord Wingate was a colonel in the British army during the early days of the mandate in Palestine. When he saw the treacherous greed of Great Britain in creating the Jewish-Arab crisis to further England's interest, he committed treason against the British government. Many books and papers have been written about Ord Wingate who organized, trained, and helped equip the first Israeli Liberation Army. Ord Wingate, like

Lord Balfour (center) and Chaim Weizmann (far right) entering the city of Jerusalem.

Lord Balfour

Ord Wingate

Heschler and Balfour, was a disciple of the Plymouth brethren movement.

In the school of dispensational premillennialism, there are tens of thousands in the Christian world today who believe that the present state of Israel is a fulfillment of prophetic expectation. Yet, among these, there are few who do not still hold the traditional replacement attitude toward the Jews, Judaism, and the rabbis. In these groups, there remains a strong zeal for the conversion of the Jew.

In a final analysis, one's attitude toward the covenants of Israel and their validity to the Jewish people will determine their attitude toward every field of theology. There are many in the traditional churches who do not consider themselves a part of the dispensational premillennial movement who recognize not only the prophetic significance of Israel, but also the validity of Israel's vital relationship with G-d through their covenants. Israel's continued survival and present success in the Jewish state is *prima facie* evidence of the validity of the Jew's relationship to G-d.

What was the significance of Jesus' words, "This cup is the New Testament in my blood, shed for the sins of many"? If it did not replace the former covenants, what relationship does it bear to them?

All of Paul's epistles are very pronounced in their expression of the relationship of that sacrifice to the former covenants. The very core of Paul's writings was the exegesis of the parallels of Jesus' work to the three covenants made to the Gentiles and its contrast to the covenants made with Israel. Beginning with the Edenic Covenant in I Corinthians 15:22: "For as in Adam all die, even so in Christ shall all be made alive." In Romans 5:12-19, he deals with the intercollated parallels between the offense of Adam in the Edenic Covenant and the reconciliation from that to a restoration of what was lost in Adam's transgression. This Edenic Covenant, we must remember, was a covenant universal in scope and one primarily concerned with the Gentile nations.

John, in his account of the crucifixion, also draws vivid parallels on the relationship between what was restored in Jesus to what was alienated in the exile of Adam from Eden. In John 18:39-40, he opens the narrative with Jesus taking the place of Bar Abbas who was a robber. In John's description, there is an echo from Eden of the disobedience of the first couple who robbed the Tree of Knowledge of Good and Evil and took the curse upon mankind from a tree. The cross, a wooden stake, was a putting back on the tree the consequence of Adam's sin in *Ben Adam,* the Son of Man.

It was not a normal procedure in Roman crucifixion to crown one with thorns. Since, however, this Jew from Galilee was being crucified for making himself a seditious king, the Roman soldiers plaited a wreath of thorns and bound them about the head of Jesus as a mock crown. John's description again echoes the Edenic curse, "Cursed is the ground for thy sake...thorns also and thistles shall it bring forth to thee.... ."

The Kabbalistic apostle John saw the *New Testament* in the sacrifice of Jesus as separate and apart from the *Abrahamic* and the *Sinaic* covenants, the *New Covenant of Moab*, and the *Davidic Covenant*. John's narrative of the death of Jesus was not a circumstance of crisis theology but was a vision of the mystique of the Adam Kadmon. "Somewhere there is an Adam, within reach of us, in need of restoration—in exile from the Garden." John saw in Jesus "that divine man in the medium of the mortal man." In Jesus, John saw the personification of that distance and space between the invisible Ten Spheres and the express image of Primal Man, the Adam Kadmon. The fleshly manifestation of *Ben Adam,* the Son of Man, in the crucifixion, was the union between the thread dangling free from the Immortal and the fiber of the soul of mortality.

The cross Jesus borrowed for this achievement was chiseled out for one "Bar Abbas, who was a robber." (John 18:39-40) There is a mystical echo in the voice of John. His eyes are hazed with the *hazun* of dreams of the misty Garden of Eden. "Bar Abbas [meaning the son of the father] was a robber." In Eden, Eve had "robbed from a tree" the fruit of prohibition. Now the Son of Man, *Ben Adam*, must be placed again upon a tree. In so doing, Jesus reached back 3,790 years to Eden. "This restoration" must be made in order to reconcile the guilt of the Adamic family in robbing the Tree of Knowledge of Good and Evil. There John saw Jesus hanging by his hands, nailed to the tree. John saw the Spheres of Mercy and Justice in the Adam Kadmon extolled above the Spheres of Majesty and Crown.

In Eden, "there was not a man to till the *ground*." (Gen. 2:5) One consequence of Adam's disobedience was, "cursed is the *ground* for thy sake. . . ." (Gen. 3:17) Cain, the son of the curse, ". . .was a *tiller of the ground*." (Gen. 4:2) The Eternal One charged Cain, saying, "What hast thou done? The voice of thy brother's blood crieth unto me from the *ground*." (Gen. 4:10) Adam's name was derived from *Adamah*, meaning the *ground* or *dust*. The Son of Man, *Ben Adam*, to the mystic John, was inseparable from that substance of earthiness.

Pilatus ordered Jesus scourged (John 19:1). The sadistic Roman soldier took no pity in laying the "cat-of-nine-tails" row upon row down the back of this treasonous, apostate Jewish king. The barbed hooks on each leash plowed deeply the thirty-nine furrows from his shoulders to his buttocks. Gaping wounds of exposed muscle and tissue gushed forth blood which Pilatus thought would satisfy the mingled mob (Luke 23:22). John made no excuse for Pilatus as did Luke. John saw the epitome of Israel's suffering, unleashed upon this one who personified Israel's historic character. As it is written in the songs of degrees or ascents, "The plowers have plowed upon my back: they made long their furrows." (Psalms 129:3)

To John, the very ground was groaning under the curse since Adam's damning day. Soil toiled and tilled, with blood spilled, by wicked hands was plowed. Briar, thorn, and thistle shrouds echo Abel's voice to say, "Damn! Damned! Vengeance damns this ground!" Who will bear this curse away? Thirty-nine furrows on his back, the *Lamed-Tet,* לט, that could wrap up and bring a magic stillness and silent hush to Abel's cry. "With his stripes," the children of Adam could be healed. John viewed the lacerations of Pilatus' scourge as deep, deep furrows running all the way back to the ground of Eden and the restoration of the fiber in mankind with that guiltless state of the First Covenant.

It was an abnormal jesting act that the soldiers made when they plaited the thorny crown. (John 19:2) John saw them cruelly wrap it around Jesus' head; yet, he saw more than just a sadistic gesture of mockery. Echoes that came from the Edenic curse, "Thorns and thistles shall it bring forth to thee," (Gen. 3:18) must be wrapped up in him for his relationship to the Edenic and Adamic covenants.

The greedy Roman soldiers took their spoil. They took all he possessed. "They took his garments and made four parts, to every soldier a part; and also his coat [Talit]: Now his Talit [prayer shawl] was without seam, woven from top throughout." (John 19:23) The only garment Jesus wore upon the cross was his own blood which dried and crusted on his groin. From death he did not flinch, but he withdrew from this indignity of exposure. "Father, let this cup pass from me." "He endured the cross, *despising the shame.*" Why was such an exposure of his naked body necessary? Through the hazy mist from Eden echo the words, "And they [Adam and Eve] knew they were *naked*. . . ." (Gen. 3:7-10)

Adam was created on the sixth day of the week. "And the Creator saw everything that he had made, and behold, it was very good and the evening and the morning was the sixth day. Thus was the heavens and the earth *finished*, and all the hosts of them." (Gen. 1:31-2:2) On the seventh day the Creator rested—in a garden of his creation.

On that same day of the week, 3,790 years later, Friday afternoon, about three o'clock, the Redeemer's cry came from Golgotha, "It is *finished!*" The Redeemer rested on the Sabbath in a secluded tomb at the back of the base of Golgotha, meaning "the place of the skull." According to Jewish tradition, Adam, Seth and Noah were buried there. Here at Golgotha is also the grotto of Jeremiah. In this aura of the Zohar, "If one can discover the secret opening in the base of the skull [Golgulet or Golgotha], one may there begin the work of restoration."

The Sacrifice of Jesus, the *New Covenant*, or *New Testament* in his blood, shed for the sins of many, was not the new covenant of Jeremiah 31:31. It went much farther back than the words of Jeremiah or Moses at Moab. It encompassed Eden. It was not to Israel, but rather to the nations of all of Adam's heirs. It followed all the tributaries of humanity back to the fountainhead, the *'Ayin Sof*, of Eden which flowed out in four great rivers.

The *New Testament*, or the *New Covenant*, spoken of by Jesus, was dramatically related to the *Edenic Covenant* and the *Adamic Covenant*. What, then, was the relationship to the third universal *covenant*, the *Testament of Noah*, and the seven laws of the *Noahic Covenant*?

Acts, chapter fifteen, answers this question explicitly. The *covenant* problem arose only after the Gentiles began to respond to the Good News. These Gentiles were not *GaiY RieYM*, or converts to Judaism. They had not received the seal of circumcision of the *Abrahamic Covenant*. Why had they not been circumcised? Because the sacrifice of Jesus was not related to them through the Abrahamic Covenant. The Abrahamic Covenant was given to Israel, not to the Gentiles!

The devout consciousness of Paul toward the plural covenants and the plurality of community can be seen in the difference of his attitude toward Timothy the Jew and Titus the Gentile. When he found Timothy, in Acts 16, immediately after the controversy on the issue of the circumcision of Gentile Christians in Acts 15, Paul circumcised Timothy because Timothy's mother was a Jewess. However, when the Judaizers sought to circumcise Titus, Paul objected to the point of physical force because Titus was a Gentile. (Galatians 2:3-5)

Dr. M. R. DeHaan, a dispensational expositionist, wrote a book called *Five Blunders of Paul*. In DeHaan's dispensational treatment of Paul's action in the case of Timothy and Titus, he denounced Paul as being "inconsistent." It is true that Paul's conduct was inconsistent with both replacement and dispensational theology on this occasion because neither recognized Judaism or that the Jew has a relationship with G-d during this time. Fortunately, Paul did not have the privilege of studying Christian theology and was unconcerned with both the replacement and the dispensational theories. Paul was, however, versed in Jewish law. He was a master in the covenants, both to Israel and to the Gentiles. His conduct was not inconsistent with either community relationship. He acted correctly both in the case of the circumcision of Timothy, whose mother was Jewish, and in the case forbidding the circumcision of Titus, who was a Gentile.

The Gentile church in Antioch had carried this debate to the Apostles in Jerusalem. This controversy in Acts 15 concerned the question of the circumcision of the Gentiles. There was no doubt in the question of the necessity of circumcision for the Jews. When the Apostles in Jerusalem saw that the decision concerned Jewish law, they all went before the Elders of Jerusalem, the Sanhedrin Court.

The decision of the Sanhedrin Court regarding the Gentile Christians and their relationship to the seven covenants of the Jewish scripture was very explicit. Their decision required no change in rabbinic logic. The Jews were to remain in full responsibility to the four covenants of Israel. The Gentiles, however, were subject to the first three covenants of universal application. Since the Gentiles were not under the Abrahamic Covenant by faith in Jesus, the obligation of circumcision was exempt and forbidden to the Gentile Christians. These Gentile Christians who had turned to G-d from serving idols were absolutely forbidden to keep *any* of the laws given to Moses at Mount Sinai. These were exclusively for Israel.

The Gentile Christians were, however, responsible to the Seven Laws of Noah. Five of those seven laws were spelled out twice in the 15th chapter of Acts. The two laws, one concerning human government and the other capital punishment, were omitted in application to Antioch and the Gentile church. The Romans were enforcing well already these two laws of the Noahic Covenant. (Acts 15:19-29)

Paul's conduct was not inconsistent with this decision of the Elders, or the Sanhedrin Court. That drama of Acts 15 was the pivotal axis of all his epistles, which were written only to the Gentile converts and were never addressed to the Jews. When one understands this distinction, he will think it more proper to retitle the book *Five Blunders of DeHaan* by the Apostle Paul.

The grave mistake of replacement and dispensational theologians is that they shuffle the mail. What Jesus said in answering questions concerning the Laws of Torah to Israel, the theologians apply to the Gentile church. Likewise, what Paul wrote to the Gentile church, they try to apply to the Jews. It is a crime in federal law to tamper with mail not addressed to you. It should be a crime to offend the Jews by trying to subject them to the Pauline letters. It is also unlawful to apply to the Gentile church what Jesus said in answer to questions about the Jewish Law.

Once one gets the proper perspective about the *covenants*, the very message of the Bible will become more vital. He can consistently ask, "Who was speaking?" and "To whom was it spoken?" When one realizes that "all the Bible was written *for* me, but it was not all written *to* me," everything will fall into its proper place.

What are usually considered the "general epistles" in the library of the New Testament are not "general" at all. For the most part, they are Jewish epistles.

James wrote to the Twelve Tribes in the Diaspora. First Peter was written to the strangers [GaiY RiYM] in the Diaspora. Peter wrote the second letter to the Gentiles "who have obtained like precious faith with us [the Jews]."

Martin Luther said, "The author of the book of James is the Devil. It should not be in the New Testament. James contradicted all that Paul taught in Romans about justification by faith." Luther did not see the distinction in the address. Paul, in Romans 1:5-6, addressed the epistle only to the Gentiles. Repeatedly, in the book, he said, "These things I write to you Gentiles." On the other hand, James, or Jacob, who wrote to the Twelve Tribes in the Diaspora, said, "If a man come into your synagogue. . . ." (James 2:2)

To his people who had a relationship through the *Abrahamic Covenant* and the responsibility to the *Mosaic Covenant* of Sinai, James said, ". . .show me thy faith without works [of the Torah] and I will show thee my faith by my works [fulfilling the commandments of Torah]." Neither Paul nor James violated the decision of the Sanhedrin in Acts 15. Paul wrote Romans, as he did the other of his epistles, to the Gentiles, while James wrote to the Jews. James' epistle was not to the Jewish Christians. There were no "Jewish Christians" in this period. His epistle was restricted to Israel. At the same time, it was unrestricted to "all Israel." He was not, as replacement theologians teach, writing to the entire church, the "New Israel." The tone and tenor of the epistle of James was as a Hassidic rabbi. We must not forget that it was James who made the appeal to the Sanhedrin (in Acts 15) to liberate the Gentile Christians from the obligations of circumcision and the observance of the Jewish Law.

The relationship of Jesus' *New Covenant* in his sacrifice was most relevant to the *Edenic*, the *Adamic* and the *Noahic* covenants which were *universal covenants to the Gentiles.* What then, if any, was that relationship to the *Abrahamic*, *Sinaic*, *Moabic*, and *Davidic* covenants which are restricted covenants to Israel?

In the *Abrahamic Covenant* there is a limited aspect of relationship to the New Covenant of Jesus. That law of limitation is restricted only to the one promise, "In thee shall all [Gentile] families of the earth be pleased." Through Abraham, and through the seed of promise, Israel produced the Messianic hope for the Gentiles. The Jews gave the Gentile world the Savior. In Galatians 3:1-5, Paul rebuked the Gentiles who sought justification by the Law of Sinai. Then, in verses 6-9, he explained the relationship of the Gentiles to G-d through the conduit of the Faith of Abraham. "Even as Abraham believed G-d, and it was accounted to him for righteousness, know ye therefore that they which are of faith, the same are the children of Abraham. And the scripture foreseeing that G-d would justify the heathen [Gentiles] THROUGH faith, preached before the Gospel unto Abraham, saying, In thee shall all the [Gentile] nations be blessed. So then they [the Gentiles] which be of faith are blessed with faithful Abraham."

Paul treated the "promise through Abraham's seed" as a channel, or conduit, for the Gentiles to have access to restoration to the Gentile covenants. Yet, this new economy and community of the Gentile church remained apart from the economy and community of Israel. This plural relationship was not in violation of Israel's responsibility to the Laws of Torah. "Seeing it is one G-d, which shall justify the circumcision [the Jews] *BY* FAITH, [actually *IN* FAITH] and the uncircumcision [Gentiles] *THROUGH* FAITH. Do we then make void [do away with or replace] the law [of Torah] through faith?

Nay! We establish [enforce] the Torah [to Israel who are under the Torah]." (Rom. 3:30-31)

Following this argument, Paul devotes the entire fourth and fifth chapters of Romans to tell how the Gentile, through the *channel* of faith in Jesus, the seed of Abraham, is transported back to the restoration of the Edenic economy. This was accomplished by the guilt suffered by the Innocent One to restore the guilty ones to innocence.

Without the hope of the patriarch Jacob's prophecy, "And unto him shall the gathering of the Gentiles be" (Gen. 49:10), the Gentiles would presently be "without a covenant relationship...without a Messiah...aliens to the Commonwealth of Israel, and strangers from the *covenants* of promise, hopeless atheists in this age." (Eph. 2:11-12) Without Israel, without Judaism, and without the Jewish people, there would have been no channel, no conduit, no way of passage for the Gentile to have access to a relationship with the Creator. That access of the Gentile is as dependent today upon Israel and the Eternal One's faithfulness to Israel's covenants as it was the day Jesus gave himself to restore the exiled Adam in each of us.

This is to say that if G-d made an eternal, everlasting, unconditional, and immutable covenant of oath with Israel through the Patriarch's faith, and Jesus of Nazareth could "do away with that relationship," as replacement theologians teach, then G-d lied to the Patriarch and the Prophets. If their covenants are so fragile and subject to abrogation, the promise of G-d to the Gentile Christian for eternal life in Jesus Christ is even less valid. The Gentile Christian must hope, if only for his own selfish interest, that the replacement theory is wrong and that Israel's covenants are still valid.

The relationship of the Gentile Christian to the responsibility of the six hundred thirteen commandments of the Law of Torah is most vividly expressed in Paul's writings. The Gentile Christian has absolutely no relationship or merit or standing in keeping the laws of Torah! The Gentile Christian who thinks that keeping the Law (and that includes the Ten Commandments) is his responsibility to gain merit before G-d, has stepped outside the perimeter of the covenant wherein G-d is doing business with the Gentiles. Every epistle of Paul drives this point home. He is guilty of stealing and robbing a most holy thing which was explicitly meant for Israel.

What Jesus said in the Gospel accounts, in answering questions about Jewish Law, was no waiver that they should be applied to the Gentile Christian. The Laws of Torah are restricted to Israel alone. Jesus did not make them universal.

A Gentile Christian who seeks to be justified or to find favor by keeping the Laws of Torah has stepped outside the perimeter where G-d does business with the Gentiles. The Jew, likewise, who forsakes that relationship he can have with the G-d of Israel through faith in the Abrahamic Covenant, and excuses his responsibility to the Laws of Torah by converting to Christianity, has jumped out of bounds from that perimeter of covenant relationship where G-d is doing business with Israel. To the Gentiles who make such a mistake, Paul addressed, "O Foolish Galatians." (Gal. 3:1) To the Jews who might make such a blunder, his words were: "Stop forsaking the synagoguing of yourselves together, as the manner of some [are doing]; but exhorting [each other in the synagogue] so much more, as ye see the day approaching [of the destruction of the Temple]. . . ." (Heb. 10:25)

What is the relationship of the sacrifice of Jesus to the New Covenant, or New Testament, given to Israel on Mount Moab? Does the "New Testament in the blood of Jesus shed for the sins of many," have any relationship to the New Covenant of Moab in the context of Jeremiah 31:31? The answer to both questions is negative. History has proved that neither the sacrifice of Jesus for the Gentile nations, nor the regathering of National Israel were either contingent upon the other.

Both replacement theologians and dispensationalists have gone to great lengths to teach that there will be a restoration of the Holy Roman Empire. All the scriptures they use to prove this theory are passages concerning the restoration of National Israel. However, since the spiritual kingdom of heaven (understood to be in Rome) had replaced the earthly kingdom of Israel, what else could they do with these prophecies?

Dispensational theologians who derailed Israel at the Cross, and somewhat rerailed them eschatologically, have never been clear on precisely what Israel's status is during the present dispensation. While the dispensationalists believe in a full restoration of Israel necessary in the fulfillment of the covenant of Moab and Jeremiah 31, they make this restoration of Israel contingent upon the Jew's acceptance of Jesus as their Messiah. Despite all the overt efforts of dispensationalists to free themselves from replacement theology, they still retain the traditional attitude toward the Jews in the church age.

The community of the Church and the community of Israel are two separate economies. The eschatology of the Church cannot be intercollated into Israel's prophetic calendar. The Church is a heavenly people with a heavenly inheritance. Israel is an earthly people with an earthly inheritance. The economy and eschatology of each community must be treated entirely separately. The regathering of National Israel, the restoration of the Jewish state, and the coming of Messiah the King to Israel cannot be mixed with the rapture and revelation of Jesus to the Church.

In summary, one's attitude toward the eschatology, or the future of Israel, and the eschatology of the Church will be determined by his view of ecclesiology, or the community of Israel, and the community of the Church. Anyone who takes a replacement theology position and spiritualizes the Scripture and considers all the covenants to Israel eradicated in Jesus will see the Church as the Israel of G-d. He will, therefore, be unable in this position to recognize the validity of the present community of Israel. On the other hand, those who accept the literalness of the Bible must, in the final analysis, recognize the validity of Israel as a distinct economy, separate and apart from the ecclesiology, or community of the Church. The community of Israel and the community of the Church are separate. Therefore, one must never attempt to intercollate the eschatology of Israel with the eschatology of the Church.

The reestablishment of National Israel in this century has brought a new dimension to Jewish-Christian relations. More and more, Christians are moving from the spiritualizing of the Scriptures to a position of literal interpretation. Israel today is neither logical nor illogical. Most of all, it is not theological. There is no place in modern Christian theology for the existence of a modern Israel. If Israel today is a product of eschatological prophetic development, this movement of

Christianity towared a rabbinic interpretation of Jesus will become more vivid as the Jewish state develops.

The next major development in Israel which will give occasion to a massive turning of Christians to a rabbinic position will be the recovery of the Ashes of the Red Heifer and Israel's ancient Ark and Tabernacle. The subsequent events in Israel will have a revolutionary effect on the Christian, the Jewish, and the Gentile worlds. Ultimately, as a result of these events, Christianity at large will come to the place of accepting the concept of the plural covenants. By way of definition, the plural covenants simply means that: ISRAEL, THE JEWISH PEOPLE, HAVE, AND HAVE ALWAYS HAD, A VITAL RELATIONSHIP WITH G-D THROUGH FAITH IN THE ABRAHAMIC COVENANT. THIS RELATIONSHIP IS SEPARATE AND APART FROM THE VITAL RELATIONSHIP THAT THE CHRISTIANS HAVE THROUGH FAITH IN JESUS CHRIST.

What is the relationship of the Christian to Israel? What is the relationship of Jesus to Israel? How does it all fit in? Where am I, who am I? What should be my response to Israel and the Jew?

Israel holds the original Passive *Covenant* or *Will* of God. The New Covenant in Jesus that made the Gentiles "Partakers of like precious faith with them" (II Pet 1:1) is a codicil or appendix resting on that original covenant of G-d-Israel relationship. If Jesus invalidated that original, then the codicil of the New Testament has no validity. Strange that many who say Jesus abrogated Israel's covenants, then turn around and try to prove their cause by the "Old Testament"!

To graft, one must wound the tree. Through faith in his wounded side, I was grafted into the olive tree of Israel's redemptive economy. Having been grafted in *among them* (the Jews), and *with them* (Rom 11:17), I partake of the root and fatness of the olive tree (Israel). Should I, a graft, be cut off — it will not harm the tree. Woe! should the tree (Israel) be cut down,. . .I perish!

"Salvation is of the Jews" (John 4:22). "In Jesus" the alien Gentile is adopted to become an*heir* of G-d and this salvation and a*joint*-heir with Israel! The Jew always had access to G-d. In Jesus the Gentile joins the Jew so *we both* (Eph 2:18, 3:6) are *fellow heirs* in their hope. Where the Jew suffers — I suffer. Where he triumphs — I triumph.

Chapter VII
THE RIDDLE OF REJECTION: KING OR KINGDOM

What the Reformation did in the sixteenth century for the Protestant world, Vatican II accomplished in the twentieth century for the Catholic. The accomplishment of both was to some degree an exoneration of the Jews in the crucifixion of Jesus. Some traditionalists, both in the Protestant and in the Catholic communities, have always viewed this exoneration as a compromise for humanitarian reasons. For example, one clergyman, in response to Vatican II, said, "When they can prove that Herod and Pontius Pilate were not Jews, they can prove to me that the Jews did not crucify Jesus. Until they do, I will maintain that the Jews are guilty of the Crucifixion." How can one answer such an argument? The texts of Scripture and of secular historians very definitely indicate that neither Herod nor Pontius Pilate was a Jew. The only answer to such a crass attitude is to repeat the words of John Lawrence, "Ignorance can be cured, but there is no hope for stupidity." Accusing the Jews of the physical act of the Crucifixion is so deeply engrained in replacement theology and liturgy that to deny the guilt of the Jews, according to the "traditional true believers," would be to deny the faith.

The wording of Vatican II, which seeks to exonerate the Jews today of the physical act of the Crucifixion, does not, however, deal with the real question. *The statements of the New Testament texts and secular history exonerate the Jews.* How could anyone today be involved in the mechanics of an event that happened twenty centuries ago? The real issue is that the Jews historically did not crucify Jesus of Nazareth. The Romans did. One Jewish rabbi asked this question concerning Vatican II, "Are we supposed to say 'thank you' to the Christians for taking a knife out of our backs that they themselves stabbed into us several centuries ago?" The criminal charge nailed over the head of Jesus, "This is Jesus of Nazareth, King of the Jews [Judaea]," was a crime against the Roman government. This title, "King of the Jews," was not a Messianic title. It was a coinage of Caesar. The Messianic title is "King of Israel."

The critical accusation against the Jews which has not yet been dealt with by the Catholic or Protestant theologians is not the issue of the Jews *crucifying Jesus* but rather of their *rejecting him*. One prominent professor in a fundamentalist seminary who advocated historic premillennialism stated the rejection problem in response to Vatican II: "No intelligent student of the Scripture or history could accuse the Jew of any special guilt in the Crucifixion. I am guilty of the Crucifixion. If I have no guilt in it, I have no benefit from it. The guilt of the Jews is not in crucifying Jesus, but in rejecting him. They rejected him then as king. They perpetually reject him as Lord. The Jews' condemnation is in rejecting their king, not in crucifying him. Any idiot who can read knows the Romans executed the mechanics of crucifying him. Any idiot who looks around today knows the Jews still reject him."

The replacement theologians produced what is called the "crisis theory," which states that G-d had Plan One for Jesus to be Savior and king of Israel. The Jews rejected him as Savior-King and crucified him. In this perilous dilemma, G-d had to sit down and figure out Plan Two where he would take the "crisis of Calvary" and salvage it by reconstructing another plan of salvation for the Gentile nations. This theory relegates the Omnipotent G-d to the position of subjection to the circumstances of an angry mob of no more than a few dozen people. It spreads the guilt of that motley crowd over millions of Jewish people. That guilt has been perpetuated generation after generation for two millennia. The crisis theologian calls this god of crisis theology a god of love.

The dispensational school, despite its distinctive direction in advocating a literal interpretation of Israel's prophetic calendar, never went so far as to divorce themselves from the replacement concept of the Rejected King syndrome. The Scofield Reference Bible, the script and commentary of dispensationalism, inserted in bold italics over Matthew 11:20: *"Jesus, rejected, predicts judgment."* In that context of Matthew, the only one who questioned Jesus' Messianic credentials was none other than John the Baptist. Yet, the Scofield editors inserted John's doubt upon the whole of the Jewish people.

Again, over Matthew 21:1, the dispensationalist, unweaned from the old traditional replacement concept, inserted *"The King's public offer of himself as King."* This context describes Jesus' entry into Jerusalem on the ass's colt, an act in itself reflecting a rejection by him of what the Jewish people expected him to do in establishing the Kingdom of Israel. If that assumption is correct—that when Jesus entered Jerusalem on the colt, he officially offered himself as king—he was certainly well accepted by the multitudes of the Jews of Jerusalem, according to that context. The people cried, "Hosanna," to the Son of David, and spread their talith's (prayer shawls) across his path as a canopy under which he rode. But!!! he certainly presented himself in a very strange manner as king—no white horse, no consort, no cavalry, and no color guard. Not even an official herald to proclaim his entry.

No, neither the dispensationalist nor especially the historical premillennialist has been able to divorce himself from the traditional replacement theological position that the Jews rejected Jesus as their king. On the other side, we may ask instead, "Did not Jesus rather reject Israel as a kingdom?" If so, what implications does this have upon theology today?

As a manner of inquiry into the question of Israel's rejection of Jesus vs. Jesus' rejection of Israel, let us examine the case in a *Beit Din*, or a rabbinic court of Talmudic law.

Some Christians may find it rather distasteful, even blatant audacity, to think of Jesus' subjection to a Talmudic examination by the Jewish law. However, since the author of this book is pleading Jesus' case in the matter, it is his prerogative to appeal the former decisions of replacement theology to what he considers the higher courts of Jewish jurisprudence. It is also justly in order to call for a change of venue that Jesus might be judged by his own laws, in his own courts, in his own country, and by his own people.

The Supreme Judge hearing this case is Rabbi Hillel the Great. Remember, it is he who codified the Seven

Laws for a Sanhedrin trial when he was only seventeen. We shall listen to those laws from Rabbi Hillel himself. They shall serve as a criterion in the matter of judgment as to whether Israel rejected Jesus as their king or Jesus rejected Israel as his kingdom. There is little doubt that Jesus himself studied in Beit Hillel in Galilee. Rabbi Hillel was executed at the age of 137 at the time that Jesus was fourteen or fifteen years old. The aged sage of Israel doubtless not only knew about the fame of the young Talmid from Nazareth, but may have even taught Jesus in that yeshiva. Hillel and Jesus were not only contemporaries but were possibly even personally acquainted.

The case is now open:

It would be most ideal to apply the Mishnaic code of the seven hermeneutical laws of Rabbi Hillel to the question. Since our purpose is to retain simplicity, such a detailed application would be out of order because of its complexity and intricacy of development. Although these laws will not be expressed in detail at each point, this chapter will follow in principle that approach. What are the seven laws of Rabbi Hillel, our Supreme Judge?

1. The first law in such a procedure states that in either question—rejected king or rejected kingdom—there must be at least a *light substance* or a *sample of the material* evidence in the texts of the Gospels as to who rejected whom. Without a sample of such evidence, there can be no premise established. This is to say: the *foam* is of the same substance as the liquid; a *crumb* is the same as the loaf; the *fragrance* is a portion of the flower and the *core sample* is the same *material* mineral content as the walls of the shaft. If there is no evidence in part—no foam, no crumb, no fragrance or no core—there is no evidence in the whole. In other words, there must be some material that bears on the question; it must clearly relate to the question; and it must contribute to the solution of the question. Hillel's first law erases all surmised and conjured-up conceptions and leaves only the facts to stand. Yet, if there is evidence in part, either for the rejected king or for the rejected kingdom, this initial principle will not relax until it has been verified by the whole. That law will carry forth and demand an interpretation to the fullest extent until it reaches a determination of which of the alternatives is the correct

one—rejected king or rejected kingdom. This first principle of Hillel is called קל וחמר, QahL WaKHoh MehR, a light or sample of the material or substance.

2. There must also be a *comparison by analogy of words*, according to the second law. If one text states or suggests that he accepted them but they rejected him, or that Israel accepted him but that he rejected them, there must be another passage sufficiently similar in content to that text that it warrants the same conclusion. If a statement is made that Israel rejected him or that Jesus rejected Israel as his kingdom, it must be supported by *corresponding particles* of evidence, either as an absolute statement or as *a fortiori* inference. If one passage of one Gospel account infers such, it should find a *parallelism of similar statements* in other passages of the same Gospel as well as in the other Gospel accounts. Only when there are *equivalent values* from opposing prospectives can a *verdict or conclusion* be positively made. This is the second law of Hillel called GiZaeRahH SHah WahH, גזרה שוה, meaning a *verdict by comparison.*

3. If we can establish a sample of *material substance* that states that Jesus rejected Israel as his kingdom rather than that they rejected him as their king, and prove that verdict by an *analytical comparison of corresponding particles*, only then do we have an established principle from that one text. *That principle derived from one verse must be applied generally.* This general application of one verse must complement, and not aggravate, the evidence of the whole. In other words, the individual verse or passage must harmonize with all other Scripture taken together. This is the third law of Hillel. This eliminates the element of contradiction of principles in a passage. This is to say that either one principle or the other is true. Either Israel rejected Jesus, or Jesus rejected Israel. They cannot both be true. The verdict will be a question of one *or* the other. One will conquer, the other will be subdued. That validity must be proved generally.

4. Hillel's third law is further tested by his fourth, which states: *A principle which is derived from two verses and is applied generally.* A repetition of evidence establishes a principle. "In the mouth of two or three witnesses shall every word be established." Compound

statements assure each other. The guilt of the rejection must be established by plurality of testimony. A conclusion cannot rest on one passage alone.

5. Hillel's fifth law is: *A general statement which is limited by a particular one which follows, or a particular statement which is limited by a following general one.* This is to say that the details are subject to the mass, and the mass is subject to the details. If a text states that Jesus rejected Israel as his kingdom, that text should be followed by a general story as to why he did so. Or, if there is such a general story in the accounts, it should be followed by a particular text that so states it.

6. Again, the sixth law of Hillel tests the fifth. It requires *an exposition by reference to another similar passage.* What is true of the fifth law must be verified by the sixth. Hillel's third and fourth laws prove the second as applied to a particular verse which must be proved by another verse. Likewise, the sixth law proves the fifth as applied to an entire narrative. They differ only in the stratum of linguistic hierarchy to which they apply. The second and the third are on the sentence level, while the fifth and sixth are on the paragraph, or narrative, level.

7. Hillel's seventh law is: *The influence which is drawn from the entire context.* This law of interpretation asks: What is the symphonic verdict of each Gospel testimony and the harmony of the testimonies of all four Gospels? If the symphonic harmony of testimony is that Israel rejected Jesus as king, the case so stands and that is the verdict. If, on the other hand, the harmonious symphonic testimony of each and all four Gospels is that Jesus rejected Israel as a kingdom, so stands the verdict! Either one or the other will be eliminated.

Yet, there is another very important principle involved in this Jewish court which non-Jews may find difficult to understand. All these laws demand a certain amount of doubt in any decision. For example, if the seventy members of the Sanhedrin were unanimous in condemning a man to death, he was set free. Why? Because such a decision would indicate that the defendant's cause was not properly represented and that his defense was not just.

The testimony of Christian theology, conjured up in the Dark Ages and peddled from generation to generation, is not admissible evidence in this court. It is not admissible because it is hearsay, is premised on opinion, is Gentile in nature, and therefore is immaterial and incompetent to deal with a distinctively Jewish question. Christian theological opinion is further inadmissible in this court because its witnesses are aliens to the judicial economy of Israel. As foreigners, they are disqualified to testify against a citizen of Israel. Only valid Jewish witnesses, such as Mark, Luke, Matthew, and John, are admitted. "In the mouth of two or three witnesses, every word shall be established." But, according to Jewish law, a fourth witness renders the evidence irrevocable.

Today, in this *Beit Din* of Jewish jurisprudence, we are not interested in the issue of the crucifixion of Jesus. Our single intention is to hear valid testimony concerning the issue of the rejection of Jesus. We have four documents which shall serve as sworn statements in the form of deposition. These documents, the four eyewitness accounts of the life and teachings of Jesus, are commonly called the four Gospel accounts.

You, the readers, are the jury or *minyan* who shall render the verdict. There are ten questions which shall be demanded in this inquisition. These questions must be firmly imprinted in your minds as you hear each testimony. Based upon Judge Hillel's seven principles of simple hermeneutical interpretation, you must render your own verdict. The ten questions are as follows:

1. Do the texts state that Israel rejected Jesus as their Messianic king? (On any level, individually, politically, governmentally, religiously, or democratically, did the Jewish people officially reject him?)
2. Do the texts infer or state that Jesus rejected Israel as his kingdom?
3. Did Jesus ever officially and formally present himself as the Messianic king of Israel, or did he even allude to such?
4. Did Jesus ever overtly avoid and evade any overtures or efforts by those who had the illusion that he was a candidate for the office of the king of Israel?
5. What did the Jews expect their Messianic king to be and to do, and did Jesus' disciples expect the same of him?
6. Did Jesus qualify as Israel's Messianic king?
7. What do the texts state concerning the attitude of the Jewish people in Israel during his time?

8. What was Jesus' response to his people's attitude toward him?
9. If Jesus had no Messianic inclination to be the King of Israel, what was his stated purpose and how does it affect the Jewish people?
10. What would be the situation if all the evidence were reversed?

There is no intention to attempt to answer each of these questions in their order. Our purpose is simply to listen to the general samples of textual evidence from the four witnesses and arrive at a particular verdict based on the seven laws of the judge, Rabbi Hillel. First, we shall examine a sample of each, then compare it to the subsequent laws.

To begin, let us observe the first question: Does the deposition of the witnesses state that Israel, the Jewish people, rejected Jesus as their Messianic king?

In reply, we ask for the first law of Hillel: *QahL WaKHohMehR*, which demands a *light substance or a sample of the material* in the textual evidence indicating such a statement. Does any text in the four Gospel accounts state that the people of Israel, democratically, governmentally, officially rejected Jesus as their Messianic king?

Before we answer hastily, we must consider the third question: Did Jesus ever officially and formally present himself as the Messianic king to the people in general or to the Elders of Israel? Again, the first law of Hillel demands a sampling of such a statement in the texts.

Despite what may have been conjured up or assumed, there is no evidence in the Gospel texts that states or makes a fortiori inference that Jesus ever represented or presented himself as the Messianic king to Israel. If there is no such statement or inference, the assumption is overruled by *QahL WaKHohMehR*. Lack of textual evidence extinguishes the thought that Jesus ever presented himself as king. Since Jesus never officially presented himself as the Messianic king of Israel, how could the Jews reject what he never offered them?

Some might insist that the forty-eight recorded signs and miracles which Jesus performed during his life were his credentials that he was their king, the Son of G-d. Then we must examine this evidence by asking a simple question. What sign or miracle did Jesus perform during his life that had not already been performed in essence by an earlier prophet who made no regal or divine claim? Every miracle that Jesus performed had already been performed in substance by earlier prophets in Israel. They all did so without any Messianic claim. *Nu!*

On the contrary, there is an incredible amount of evidence that Jesus himself rejected and deliberately avoided any remote inference of his coming to be their king. If textual evidence indicates this, as required by Hillel's first law, it affirms the fourth question. To name a few observations of his overt rejection of Israel as his kingdom, we might note the following: he never stated that he had come to be Israel's Messianic king; he definitely stated, "My kingdom is not of this age." Each time it was suggested that he might be the Messianic king, he "passed through the midst of them and passed by," which means he disappeared not only from their presence but evacuated his followers from that entire region. Jesus not only avoided publicity, he acted aggressively to minimize his popularity among the people of Israel. There are sixty-four references in the four Gospels where Jesus restricted his popularity. This is most vividly brought out when he heals a person, "... and charged them straitly that they should tell no man."

The followers of Jesus—not only the twelve but the multitudes, as well—followed him under the illusion that he would be the Messianic king of Israel. Jesus never encouraged or gave even an allusion to anything that would cause them to suspect that this was his ambition or purpose. On the contrary, he made repeated statements and allusions in which he states his purpose as the anointed one of G-d to be the savior of the Gentile world. The reader will find not one inference in the New Testament where Jesus is king of the church. His relationship to the Gentile world was that of a savior and a redeemer. His relationship to the Gentile church is that of a bridegroom to his bride. Eschatologically, the Scripture refers to the church as his royal consort. Never does it present Jesus in a regal relationship to the Gentile world or to the church. Every relationship he has to that community is organic in nature. As a shepherd to his flock, as a vine to the branches, as a sower to the seed, as a wound in the side of an olive tree (Israel's spiritual economy) wherein is grafted the wild olive branches (Gentiles), so is his organic relationship to the Gentile believers. The church is a hybrid mutation in its economy between Israel and the Gentile world. Its relationship to him was parabolically expressed as a pearl of great price. Even the pearl is an organic substance created by the secretions from the wounded side of the oyster. So the Gentile church is a by-product of Jesus' wounded side.

There is no relationship or parallel between the soteriological Gospel of Jesus to the Gentiles and the community of Israel in their hope of a coming Messiah. Israel's hope is for a majestic king from the regal house of David. The salvation of Israel is a national salvation. In this relationship the Messiah of Israel is more a kinsman-redeemer than a divine savior. His relationship to the people of Israel will be as a great teacher who will answer all unanswered questions. He will be the judge to execute justice upon the Gentile nations, not to be their savior in a Christian soteriological sense. Jesus, the Messiah to the Gentiles, said, "I have not come to send peace upon the earth but a sword." Yet, through faith in him, the Gentile receives the fullness of peace internally. On the contrary, Israel's Messiah is expected to come by the power of the sword and to conquer the enemies of Israel and to bring upon the earth an external but everlasting peace among nations. The very nature of Israel's Messianic expectation is in strong contrast to the Messianic realization of Christianity in Jesus.

Christianity has erased the distinction between the majestic Messiah of Israel and the Messianic suffering savior who would call out from among the Gentiles a people for his name. They made the suffering savior a sort of spiritual king over a spiritual kingdom. The church, therefore, by the fourth century, evolved into a political force under Constantine. The Dark Ages immediately followed. Crusades and holy wars ensued. One monarch after another reigned by "divine right" and waged murderous wars in the name of Jesus Christ to gain political ends. Until the beginning of the twentieth century, and even to this day, many nations impose their authority as "Christian nations" upon their subjects. The world has known no greater monstrosities than have been executed in the name of the perpetuation of so-called Christian governments. The Christian faith, as taught in the New Testament, is not a political force and has no national character. Even in America where separation of church and state is such a vital premise in the Constitution, there is a strong erroneous assumption that the United States is a Christian nation. One will observe that in every movement where American Christian nationalism is emphasized, anti-Semitism is rampant. Christian nationalism has always viewed the Jew as an enemy of the state. They interpret the Jews as being treasonous because they *do not accept Jesus* as their Lord and Savior. The very concept of Christian nationalism, or the church as a political force, is totally foreign to the New Testament concept of the Christian faith. When the replacement theologian replaced the church in lieu of national Israel, Christian nationalism was an inevitable result.

In the simple grammatic analysis of the Gospels, there is no suggestion by Jesus of his intent for Christianity to be a political force. Neither is there suggestion that his purpose was to be the political monarch of Israel. He did not offer a kingdom to Israel which they rejected; instead, they offered him a kingdom which he rejected. There is no suggestion that Jesus had Plan One to be the king of Israel and an optional Plan Two which was to be the savior of the Gentiles. From the beginning as well as throughout his entire ministry, he repeatedly emphasized that his purpose in coming into the world was a cross and not a crown—an altar, not a throne.

The Christian must realize that had Jesus accepted any one of the several propositions from Israel to be their king, he would never have died. Had he lived forever, Israel's triumph would have been certain, but there would not have been a cross and an empty tomb to bring the Good News of the Gospel to the Gentile world. As the disciples watched the crucifixion, they saw no good news whatsoever. They were bewildered, frightened, and in terror at the news of an empty tomb. These things were totally alien to the Messianic expectation they focused on Jesus, which was, in essence, the Messianic expectation of Israel. With the news of the resurrection, some of the disciples remained hidden behind locked doors. The death and resurrection, too, was totally alien to their expectation of the Messiah of Israel. Luke 24:13-35 relates the story of two disciples who fled Jerusalem when they heard the news of the empty tomb. En route to Emmaus, about seven miles from Jerusalem, they met a stranger on the way. Not knowing that the stranger was Jesus incognito, they began relating to him the tragic events which had just happened in Jerusalem. When he asked them what events had made them of such *sad* countenance, they answered, "Concerning Jesus of Nazareth, which was *a prophet* mighty in deed and word before G-d and all the people [of Israel] and how the chief priests and their rulers delivered him [to the Romans] to be condemned to death and they [the Romans] have crucified him. But we trusted that it had been he who should have redeemed Israel: and besides all this, today is the third day since these things were done. Yea, and certain women of our company made us astonished, which were early at the sepulchre; and when they found not his body, they came saying, that they had also seen a vision of angels, which said that he was alive. . . ." Peter and the other disciples misunderstood the events of the resurrection as a second hope for the political salvation of national Israel and the establishment of the Davidic kingdom immediately. In Acts 1:6, they asked him, "Wilt thou at this time restore again the kingdom to Israel?"

Concerning this, Dr. Frederick Schweitzer points out, "Jesus had an excellent opportunity to divorce himself from any connection with restored national Israel had he chosen to do so. If Jesus had planned for the church to replace Israel, this would have been an excellent opportunity for him to have stated such. Jesus' answer to his disciples was: 'It is not for you to know the times nor the seasons which the father had put in his own authority.' Since Jesus did not disassociate himself with the idea of a restoration of national Israel at a later time, it is difficult to understand why Christians today are not more emphatic with the present Jewish state."

Despite Jesus' instructions to his disciples, "As you go among the Gentiles, teach them . . . ," it took Simon Peter and the other disciples many, many years to take that message to the first Gentiles. It is evident that Peter never grasped the meaning of the cross to the Gentiles until after the destruction of the Temple.

The mother of James and John, in Matthew 20:20-28, and in Mark 10:35-45, requested of Jesus that he would grant her sons the right to sit on the right and left side of his throne when he established his kingdom. Mary certainly was not thinking of a spiritual kingdom when she made this request. There are several references of contention among the disciples over their place as "knights of the round table" when Jesus would overthrow the Romans and Herod and establish what they expected in the restoration of the kingdom of Israel.

The illusion on the part of the disciples that Jesus would be their Messianic king does not indicate that Jesus ever made that illusion. When each such assumption occurred, he rebuked their aspirations and plainly stated that the motive of his life was not to be the king of Israel.

The third question: Did Jesus ever officially and formally present himself to Israel as their Messianic king, or did he ever allude to such? Remember, Hillel's laws demand evidence of such, either in a textual passage or in a narrative.

When G-d sent Moses to deliver Israel from Egypt, he gave him specific instructions to present his credentials to the Elders of Israel, Exodus 3:16. Moses did not preach on a soapbox at the street corners of Pithom and Raamses. He officially and formally presented himself as their deliverer. This is what the people of Judaea demanded of Jesus in John 10:24, "How long dost thou keep us in doubt? If thou be the Messiah tell us plainly." They wanted evidence by an official presentation as Moses had given the Elders in Egypt—especially if he is the "prophet like unto Moses." Yet, Jesus had not done so. His answer was simply, "You are not my sheep, I am not your shepherd."

If there is no textual evidence in the depositional records of the four Gospels that Jesus ever presented himself officially and formally as Israel's expected Messianic king, how then can the Jews be accused of rejecting him? The Jews never rejected Jesus as their king because he never proposed to them that he was their king. The charge that the Jews rejected Jesus as their king is dismissed by Rabbi Hillel's first law because of the lack of a *sample of material evidence* in the text.

The fifth question: What did the Jews of Jesus' day expect the Messianic king of Israel to do? Judaism has not changed its Messianic expectation; the traditional Jews today expect the same as those of Jesus' day. His disciples and the multitudes expected the same of Jesus.

The Jews expected the Messiah, the son of David, king of Israel, to appear at a time when the nation was in great political stress. He would reveal himself at a time when Israel's very existence was threatened. The coming of the Messiah would find not only external and alien oppression upon Israel, but would find a time of internal decadence when the Temple, many priests, and many judges of the Sanhedrin would be apostate from the traditional concepts of Judaism. In this dark hour, the Messiah would appear, purge Israel of its internal apostates, execute judgment and destroy the Gentile nations that brought about the external oppression. He would never die but instead would destroy death. He would establish a kingdom of peace which would be universal. The earth would be restored to its original Edenic state. This is what Judaism has always expected of a Messiah. This is what the disciples of Jesus and the people of Israel expected Jesus to do. All the conditions that should precede the revelation of Israel's Messianic king were present under the alien Roman rule and apostate monarchy of the Herodian family of the latter Second Temple period. Jerusalem was then at the threshold of destruction. The disciples and multitudes in Israel expected Jesus to execute all the activities of the Messiah. But, Jesus explicitly stated that he had *not* come to usher in the age of righteousness.

The sixth question is: Did Jesus in any way fulfill or pretend to accomplish the traditional expectation of Israel for their Messiah? If Jesus did not accomplish that traditional Messianic expectation of Israel, why then should the Jews be accused of rejecting him, when he did not, in one single phase, fulfill the requirements of the Messianic king of Israel? If Jesus had done what his disciples and the masses of Israel expected him to do, both they and the Jews throughout history and even today would accept him as their Messianic king. He did not; therefore, they did not and do not so accept him and shall never accept the Jesus of the Christian concept as their savior or king.

The expected response from the average Christian is: "Oh! When Jesus comes again, he will do all that." One can be assured that when such happens, every Jew will recognize it without the assistance of a Board of Missions to the Jews.

Jesus did not fulfill what Israel expected in the Messiah king. He did not fulfill the expectation of his own disciples. What is more, he made no attempt to do so. That was not his intention or purpose. Jesus did not fail to qualify as Israel's Messiah; he never attempted to qualify!

The seventh question: What was the general attitude of the people of Israel toward him? This is a good Jewish question that demands a good Jewish answer. "Which people of Israel?" He had friends and followers among the Pharisees and he had enemies among them. He had friends and disciples who were priests, and he had enemies who were also priests. There were many on the Sanhedrin Court who were for his cause and some who were not. The same was true of the rank and file of the people of the land. The Zealots, the Zionist movement of that day, supported him. Simon the Zealot was one of the Twelve. They supported him according to Luke 19:11 because they thought "the Kingdom of G-d should immediately appear." The Sons of Zadok, who were the legitimate priests before their expulsion by Herod The Great, supported Jesus because he was their only immediate hope of regaining the priesthood. John the Baptist and other Qumran disciples were among these. Jesus himself was a Pharisee. By and large, the Pharisees did support him. There is no record of any Sadducees following him. A *Tsadushi*, or Sadducee, would not be expected to follow a *Parushi*, or Pharisee. The common people were under the distress of Roman taxation and daily abuse. They all hated Caesar and Pilatus; yet, they respected both out of fear. That Arab king and his family who were Roman puppets, the Herodians, were detested by every Jew, except those who economically benefited by Herod's throne. If Jesus could overthrow the Romans, the Herodians, and the powers vested in Herod's apostate priesthood, the vast majority of the Jews of that time would have been more than pleased.

But then Jesus did have his natural opponents. The Romans, the family of Herod, the apostate priests, the Sanhedrin (especially the forty-seven Sadducees and those Pharisees who, by their office, benefited by the Herodian status quo), and every person who was economically dependent on the regime in power, were threatened by the very strong probability that Jesus would attempt a *coup d'etat* and overthrow the existing powers. Not only would they very likely lose their jobs and positions, they would probably lose their heads. Naturally, they did not want Jesus to rock the boat. If such a coup were successful, they were finished. If it were not successful, the Romans would come and destroy the whole system anyway. The puppet governmental system and all involved in it directly and indirectly were threatened by this rabbi from Nazareth. In all, they represented only a few thousand people, a small percentage of the whole nation, but they were the power axis of the alien Roman government.

Up north was Galilee where Herod Agrippi was king. Down south was a separate country, Judaea, where Herod Antipas reigned. Any one from Galilee was a foreigner, a "damn yankee," when he came into Judaea. In modern vernacular, he needed a passport, a visa, and a military pass to be there. The old stigma of Ephraim and Judah was very much alive. Galileans were known rebels. Pilate had shortly before "mingled their blood with their sacrifices," Luke 13:1. The rebellion against Rome of Theudas and Judas, the Galilean mentioned in Acts 5:34-42, with many others, originated in Galilee. The Judaeans preferred that the Galileans go home and stay home to make their revolt.

The words of Jesus of Nazareth, the man from Galilee who spoke of "my kingdom," "the kingdom of heaven," or "the kingdom of G-d," were not void of political overtones. Even the armed revolts in Galilee, with thousands of rebels, had failed against the Romans. How much more this pacifist rabbi who talked about "turning the other cheek," "not hating," and "rendering unto Caesar what is Caesar's." This man from Galilee only meant trouble to the Judaeans. One whose arsenal was "He that killeth with the sword shall die by the sword," offered little hope to liberate Israel from the Romans.

In John 7:1 is a most misleading and overt mistranslation. "After these things Jesus walked in Galilee: for he would not walk in Jewry because the Jews sought to kill him." This is another attempt of replacement translators to implant bigotry in Christians toward the Jewish people and Judaism. When the average Christian reads this text as translated, he associates "Jewry" with Judaism and the "Jews" with the people who go to synagogue today. The Greek text reads "...Jesus walked in Galilee: for he would not walk in Judaea because the Judaeans sought to kill him." It was a question of geography, not religion. To many Judaeans, Jesus was a carpetbagger from up north who would bring about their destruction by the Romans. This is not to say that all Judaeans felt this way, for even the common people of Judaea were his followers; but again those of the status quo were afraid of the threat of a *coup d'etat* by the man of Galilee.

There are thirteen textual references in the Gospel accounts which give either a direct statement or *a fortiori* inference about the attitude of the Jews in Israel about Jesus. In Mark 11:18, for example, when Jesus had purged the Temple of moneychangers the second time, the Judaeans displayed a divided attitude: "And the scribes and chief priests heard it, and sought how they might destroy him: for they feared him, because *all the people* was astonished at his doctrine," "...and the common people heard him gladly." Mark 12:37. Theologians have treated all the Jews of history with the same crass, stereotyped attitude as though they all reflected the philosophy of the few scribes and chief priests who were in the Roman-Herodian regime. The "common people," the multitudes who followed Jesus, all those who were sympathetic to him, those who numbered in the hundreds of thousands, the theologians have treated as "Christians" and not as Jews. Yet, every last one *was* a Jew! Even worse, as Dr. Roy A. Eckert pointed out, "Many Christians consider even Abraham and David as Christians and not as Jews."

The consideration of the eighth question—what was Jesus' response to his people's attitude toward him?—must be measured by the fourth question: "Did Jesus overtly avoid and evade any overtures or efforts by those who had illusions that he was a candidate for the office of Messiah of Israel?"

Though it was impossible to avoid the answer to this question in considering those texts which stated the Jews' attitude toward him as king, Jesus' rejection of the crown of David is most subtle. When they read the Gospels, many Christians wonder why Jesus was so hush-hush about his own popularity.

In Mark alone, there are seven texts in which Jesus tried to muffle his fame. He healed a leper, and said, "See thou tell no man." 1:44. He cast out unclean spirits and "straitly charged them to not make him known." 3:12. He raised Jairus' daughter and "charged them to tell no man." 5:43. He opened deaf ears, 7:36, and opened blind eyes, 8:26, and "charged them to tell no man." Simon Peter said, "Thou art the Messiah...and Jesus charged them that they should tell no man of him." 8:30. After the transfiguration in 9:9, "He charged them that they should tell no man." Seven times this occurs in Mark.

What kind of game was he playing? If he had

ambitions to be the king of Israel, he needed a few lessons in "how to win friends and influence people." Jesus smothered his popularity in Israel because he had no ambition to be their king. His rejection of fame was itself a rejection of Israel as a kingdom.

Luke cited three references where Jesus charged them that they should not make him known. In 4:41-42, 8:56 and 9:21, Jesus forbade his fame to be known. Like Mark's, these concerned the unclean spirits, Jairus' daughter, and Simon Peter's confession.

Matthew gives only four such statements, but he also gives the explanation as to why Jesus did so. In 9:30, he charged the blind man, "See that no man know it." The multitudes were charged that they should not make him known," 12:16..."That it might be fulfilled which was spoken by the prophet Isaiah," verse 17..."He shall show judgment to the Gentiles," verse 18, ..."and in his name shall the Gentiles trust." Here is the heart of the matter. If Jesus had let his popularity and fame spread freely about, the Jews would have been more determined to make him king. And this was not his purpose. If he did not purpose to establish his kingdom, what was his purpose?

Matthew also refers to Peter's confession and the transfiguration in 16:20, 28, charging them they should tell no man. John omits any such statements about Jesus' cloak of secrecy about his miracles.

The survey of the depositions of the Midrash of Mark and the testimony of Luke, the Gemarist, gives the genealogy of Jesus all the way back to Adam. In this genealogical regression beyond David, Judah and the Patriarchs, the relationship of Jesus is beyond the scope of Israel's economy. Luke's genealogy is universal, showing the relation of Ben Adam, the son of man, to Ben Adom, humanity in general. Luke opens his account in chapter two with the birth of the Lamb in a manger, not the birth of a king in a palace. In 2:10-14, Luke records the angelic anthem of "...Good News [Gospel] of great joy which shall be to all people." Note that all people is "Am Ha Olam," the peoples of the world. There was no verse in the angelic hymn for a king of Israel, but rather "good news" for *all the Gentile nations*.

In Luke 2:25, the physician charts on the case record the testimony of Simeon Ben Hillel the Great. He was the son of Rabbi Hillel of Beit Hillel whose principles we are applying to this analysis. Simeon Ben Hillel the Great was also the father of Rabbi Gamaliel who defended the Apostles in Acts 5:34-39 who was also the tutor of Rabbi Saul of Tarsus who became Paul the Apostle (Sent One) to the Gentiles. The Gentile Christians might be surprised at what they call the massive amount of New Testament Pauline truth which in actuality is a quotation from Hillel, Simeon and Gamaliel.

According to Doctor Luke, when Rabban Simeon Ben Hillel the Great made a traditional rabbinic blessing over the baby Jesus, after the traditional *B'Rucha*, he said, "...mine eyes have seen thy salvation which thou hast prepared before the face of *all people* [GahM HaGoHLahM]; a light to lighten the *Gentiles*, even the glory of thy people Israel. And Joseph and his mother marveled [could not understand] at those things which were spoken of him. Then Rabbi Simeon blessed them [with the traditional blessing] and said unto Mary his mother, Behold, the child is set for the fall and rising again of many in Israel; and for a sign which shall be spoken against."

Simeon states clearly that the purpose of Jesus was not to be the Redeemer of Israel. He was to be a light reflected, not rejected, to the *Gentiles*, for the salvation of *all people*.

In Luke 3:6, John the Baptist asserted that Jesus was to be the savior of all mankind instead of the Messianic king of Israel: "*All flesh* shall see the *salvation* of the Lord." Again, in Luke 4:16-21, Jesus came to the synagogue in his home town of Nazareth. As was his custom, he stood up and began reading the Haftorah, which was the prophetic passage of that Sabbath day's Torah reading. Without finishing the complete verse of Isaiah 61:1-2, he stopped and sat down. His omission is noteworthy because he stopped with the thought, "...to proclaim the acceptable year of the Lord...." He did not read the remainder of the verse, which says "...the day of vengeance of our God." Messiah, king of Israel, will execute vengeance upon the enemies of Israel. Jesus had not come to be the Messiah of Israel. Even though it was very unusual to do so, he stopped reading in the middle of the verse, rolled up the scroll, gave it back to the *Khazin*, or cantor, and sat down saying, "This day is the Scripture fulfilled in your ears." This very omission is the rejection of the kingdom by him. The response of the people in the synagogue was dynamic.

The learned Jew who reads this passage will see things the casual Christian reader might overlook. "Every eye was fastened upon him...and they all bare him witness...." Amen, Amen, our hometown boy has made it! They wondered; they were in awe at the gracious words that proceeded out of his mouth, and they said, "Is not this Ben Yoseph?" On the simple level, such as Mark wrote, the Christian reader would think they spoke of Joseph the Carpenter; but the title Ben Yoseph, or Son of Joseph, is a *Messianic title*. In Judaism there is the expectation of two Messiahs. One is to be the descendant of the patriarch Joseph as we read in Genesis 49:24. The other is to be the descendant of Judah, Genesis 49:10, the son of David, by nativity. The former, "from thence," (the inheritance of Joseph, Galilee) is to come the "Shepherd the Stone of Israel," or the Northern Kingdom. The ignominy of Nazareth can now be erased. The question, "Can anything good come out of Nazareth?" can now be answered. The hometown boy from the carpenter's shop could heal the shame of this infamous village. "Physician heal thyself: Whatsoever we have heard done in Capernaum do also here in thy country...Amen!" Then, with somewhat of a sneerish note in the imperative, Jesus continued, "No prophet is accepted in his own country. Many widows were in Israel in the days of Elijah...but who was saved? The widow of Serepta Sidon [a Gentile]. Many lepers were in Israel in the time of the prophet Elisha and none of the Israeli lepers were cleansed except Naaman the Syrian [another Gentile]."

To his hometown people, Jesus, in a most vicious manner, crushed their ambitious expectation that he had come to be a redeemer of Israel that they might boast of him, "Our hometown boy." So cruel were his words that they were "...all filled with wrath and led him to the cliff of the hill whereon the city was built to cast him off headlong." This is the same parochial syndrome that eats its way through every institution today: If you are not going to be our Messiah, you are not going to be anybody's Messiah, especially the Gentiles!

This action in his hometown, his rejection of them as a kingdom in order to be the Savior to the Gentiles, and their repulsion of him because he was to be a savior of the

Gentiles, were all prophetic actions of future community relations. Later the apathy reversed; and it was the community of the Gentile Christians who repulsed the Jews from their synagogues, in spite of the fact that it was the Jews who gave the Christian faith to the Gentile world.

Luke, in an aristocratic manner, illustrates the rejection of Israel as the kingdom by Jesus in order that he might be the savior of the Gentiles instead by the prophetic narrative of the salvation of the widow of Sidon and Naaman the Syrian. Luke 4:22-30.

Again Luke immediately accounts (Luke 4:40-42) that when the rabbi from Nazareth performed exorcism of casting out devils at Kfar Nahum (Capernaum), the demons cried out, "Thou art Christ the Son of G-d. And he rebuking them permitting them not to speak [that] for they knew that he was Messiah. And when it was day he departed and went into a desert place." One must note that when he departed into a desert place or left that country, it was always when he had been publicly acclaimed as Messiah. He avoided the publicity and ran from that acclaim. He rejected any such tenor. He had not come to be the Messiah of Israel—nor was he a candidate to be the king of Israel. He made no campaign for it and absolutely rejected any suggestion of such an idea. Jesus abdicated the very suggestion of being king of Israel. In the dictum of the Hebrew Epistle, in 12:1-2, "Who, instead of the joy that was set before him [as the crowned prince of the house of David and the glory of that kingdom to come], he chose *instead* to endure the cross [for the Gentile world] and despised the shame and indignity of being stripped naked and hanged on the Roman stake."

In Luke 7:1-10, the narrative of the healing of the servant of the Roman centurion is a classic illustration of the Gentile position before the cross. The Gentile centurion was not a pagan, but was what the Jews called a *Y'Aeyr Adoni*, a "fearer of G-d of Israel." Despite this fact, the centurion was unworthy to approach Jesus. The favorable response of Jesus to the centurion's word was, "I have not found so great faith, no, not in Israel!"

In the raising of the daughter of Jairus in Luke 8:56, Jesus again "charged them that they should tell no man." In Luke alone, there are twenty-one such assertions that

Jesus did not purpose that Israel should expect him to redeem Jerusalem and that nation. The scope and purpose of his coming was to be a savior of the Gentiles.

Moses performed two signs to the Elders of Israel as credentials that G-d had sent him to be the redeemer of Israel out of Egypt. Moses cast down his staff and it became a serpent; he took up the serpent by the tail and it again became a staff. Again Moses put his hand into his bosom; it came forth leperous. He repeated the procedure and it came forth clean.

The miracles of Jesus were of a different nature. He never performed a miracle to prove to the Sanhedrin or to the people that he was their national deliverer. The signs Jesus performed were not appeals to the nation but were responses to the personal needs of the people. Jesus never fed the full or healed the whole. "The well need not a physician," but he made the blind to see, the deaf to hear, and the lame to walk. He ministered to the need of the individual, not to the nation. When the national leaders, Herod or the hierarchy demanded a sign of Messianic credential, he refused to demonstrate. On the contrary, Luke points out that upon this request, Jesus said: "...this is an evil generation: they seek a sign; and there shall no sign be given it, but the sign of Jonah the Prophet. For as Jonah was a sign *unto the Ninevites*, so shall the Son of Man be to this generation." (Luke 11:29-30) The emphasis which Jesus gave of the sign of Jonah to the Ninevites was that prophetic enigma that he was to be a Savior *to the Gentiles* through the message of the experience of Jonah who was sent from Israel *to the Gentiles*. This was the only sign that would be witnessed by that generation of Israel. They could see that the Gentile would receive the message of the Prophet. Luke, in an allegorical method, draws the vivid picture that it was Jesus who rejected Israel as a kingdom and not Israel who rejected him as king. With all the metaphor of the Gemaric principles, he makes the allusions through the graphic historical narratives of the widow of Sidon, of Naaman the Syrian and of the Ninevites, who were all Gentiles.

In Luke 17:20, the Pharisees demanded of Jesus when the kingdom should come. He answered them that "the kingdom of God will not come with your observation." That is to say, you will not witness the kingdom you expect from G-d in your generation or lifetime. His own disciples found this rather appalling. "Then he took unto him the twelve and said unto them, Behold we go up to Jerusalem, and all things that are written by the prophets concerning the Son of Man shall be accomplished. For he shall be delivered unto the Gentiles, and shall be mocked, and spitefully entreated, and spitted on; And they shall scourge him, and put to death; and the third day he shall rise again. And they understood none of these things: and this saying was hid from them, neither knew they the things which were spoken." Is it not strange that his own twelve could not comprehend the idea that he would not redeem Israel? Jesus seemed to make exception to this in addressing Zacchaeus, (Luke 19:9-11) "...this day is salvation come to this house, *forasmuch as he also is a son of Abraham.* For the Son of Man is come to seek and to save that which was lost. And as they [the disciples] heard these things, he added and spoke a parable, Because they thought that the kingdom of G-d should immediately appear." The disciples assumed that the redemption of Jerusalem and Israel would be accomplished immediately, despite what Jesus had so recently said about the Roman crucifixion and his resurrection. Therefore, Jesus gave them a parable of a nobleman who went into a far country to receive for himself a kingdom and to return. Jesus, in this parable, is restating that he is not going to redeem Israel in that generation but instead is going to the Gentile nations.

In Jerusalem (Luke 19:47-48), "Jesus taught daily in the Temple." He was at home there. He worshipped and offered sacrifices there. It was his place. The Chief Priests saw Jesus as a threat to their well-established dynasty. They feared Jesus because of the rumors that he would now immediately establish the throne of David, rumors which his disciples believed vehemently. This was well verified by Jesus' actions as he drove the merchandising vendors out of the Temple. This rumor was now action. Herod and Pilatus and the apostate priests who were collaborating with those merchants saw they would be next to be driven out. Luke 19:47-48 states: "...but the Chief Priests and the scribes and the chief of the people sought to destroy him. And could not find what they might do: for all the people were very attentive to hear him." Look at the phrase, "sought to destroy him," in verse 47. Christian theology has stretched and magnified that statement, applying it to all

Israel of all ages. They even apply what Luke said about the apostate priests to every Jew of every contemporary generation. The theologians have ignored completely in verse 48 that all the people of Israel were in affirmation to Jesus. Verse 48 has been minimized, ignored, and dismissed.

Unfortunately, the replacement theologians have succeeded in making most Christians think of Herod, Annas, Caiaphas, and their supporters from among the Pharisees as the legitimate Jewish leaders of that day. The Jewish Talmud spells out the anathema that befell the nation as a result of the apostate priests: the "fox" or "dog" Herod and the "bloody" Sanhedrin. Christian commentators and translators associate the Jewish leaders throughout history and today with that illegitimate non-Jewish government of the late Second Temple Period.

A prime example of this is in the recent "Living Bible." Mr. Ken Taylor lumps all the groups as the "priests," "Pharisees," "Sadducees," "Sanhedrin," and even the "crowds" into one category—"the Jewish leaders." In the mind of the average layman today, Jewish rabbis, Zionists, Israeli political leaders, and the directors of Jewish institutions are painted with the same brush and red paint as are Herod, Annas, Caiaphas, the Pharisees, Sadducees, and even Pilate and the crowd in the Passion story.

Here, too, is a thought for the betrayal: "Jew-das Iscariot." Jesus chose the Twelve. Ten of the *minyan* were ethnic and religious Jews. Two were not ethnic Jews but were Jewish proselytes. Simon the Canaanite was not ethnically a Jew, but was a son of Cushi. Ethnically, Simon the Canaanite was a Negro. One of the group chosen by Jesus was a black convert to Judaism.

Judas Iscariot likewise was not a Jew. His last name was not Iscariot. Ish-Kirot means he was a foreigner, an alien to the ethnic family of Israel. *Ish* means man and *Kirot* means he was a citizen of Kir, or Kirot. There was a city in southern Judaea called Kirot. It was Jewish. In southern Moab, across the Dead Sea, was another Kir or Kirot. If Judas, son of Seemon, had been from Kirot in Judaea, he would have been called Judas Mi-Kirot, as Mary from Migdol was called Mary Magdalena. Since Judas was a foreigner who had converted to Judaism, he was a *gayer*, and was designated as the man of Kirot, or Ish-Kirot.

Judas Ish-Kirot was not ethnically a Jew; he was a Moabite Arab. This might suggest a new dimension in the story of the betrayal. His concern over the purse and hush-hush conduct in the entire narrative could even suggest that he was a stooge for the Romans or a stool pigeon for his brother Arab, Herod. Again, that Judas would ask the meager price for a woman, or thirty shekels of silver, out of the non-negotiable silver shekels of the Temple treasury, leaves much to be answered about his relationship with the imposter priests of Herod's appointment. He asked a price which he could not spend; and according to Jewish law, a price they could not pay, though they did. The price for a woman became the price of blood, *aceldama*, Asha Ldama, אשה לדמה. That price bought a field at the foot of the Mount of Wickedness where Solomon housed his strange wives and concubines. It was to be the burial place for strangers.

The other disciples of Jesus expected him to establish the Kingdom then and there. When they followed him, they believed he would be Messiah king. Despite the fact that they had seen him again and again reject the proposition of the Kingdom, they still held fast to that expectation. Only in the last three weeks of his life did he begin to teach them that he would go to Jerusalem and die. They could not see it, comprehend it, or accept it. The Good News they were looking for was the redemption of Israel, not the redemption of the Gentiles. They watched him from afar as he dramatically acted out each part of the plot he had forspoken. Was the Betrayal, the Mock Trial, the Crucifixion, and the Burial good news to Israel or to his disciples? By no means was that good news! It was bad news for Israel and the multitudes who were attentive unto him. It was bad news to the disciples who had "forsaken all to follow him." The only ones who saw any good news were those apostate profiteers who were threatened economically by his existence. They represented only a small handful of the inside "Mafia" controlling the Herodian dynasty and priesthood.

Pontius Pilate was the Roman governor. The Herodian dynasty were Edomite Arab overlords. Herod's self-appointed priests were not the legitimate lineage by

Jewish law. The Pharisees were divided over Jesus, who was himself a Pharisee. Those in the "Mafia" syndicate system, either for profit or fear, were opposed to Jesus' jeopardizing the status quo. Other Pharisees were his avid disciples. The actual rulers of the people were themselves not Jewish leaders. They were despots over the Jewish leaders and people. These despots murdered the true Jewish leaders as they murdered Jesus. Jesus was one of many who had fallen by the sword of Rome or the Herodian dynasty.

Rebellion was seething in all the land. The Zealots, the Zionists of that day, opposed both the Herodian Tetrarchs and the Roman government. The Essenes and the sons of Zadok were in opposition to the apostate priesthood. The Talmud describes the Sanhedrin of that day as the "destructive Sanhedrin." The times and conditions were all there for the appearance of Israel's Messianic king. Jesus rejected that timely opportunity to be the Redeemer of Israel—even though he met all the qualifications.

Jesus had the right pedigree to be the king of Israel. The blood of King David flowed in his veins. Furthermore, anyone who could take five biscuits and two sardines and feed 5,000 families would be able to feed an army. He who could heal the wounded and raise the dead would not be defeated in a war of liberation. After each battle he would be able to restore his troops to a non-casualty status. Anyone who was courageous enough to walk into the Temple and overturn the moneychangers' tables and drive the Temple merchants out with a string whip, would doubtless be ready to purge the apostate priests at the appointed time.

The age-old struggle between Jacob and Esau wrestled in the bosoms of Jesus and the Herodian kings. He was the son of Jacob; they were the sons of Esau. The Jewish-Arab crises of the twentieth century smoldered in the bosoms of the Herods against Jesus. He showed no affinity for the Herods or their regime.

The Jews of Jesus' day, except for that very small corrupt heirarchy of Herod's court, the priesthood he had appointed, the Sadducees of the Sanhedrins and Pilate's mercenary servants, were hopeful that Jesus would deliver and save Israel from the dilemma that was before it. It was his popularity among the masses of Jewish people in Israel that made him a threat to the destructive Sanhedrin, to the apostate priesthood, to the Herodians and to the Romans. Jesus was not crucified because the Jewish masses were rejecting him. Had that been the case, he would have been no threat to the anti-Jewish leaders of his day.

Jesus of Nazareth stirred the hearts of the Zionists in Israel. Their blood boiled against the imposed alien hierarchy. Jesus was crucified because he was an enemy of Caesar. He was crucified because the Jews heard him, followed him, and believed he would be their Messianic king. No, Jesus was not crucified because the Jews rejected him as king. He was crucified because the Jews accepted him as their king!

No man ever had the qualifications and opportunity of timeliness to be Israel's Messianic deliverer as did Jesus of Nazareth. No man ever had more popular support to that candidacy than did he. Yet, he was altogether indifferent to it. He predicted in detail the destruction of the Temple, Jerusalem, and the Jewish State, yet he did nothing to avert it. He did not overthrow the Romans and free Israel from the alien rule of the Herodians as the Messianic king of Israel was and is expected to do. He did not purge the apostate priests and restore the valid sons of Zadok to their divinely appointed hereditary office. He did not destroy the Gentile nations which came against Jerusalem, nor did he establish world peace as the Messiah of Israel is supposed to do. He did not resurrect all the dead and restore the earth to its Edenic state. Rather than "abiding forever" and destroying the Romans, the Romans destroyed him. Jesus of Nazareth did not fulfill the expectation of the Messianic king of Israel. He did not fulfill the expectation of his own disciples and the multitudes who followed him. He did not qualify by performance to do what the Jews have always expected the Messiah to do. That is why the Jews have never and will never recognize Jesus of the Christian message as the Messianic king of Israel.

The *Last Supper* is not the *Passover*, nor is the *Passover* the same as the *Last Supper*. They are never synonymous. When they began to ignore such distinctions as these, the Christian commentators created many unsolvable problems. Mark, Luke, and Matthew record the events of the night of *Passover* without mention of the *Last Supper*. John does not mention the *Passover* at all. He alone relates the story of the *Last Supper*.

What is the difference between the *Last Supper* and the *Passover*? Everything is different between them. The tenth day of the month of Nisan or Aviv initiated four days of "preparation for Passover." That night, at the sunset which inaugurated the tenth day of the month, the Jews ate leavened bread with fermented foods. The feast on that evening, beginning the tenth day of the month, was called the "Feast of the First Night." Twenty-four hours later, sunset the next day, which was the eleventh of Aviv, they had another "Feast of the Second Night." Then, too, leavened foods were eaten. The following evening at sunset, the twelfth of Aviv, they ate the "Feast of the Third Night" and again with leavened foods. The thirteenth day of Aviv was the last feast at which leavened bread could be eaten. Therefore, it was called the *Last Supper*.

The fourteenth of Nisan, or Aviv, is the Passover. No leaven in any form could even be in their homes. Mark, Luke, and Matthew each mention articles of Passover: the unleavened bread, four cups of wine, the *Afikoman*, and the closing hymn of the "Chad Gad Yah." These narratives open with Jesus' words: "With desire have I desired to eat this Passover with you before I suffer." Luke 22:15.

The night before Passover, the night of the Last Supper, John makes no inference of any Passover item. On the contrary, he relates that Jesus "tore" the leavened bread instead of "breaking it" as a matzo. Jesus dipped the leavened bread, *Tzomach*, into a "sop." From that table, Judas Ish-Kirot went out and covenanted with the priests for the price of a woman—thirty pieces of silver. (Lev. 27:4) Had it been Passover, the priests would have made no such transaction.

The following chart will illustrate the difference between the Last Supper and the Passover.

Jesus ate the traditional Jewish Passover, as Jews always eat the Passover, on the fourteenth day of Nisan, or Aviv. Luke 22:14-20 relates that story while John, Chapters 13, 14, 15, 16, and 17, transpired around the table of the Last Supper on the thirteenth of Nisan. The time element is made very clear in John 13:1: "Now [just] *before* the feast of the Passover . . . ."

Four cups of wine were served at Passover. The first was a toast to *Remembrance*, the second a toast to *Redemption*, the third to *Salvation*, and the fourth a cup

INSTITUTE OF JUDAIC-CHRISTIAN RESEARCH

Luther C. Peak, President
8554 Santa Clara Drive
Dallas, Texas 75218

©

Vendyl M. Jones, Executive Director
P. O. Box 35 Tyler, Texas 75701

ORDER OF SEQUENCE OF EVENTS OF PASSION WEEK BY JEWISH CALENDAR

Jewish Day starts at Sundown of Preceding Day

Day of First Month of Nisan or Aviv	9th	10th	11th	12th	13th	14th	15th	16th	17th thru 21s
Day of Week	First	Second	Third	Fourth	Fifth	Sixth	Sabbath	First	
Name of Day	Sunday	Monday	Tuesday	Wednesday	Thursday	Friday	Saturday	Sunday	
Day of Preparation Before Passover		1st	2nd	3rd	4th				
Name of Feast of Preparation		Supper of First Night	Supper of Second Night	Supper of Third Night	LAST SUPPER				
Hebrew Name of Feast Days of Passover						Pasach	Matzo	Hag-Shemen or Roshath	
Name of Feast by Translation						Passover	Unleavened Bread	Feast of Oil or First Fruits	
Day of Passover						First Day	Second Day	Third Day	Till 8th Day
Scripture References		E X O D U S 1 2 :	1 - 3			Ex. 12:6, 18 Lev. 23:5	Lev 23:6-8	Lev 23:10-14	
				Mk 14:1	Mk 14:10 Mk 14:12	Mk 14:17-15:41	Mk 15:42-47	Mk 16:1-13	
				Lk 22:1	Lk 22:7-13	Lk 22:14-23:55 1st Day	Lk 23:56 2nd Day	Lk 24:1-12 24:13-49 "Today is..." 3rd Day v.21	
				Matt 26:2-16	Matt 26:17-19	Matt 26:20-27:61	Matt 27:62-66	Matt 28:1-20	
8th Day of Aviv Sabbath Jn 12:1-11	Sunday 1st Day Jn 12:12-50				Jn 13:1-17:26	Jn 18:1-19:42	(Jn 19:31-)	Jn 20:1-25	8th Day Jn 20:26-31

in toast to the coming *Messiah* who would deliver Israel. When they came to that final toast to the Messiah, Jesus refused to drink with them. "Take this cup [of Messiah] and divide it among yourselves; for I say unto you, I will not drink of the fruit of the vine, until the Kingdom of G-d shall come." (Luke 22:17-18) Jesus refused to drink the "cup of the Messiah," and in that action he was again rejecting the kingdom of Israel. In Matthew we shall see a greater development of this Passover. After the recovery of the hidden matzo, the *Afikoman*, which Jesus symbolized as his broken body, the disciples opened the door, as is the tradition, to welcome Elijah. When Elijah did not come, the door was left open and they sang the traditional incantation: "Praise the Eternal, *all nations*, Laud Him, *all peoples*, For great is His mercy toward us, And the faithfulness of the Eternal is forever, Hallelujah—Praise the Eternal." When the song was ended, the door remained open; Jesus took the "Cup of Elijah" and blessed it. This cup contained the essence of the first four cups: the "Cup of Remembrance," the "Cup of Redemption," the "Cup of Salvation," and the "Cup of Messiah," which Jesus had refused. With the door open (indicating an invitation to the Gentiles), Jesus lifted the "Cup of Ali Novi" and said, "This is my blood of the New Testament which is shed for the sins of many. . . ." (Matthew 26:28) He did not say, "shed for the House of Israel and the House of Judah" as in Jeremiah 31:31; instead, he said, *"Shed for the sins of many,"* meaning *for the Gentiles*, outside the Commonwealth of Israel. It is through the Open Door of Elijah, who was the savior of the Gentile widow of Sidon, that the access of the Gentiles was made, as seen through the "Cup of Elijah." That cup symbolized the blood of the New Covenant to the Gentiles. By the cross of Jesus, the covenantless, hopeless, G-dless, pagan Gentiles could find a relationship with the G-d of Israel through the open door and the *Silver Chalice* of Elijah. The chalice contained all the cups—remembrance, salvation, redemption, and the cup of the Messiah. This open door invited the Gentiles to an access and communion to the fellowship with the G-d of Israel and his people.

For that relationship to be accomplished, Jesus had to refuse to drink the Fourth Cup, the toast of the Messianic Kingdom of Israel. He refused the crown in order to take the Cross, rejecting Israel to save the nations.

In Luke 24, note again the attitude of the Jewish couple on the Emmaus road. This was not two men but rather Cleopas (Cleopas of John 19:25) and his wife Mary, the aunt of Jesus. What did they expect of Jesus originally and what was their response to the resurrection? When they were told of the resurrection, the disciples were bewildered. This was more than they could comprehend. Two of them made their escape from this crisis by departing Jerusalem and going to Emmaus. When they met Jesus incognito, they emphatically stated to the stranger that Jesus had failed to do what they had expected him to accomplish as their Messianic king. Their disappointment was expressed in these words: "...we trusted that it should have been he which should have redeemed Israel."

The reply of the stranger was stranger still. He spoke of the "suffering Messiah...Their hearts burned within them." They yet saw no good news in his words. To them this stranger was not fully aware of the circumstances. The day was far spent and they constrained him to abide with them in Emmaus.

A table was set before them. The stranger took the bread and broke it. The traditional "motza" was uttered from his lips, *"Baruch ata Adonai, Alohaynu melech ha Olam, Ha motza lechem men ha aretz, Amen!"* The stranger, in the traditional Jewish manner, stretched forth his hands, handing each of them a portion of the broken bread. As they took the matzo from his palms, they were agasp! There engraved in each palm was a nail-etched yod, a bloodless wound! As they looked upon the two yods in his palms, their eyes were opened. "He was made known unto them in the breaking of the matzo." The hands that only three nights before at the Passover table had taken the *Afikoman* now handed them another matzo. Looking upon those hands, they now saw his wounded palms. As their eyes were loosed and they recognized him, he vanished from their sight.

The couple immediately pressed their way back to Jerusalem, to the hiding place of the disciples. They related their story and how he was made known unto them in the breaking of bread. As they recounted their experience, that same stranger stood again in their midst. Two simple Hebrew words left his lips, *"Shalom aleichem!"* Peace be upon you!

Upon Jesus' appearance to his disciples in Luke 24,

Luke accounts their reaction not as that of joy and happiness, "but they were terrified and afrightened, and supposing that they had seen a spirit."

In the course of that conversation, when Jesus had eaten with them, he had made a declaration that was for the first time completely alien to Jewish tradition.

Israel's mission was to be a witness that there was one G-d to the pagan, polytheistic, Gentile nations. At no time was Israel commissioned to convert Gentiles to Judaism. The only message the Prophets had to the Nations was a message of judgment. It was never a message of salvation and repentance. Nineveh repented at Jonah's preaching but his message was judgment, not salvation. The Law of Torah alienated the Gentiles. G-d's message to Israel was exclusively for Israel. Each section of Torah opened with the words: "And the Eternal One spoke unto Moses again saying, speak unto the Children of Israel." That address excluded all Gentile nations. The Gentiles were condemned by the Law since they were excluded from the Law. The Gentile is not condemned because he broke the Commandments. He is condemned by not having had the privilege to keep or to break them. Gentiles are outlaws because they are lawless, needing and seeking a refuge, but not in the Law of Moses. The Law was a schoolmaster to drive the Gentiles to the Cross. It contained no salvation for the Gentiles nor any hope for the Gentiles. Instead, the Law was justice and judgment. The Law was condemnation, not commendation. Judaism was never and has never sought to convert Gentiles to Judaism.

Now, Jesus tells his disciples to do something that was indeed strange to their ears. They were to be ambassadors from Israel to take a message of salvation *to the pagan nations*. In Luke 24:45-49 was a message of "repentance and remission of sins to be preached in His Name among all [Gentile] Nations, beginning in Jerusalem and Judaea and unto the uttermost part of the world.'" Preaching faith in his name was the message from Jerusalem. The disciples were to be the witnesses of these things. That was to be the message of the "suffering and resurrection of Jesus from the dead" for the remission of their sins. This message was not *to* Israel, it was *from* Israel! It was not a message of "Good News" to the Jews. The preaching of the cross was not *for* the Jews, it was a message *by* the Jews. They got the message out. "By the Jews first and even the Greeks," according to Paul's statement in Romans 1:16. They did their job; had they not, there would not have been a Christianity. The Jews of the first and second century fulfilled their responsibility. It was not until the Council of Nicea that the message from Israel was aborted by the Church.

There are at least twenty-one direct references in Luke which teach that it was not Israel who rejected their king. The references clearly state that Jesus rejected Israel's kingdom. Mark gave seven simple statements concerning that case. Luke gave three times as many. In Matthew occur fourteen such assertions. John gave only one.

The interrogation continues. The investigation of the depositions of the four witnesses adds more answers to the ten questions of our inquiry. Examine now the deposition of the regal Midrashic, Matthew. He makes only one reference in 12:23 to the applause of the people for Jesus. "All the people were amazed, and said 'Is this not the son of David?'" The words "Ben David" are strictly a patronymic title attributed to the Messianic King of Israel. Other than that single reference, Matthew rests on the assumption that Jesus was favored by the people. Mark made much over the *common people's* applause because he was a commoner writing to the commoners. Matthew, however, was of the aristocracy and was in a strata which was less given to the occasion of applause. The tax collector friends were all of that Herodian system.

In the angelic announcement to Joseph in Matthew 1:20-25, there is the statement: "...thou shalt call his name Jesus for he shall save his people from their sins." Who are "his people"? The casual reader will naturally say Israel. However, when the text is translated to Hebrew, we see a strange message; *laon autou*, in Greek, becomes *amin otto* in Hebrew. This reference immediately relates to a passage of Messianic speculation from Genesis 49:10: "Unto him shall the gathering of the peoples [Gentiles] be." Matthew's opening statement relates the naming of the child *Yeh-Oshua*. This name is found in Numbers 13:8 and 16, where Moses sent the spies from each tribe into the land of Israel. From the tribe of Ephraim there was Oshea, son of Nun, whom Moses renamed *Yehoshua*, which meant "the Eternal One's salvation." Joshua, the son of Nun, and Jesus had the same name. Rabbi Max Landman points out that Jesus' name was Emmanuel, but he was called Yehoshua in designating his office as the Savior.

The angel told Joseph that the child's name would be called Jesus, or Yehoshua, because he would save his people from their sins. That is as Luke later said: "That repentance and remission of sins *in his name* should be preached among all nations, beginning at Jerusalem." Israel is the *source*, not the *object*, of the Gospel.

Jesus not only avoided popularity, he sometimes overtly went out of his way to be unpopular. This can be seen in the different, and sometimes opposing, things he preached at various times and places.

In an "inference of an analogy of words," Matthew indicates that Jesus did all in his power to smother any ray of hope that he was to deliver Israel in that age. "My kingdom is not of this age" was not an evasive statement of expediency before Pilate. It was the tenor of his entire ministry.

The Yeshiva Beit Hillel was in Galilee. There the spirit of the law was emphasized. Yeshiva Beit Shammi was in Jerusalem, where the intensity of the letter of the law was stressed. If Jesus had any Messianic inclinations toward gathering a massive public support for his coronation as king of Israel, it would have been politically expedient for him to preach the "spirit of the Law" as Hillel while in Galilee, and the intensity of the "letter of the Law" as Shammi while in Jerusalem. The inference from the analogy of words clearly indicates otherwise. When in Galilee, where Hillel was popular, Jesus preached an intensity of the letter of the Mosaic Law that far exceeded the standards of Rabbi Shammi. This can be vividly seen in the Sermon on the Mount in Matthew, chapters 5-7. For example, let us look at a few illustrations from the Sermon on the Mount in Matthew's Midrash on the subject: "...I say unto you, that except your righteousness shall exceed (the righteousness) of the Scribes and Pharisees, ye shall in no wise enter into the Kingdom of Heaven. Ye have heard it said by them of old time, 'Thou shalt not kill,' and whosoever shall kill shall be in danger of the judgment, but I say unto you that whosoever is angry with his brother without a cause shall be in danger of the judgment. Ye have heard it is said of them of old time, 'Thou shalt not commit adultery.' But I say unto you, that whosoever looketh upon a woman to lust after her hath committed adultery with her already in his heart. And if thy right eye offend thee, pluck it out, and cast it from thee: For it is more profitable for thee that one of your members should perish and not that the whole body be cast into Hinnom. . . ." (Matthew 5:20-22, 27-30)

These standards of interpretation far exceeded the intensity of interpretation that was demanded by Rabbi Shammi's "Letter of the Law." This kind of preaching would have gone over well in Jerusalem where Shammi was more popular, but this kind of homiletical conduct was most unpopular in Galilee.

Amazingly, Jesus' preaching in Jerusalem was precisely opposite from his preaching in Galilee. In Jerusalem he preached Hillel's spirit of the Law equally emphatically as he had preached Shammi's letter of the law in Galilee. This might be observed in Mark's deposition, 12:28-34: "And one of the Scribes came, and having heard them reasoning together and perceiving that he had answered them well, asked him, which is the first Commandment of all? And Jesus answered him, The first of all the Commandments is, Hear, O Israel: The Lord our G-d is One: And thou shalt love the Lord thy G-d with all thy heart, and with all thy soul, and with all thy mind, and with all thy strength: this is the first Commandment. And the second is like, namely this, Thou shalt love thy neighbor as thyself. There is none other Commandment greater than these. And the Scribes said unto him, Well, Master, thou hast said the truth: for there is one G-d; and there is none other but he: And to love him with all thy heart, and with all the understanding, and with all the soul, and with all the strength, and to love his neighbor as himself, is more than all whole burnt offerings and sacrifices. And When Jesus saw that he answered discreetly, he said unto him, Thou art not far from the kingdom of G-d. And no man after that durst ask him any question."

From these examples, we may draw an inference from an analogy of words that Jesus overtly rejected Israel as a kingdom. If Jesus preached Shammi in Galilee where Hillel was popular, and preached Hillel in Jerusalem where Shammi was popular, he certainly was not trying to win friends and influence people. Politically this was a blunder, or else he deliberately discouraged the idea that he was a candidate to be Messiah, King of Israel. On the other hand, there is never an "inference by an analogy of words" that suggests that he was a candidate to be Israel's Messianic king.

Jesus said, concerning the faith of the Roman centurion, "I have not found so great faith, no, not in Israel. . . ." (Matthew 8:10-12) Then Matthew gives a very interesting observation, ". . .that many [Gentiles] shall come from the east and west, and shall sit down with Abraham, Isaac, and Jacob, in the Kingdom of heaven." In verse 12 he predicts that during this time of the calling out from among the Gentiles, a people for his name, the people of Israel would be suffering in the diaspora. "But the children of the kingdom shall be cast out into outer darkness; there shall be weeping and gnashing of teeth."

In Matthew 12:15-16, ". . .he withdrew himself from thence; and great multitudes followed him." "And charged them that they shall not make him known." This is not characteristic of one who was seeking popularity and the Crown of the Kingdom of Israel. By quoting Isaiah 42:1, Matthew explains in 12:21 why Jesus withdrew himself and charged them not to publicize him: ". . .He shall bring forth judgment to the Gentiles. In his name shall the Gentiles trust." This answers the ninth question stating the purpose of Jesus as the Messianic Redeemer of the Gentiles.

In Matthew, chapter 13, we find seven parables of the Kingdom of Heaven. In this section the interpretations of the symbolisms are made by Jesus himself in verse 38: "The field is the world," *not Israel.* Israel is symbolized by the "Vineyard of the Lord" in Isaiah, chapter 5. Jesus did speak of the vineyard parables concerning Israel, but the parables of the field concern the non-Jewish world. Jesus dealt with the harvest of the field, the tares of the field, and the treasure hidden in the field. All these develop various aspects of the "Good News" to the nations. In these parables Jesus was setting forth the sovereignty of G-d regarding the salvation of the Gentile nations. The purpose did not involve the rejection of the king by Israel, but instead the rejection of the kingdom of Israel by Jesus so that he might be the Redeemer of the Gentiles. The discussion of these seven parables in Matthew 13 immediately follows the account in Matthew 12 of the "Sign of Jonah," who brought salvation to the Gentiles.

"Come ye apart and rest," Jesus said to the Twelve. They had spent themselves almost three and a half years now with no vacation, no ease, no relaxation. The greatest work is still before him; yet, he and the disciples are all exhausted. They turn northward away from the press of Galilee. They walk along the Jordan Valley, around Lake Hula and proceed toward the foot of Mount Hermon. There they arrive at the resort town of Baniyas, called in that time, Caesarea Philippi. Here, the pedestal of the high rock cliffs are two caverns of mammoth size. From these cavern conduits gush cold artesian waters from the snows of Mount Hermon. Tall cedars tower to colonnade the clear blue sky. Flora, a thousand specimens, carpet the cove. Rocks are wrapped with green moss and fern. A gentle turf blankets the banks along the waterway. Tons of water per second cascade down the steep descent, forming a headwater of the river Jordan. Like the Garden of Eden, a blue haze fills the air with a fog, beribboned with rainbows moving with the sun. (Ah, such solitude! Here the Adam that is in each of us reaches out to find what was lost in the exile from that primal garden.)

Jesus and his disciples lie on the grass by the living musical waters. They peer upward through the towering cedars at the ceiling of heaven's cathedral. Such recluse from the multitudes! In these cool shadows of the springs of Baniyas, the Thirteen are sprawled about in half a slumber. Jesus breaks the silence with the query: "Who do the Sons of Adam say that I, the Son of Adam, am?" Casually, one answers, "Some say that you are John the Baptist." Another says, "Some think you are Elijah!" Simon Peter adds, "Others say that you are Jeremiah or one of the Prophets."

Jesus leaps to his feet. "Speak for yourself [Peter]! Who do you say that I am?"

Simon and the eleven, following the crescendo of vigor, leap up with their rebbe. Why is the imperative so sharply put to them? Each searches himself for the right answer. Surely they follow him, believing that he is the Messiah, King of Israel. Each of them expects that as soon as Herod and the Romans are expelled, they shall sit at His Royal table in the Palace of Jerusalem. For these three and a half years, he has avoided the Messiah King question. The people are now cooling down in Galilee, "He is just another prophet." He has repeatedly refused the crown there. Maybe in Jerusalem, perhaps in "Ariel, Ariel, the city where David encamped," Jesus will make a triumphant regal entry. There, Messiah, Son of David, will reveal himself. Only a few days now till Passover. They are going to Jerusalem after leaving this haven. Maybe this is the year in Jerusalem we can sing:

The year is come, the year is come,
The Messiah has arrived
The Son of David, Son of the Highest, the
  expected.
Have Mercy on us! Have mercy on us!
  Have mercy on us!

Now, Jesus, in an imperative tenor, commands them, "Speak for yourselves! Who do you say that I am?" Simon quickly answers, but his answer is not exactly what he has been thinking. Until now, Simon has only thought of Jesus as Meshiach Ben David, the political king of Israel. But now, only two words leave his lips—two words that leave his lips numb and the eleven disciples stunned—"Meshiacha Ben-ElKhai," you are the Son of the Living G-d.

There is a display of astonishment by Jesus at Peter's words. "Blessed art thou Simon Bar Yonah for flesh and blood hath not revealed this unto thee but my Father which is in heaven."

This statement of Peter's, "Thou art the Messiah of the Living G-d," comes at the very end of Jesus' ministry. Jesus had never told the disciples anything like this about himself in these nearly three and a half years. No other man had ever even suggested that he was a divine person. There was speculation in the highest mystical concepts of the Kabbalah that the Messiah, after a sort, would be a manifestation of the Adam Kadmon, or a personification of that Essence in whose image the first Adam was created, but Jesus had never made any such allusion, except in the faint suggestion of the title, "the Son of Man," or "Ben Adam." In this he could have referred to either the first man, Adam, or to the primal manifestation of the Adam Kadmon of the ten intransitive spheres.

"Flesh and blood hath not revealed this to thee [Peter]." This means simply, "Peter, I have not told you this, neither has any other man." In the misty haze of Baniyas, Peter had drawn a statement from the heights of Jewish mysticism and projected it upon his rebbe. Simon, Jesus had renamed Cephas, or Tsafat (Tsaphat). Tsafat, as noted in chapter three, means a particular kind of stone. The tsafat is the stone which crowns a colonnade, or pillar, upon which the beams of the roof rest. The concept of the Messiah to Simon, as to all the Jews, was the Son of David. The statement by Peter, or Tsafat, was a crowning application. That tsafat statement, "Thou art the Messiah, the Son of the Living G-d," was to be the crowning pillar in the message to the Gentiles. Tsafat, Cephas or Peter, was the one who was to deliver that message to the Gentiles.

What did this statement, "Thou art the Messiah, the Son of the Living G-d," have to do with the Jews in their Messianic expectation? It had absolutely no place in the Messianic speculation of Israel. There was no intent on the part of Jesus that such a declaration should ever be made to the Jews. The twentieth verse plainly states that the crowning statement of Peter, or Tsafat, (Cephas) was not to be declared to the Jews. "Then charged he his disciples that they should tell no man that he was Jesus the Messiah."

Matthew 16:20 is another "obscure passage" which the Christian commentators and replacement theologians never seem to have time and space to explicate. Good preaching from pulpits about the Messianic acclaim of Jesus seems always to stop short of verse 20..."Tell no man...." It is so easy to ignore those statements in the texts which are not conducive to our theology with a sanctified ignorance.

Why did Jesus charge the Twelve not to tell *his own people* that he was the Messiah? Because it would have been inconsistent with the purpose of his coming to be the Savior of the Gentiles. Furthermore, it would have violated the very trend of his preaching for over three years in which he had overtly avoided such Messianic claim to Israel. In addition, he came for a cross, not for a crown. He could not obtain both a cross of sacrifice for all mankind and also wear the crown of Israel. As the Lamb, he came to be the sacrifice; hence, he could not be the majestic Lion of Judah. As in Revelation 5:1-6, John wept much because no man was found worthy to open and to read the seven-sealed book. The emphasis on John's weeping was not that there was no man worthy to open the book, but rather that the one John knew to be worthy was not found. When the elder directed John's attention to the throne and said, "Behold the Lion of the tribe of Judah hath prevailed and is worthy. . . ," John turned; and instead of seeing a lion, he beheld a Lamb, as if it had been slain.

Note the striking relationship that Jesus makes at Caesarea Philippi to Peter in his role as the bearer of the Gospel to the Gentiles. "Simon, son of Jonah," is an allegorical nominative of address. In Simon, we see the deeply embedded character of the prophet Jonah. Jonah did not cherish the idea of taking the Word of the Eternal One to Nineveh. In fact, he fled to Joppa to evade that commission. Jesus had commissioned Peter to head the program to take the Gospel to the Gentiles, in Matthew 28:19-20. However, almost a decade and a half later, we find Simon Peter resting on his laurels on the housetop of one Simon the Tanner in Joppa, the very place where Jonah had also fled to avoid a similar commission.

There is a concept in Judaism called *gilgul ha nefesh*, or the "cycle of the soul." This is, after a fashion, a reincarnation of the spirit of an earlier prophet in a later one. The case is clearly illustrated in John the Baptist who was "Elijah come in the spirit." Simon Peter embodied the spirit and attitude of Jonah. Both Peter and Jonah made Joppa the starting point of their missions. They were both reluctant at the idea of their visions. In Acts 10, when Peter saw a Jewish prayer shawl (Talit) let down from heaven, knitted (or fringed) in the four corners, and filled with all manner of unclean beasts, he reacted in a typically Jewish fashion, "Nothing common or unclean hath ever entered my mouth." It appeared both to Jonah and to Peter that there was some contradiction in the character and nature of the G-d of Israel that he would send a Jewish prophet to the Gentiles. Why could not G-d raise up a Gentile prophet to speak to the Gentiles? Jonah was disgruntled about the repentance of the Gentiles at his preaching. Likewise, Peter found himself confronted with a dilemma about what to do with the Gentiles who turned to G-d at his preaching.

Peter obeyed the vision to go to the Gentiles when he went with the three men who took him to the house of Cornelius, the Roman centurion. However, the text reflects Peter's astonishment and hesitancy to tell the Gentiles about the "Good News." This was possibly fourteen or fifteen years after the ascension of Jesus and

His commission to share the Gospel with the Gentiles. Peter had the keys and only he could use them. He did use them at Pentecost as seen in Acts 2:21, by quoting the prophetic decree by Joel the Prophet: "And it shall come to pass that whosoever [anyone—all the Gentiles] shall call on the name of the Lord shall be saved." Again he used the keys in the narrative of Acts, chapter ten. Peter said to Cornelius, "Ye know how that it is an unlawful thing for a man that is a Jew to keep company, or come unto one that is of another [Gentile] Nation; but G-d hath showed me that I should not call any man common or unclean...of a truth I perceive that G-d is no respecter of persons; But in every [Gentile] Nation he that feareth him and worketh righteousness is accepted of him. The message which is now being sent out by the children of Israel, preaching right now to you [Gentiles] Peace through and of Jesus Christ." (Acts 10:22, 34-35)

Despite all he had said, Simon Bar Jonah, like the prophet Jonah, did not know what to do with those Gentiles who were accepted by G-d through faith in the preaching of Jesus Christ. This dilemma of Peter, like Jonah under the gourd vine, was depicted by Acts 10:47: "Can any man [of you Jews from Joppa] forbid water of the Jewish Mikvah [baptism], to these [Gentiles who have received the seal of the faith and Spirit of the Holies] as even we [have]?" (The Gentile who converts to Judaism must go to the Mikvah and be immersed, according to Jewish law.)

Peter's question is a statement of doubt about his own conviction that this was really in order; that is, "Vat are ve going to do with dese Gentiles?"

Many years later, Peter was still having problems as to how to deal with the Gentiles. In Galatians 2:11-21, Paul rebuked Peter for his inconsistency and dissension against those Gentiles who had found salvation. Jonah the Prophet had the same problem after he had seen the salvation of Nineveh instead of their destruction. He bitterly cried against G-d: "And G-d saw their works, that they turned from their evil way; and G-d repented of the evil that he had said that he would do unto them; and he did it not." (Jonah 3:10)

"And he prayed unto the Lord and said, I pray thee, O Lord, was not this my saying when I was yet in my country? Therefore I fled before unto Tarshish: for I knew that thou art a gracious G-d and merciful, slow to anger, and of great kindness, and repentest thee of the evil." (Jonah 4:2)

Jonah, like Peter, was distressed about what to do with the Gentiles. Jesus chose Simon Bar Jonah to do a whale of a task! Peter was about as anxious to take his message of salvation to the Gentiles as Jonah had been to take the message of judgment to the Ninevites. To say the least, Peter was not jumping up and down about organizing an evangelical crusade to share this good thing they had going in Jerusalem with the Goyim (Gentiles). Peter had a hang-up, a mental block, a deterrance of heart, because he had always been taught that the pagan Gentiles had no place in the economy of G-d. "*Ya'achov, Ya'achov—* Osee, Osee, Jacob is Jacob and Esau is Esau."

When they speak about each other, some Jews can have as much sarcasm in the way they pronounce "goyim" in reference to the Gentiles as do the anti-Semitic Gentiles in the way they pronounce the word "Jew." This is to say that the Gentiles have no monopolies on arrogance, prejudice, and ethno-centric complexes. The Jews surely are entitled to some reprisal against the Gentiles, and especially the Christians, because of their lot in history. This does not, however, justify the Jew's attitude that every Gentile and every Christian participated in slamming the doors on gas chambers during the holocaust. It is, in fact, a violation of every concept of Judaism to do so. As Max I. DiMont points out, there were seven million Christians who died with the six million Jews in the camps, many of whom died because they had tried to aid the Jews. They seemed to be the ones really forgotten.

These Jewish attitudes against the Gentiles were personified in the prophet Jonah and his protege, Simon Peter, and that long before the holocaust, the Inquisition, and the crusades.

In our examination of the deposition of Matthew, we have analyzed well over three years of the ministry of Jesus. The evidence is that at that point in time, none of the people of Israel thought of Jesus as their national Messiah. Those occasions when they tried to force him to be Messiah had been well suppressed by Jesus' rejection of the crown of Israel. Here, only a few weeks before his death, he was considered no more than a rabbi and a prophet.

Peter's confession brought about the urgency of a full explanation of Jesus' role as a savior of the Gentiles against the background of the kingdom of Israel. This is what the following context, the transfiguration, was all about.

At Caesarea Philippi, Jesus told the Twelve that there were some standing there with him who would not taste death till they would see the Son of Man coming in his Kingdom (Matthew 16:28). For this regal preview of coming attractions, Jesus took three of them south, over one hundred miles to Mount Nebo, "a high mountain apart [that is, apart or outside the land of Judah and Galilee]." This is Mount Nebo, not Mount Tabor. Here in Nebo, about six days' leisure journey south of Mount Hermon where Moses was buried and where Elijah ascended, Jesus called a reunion with Peter, James, John, Elijah, Moses, and himself. Jesus transfigured himself through a metamorphic change and appeared as the Messiah king of Israel. With Moses and Elijah, he discussed his decease, or death, which would be accomplished in Jerusalem. Again, we come to one of those famous, obscure, overlooked, remote, and ignored verses in Matthew 17:9: "And as they came down from the mountain, Jesus charged them saying, Tell the vision to no man, until the Son of Man be risen again from the dead."

When Simon saw the regal Messianic transfiguration of Jesus, he thought the Messianic Age had arrived. With Moses and Elijah, the kingdom was come. With Moses and Elijah, he saw the resurrection and all was now history in Peter's mind. Now, all Gentile nations would come up to Jerusalem and keep the Feast of Tabernacles each year, according to Zechariah 14:16-21:

> And it shall come to pass, that everyone that is left of all the nations which came against Jerusalem shall even go up from year to year to worship the King, the Lord of hosts, and to keep the *feast of tabernacles*. And it shall be, that whoso will not come up of all the families of the earth unto Jerusalem to worship the King, the Lord of Hosts, even upon them shall be no rain. And if the family of Egypt go not up, and come not, that have no rain; there shall be the plague, wherewith the Lord will smite the heathen that

> come not up to keep the *Feast of Tabernacles.* This shall be the punishment of Egypt, and the punishment of all nations that come not up to keep the *Feast of Tabernacles.* In that day shall there be upon the bells of the horses HOLINESS UNTO THE LORD; and the pots in the Lord's house shall be like the bowls before the Altar. Yea, every pot in Jerusalem and in Judah shall be holiness unto the Lord of hosts; and all they that sacrifice shall come and take of them, and seethe therein; and in that day there shall be no more the Canaanite in the house of the Lord of hosts.

Since it was evident with the presence of Moses and Elijah that the resurrection had occurred, Peter thought it was time to set up the "Sukkot" (Tabernacles), according to Leviticus 23:34-44. To Peter's dismay, Jesus was only giving Peter, James, and John a preview of the Messianic Kingdom of Israel. The subject of discourse between Moses, Elijah, and Jesus was his decease, or death, which was to be accomplished very shortly in Jerusalem. Since Jesus had not come to establish the Messianic Kingdom of Israel, but instead to die for the Gentiles, he charged these three disciples not to tell any man the vision until after he had been put to death and had been raised again. That message was then given to the Gentiles by the children of Israel. There would be a new economy, or dispensation, of community whereby with that message of death, burial and resurrection, there would be a calling out from among the Gentiles a people for his name. That message was not *for* Israel, but was *from* Israel; therefore, he charged them not to tell any man. Israel did not reject Jesus as their king—he rejected Israel as his kingdom. Yet, there is the presence of Israel in the Messianic kingdom. Israel's presence in the kingdom is not because they have all converted to Christianity. The reverse is the case. It is the Gentiles who will be coming up to Jerusalem to observe a Jewish feast each year.

Each of the four Gospel accounts gives record of what is called the Triumphant Entry of Jesus into Jerusalem. Matthew, in his Midrashic manner, puts much emphasis upon the prophetic adage, "Behold thy King cometh," from Zechariah 9:9: "Rejoice greatly, O daughter of Zion; shout O daughter of Jerusalem; behold thy King cometh unto thee; he is just, and having salvation; lowly, and riding upon an ass, and upon a colt the foal of an ass."

There are two observations we might make about this citation of Matthew from Zechariah's prophecy. First is the paradox of the Jewish expectation and hope in the Messiah's advent. The Jews expected the Messiah to appear in a time of great national distress, riding on a great white horse. John, in his apocalyptic vision of Rev. 19:11-16, best expresses this expectation:

> And I saw heaven opened, and behold a white horse; and he that sat upon him was called Faithful and True, and in righteousness he doth judge and make war. His eyes were as a flame of fire, and on his head were many crowns; and he had a name written, that no man knew, but he himself. And he was clothed with a vesture dipped in blood: and his name is called The Word of G-d. And the armies which were in heaven followed him upon white horses, clothed in fine linen, white and clean. And out of his mouth goeth a sharp sword, that with it he should smite the nations; and he shall rule them with a rod of iron; the fierceness and wrath of Almighty G-d. And he hath on his vesture and on his thigh a name written, KING OF KINGS, AND LORD OF LORDS.

According to this expectation, the Messiah should have ridden into Jerusalem on a great white horse. The words of Zechariah were indeed strange, but not unlike many other apparent contradictory passages concerning the coming Messiah. From the earliest dawn of Messianic expectation, the Scriptures were very vague about his promised appearance. On the one hand, he was to be the Triumphant King who would never die, while on the other, he was the Suffering Servant put to death, but without a soteriological significance. He was the "Scepter of Judah," the regal descendant of Judah through the posterity of David. Concerning the latter, he was called the son of Joseph, Judah's younger brother, "The Suffering Shepherd, the Stone of Israel." As the first, he was the majestic Redeemer of Israel. As the latter, he was the Suffering Messiah. In rabbinic commentary, the nature and person of the Suffering Messiah, called *Mesheach Ben Yoseph*, is vague and undefined. As a result of this ambiguity, long before the time of Jesus, the Sages of Israel had concluded that there must of necessity be two Messiahs, one a "Suffering Messiah," and the latter, the "Majestic Messiah." John speaks of two such pseudo-Messiahs in the Apocalypse. To understand this, one must understand the aspect of the word "Messiah." In Hebrew, "Messiah" has not the connotation that the Christian means when he uses the word Messiah or Christ, "the Anointed." When the Christian uses the word Messiah or Christ, he has a solitary connotation in mind—Jesus only. The Jew must learn to appreciate this since the only concept of Messiah to the Christian is in that experience of faith in Jesus Christ. Without faith in him, there is no knowledge of Christ to the Gentiles. The Christian must appreciate also that the Hebrew *Mesheach* means "anointed." In the Hebrew concept, Moses was *Mesheach*, Aaron was *Mesheach*, the Elders of Israel and all the priests were *Mesheachim*. David was the Lord's anointed, or *Mesheach*. Israel, as a nation, is the Anointed nation, or the Messianic nation; therefore, it is not a problem, from the Jewish point of view, to expect two Messiahs. One who would come riding on a great white horse and another riding on the colt of an ass. Not only these two, but any man anointed of G-d for a special purpose, is the Messiah.

When Jesus approached Jerusalem, the people thought he would immedately establish the kingdom of Israel. They expected a majestic, triumphant entry on a great white horse. The multitudes went out of the city to meet him, lifting up their *talits*, or prayer shawls. They tied the *tsitsits*, fringes, to the tips of palm branches, making a canopy, or *huppah*, for him to ride under into the city. This train of canopies stretched over the road all the way from the Mount of Olives, through the brook Kidron, and up to the Golden Gate, which entered into the Temple area. They were all singing: "The year has come, the year has come, The Messiah, Son of David has come, Have mercy on us, have mercy on us, have mercy on us."

Yet, when Jesus made his appearance, he did not come riding on a great white horse as the majestic king, the Son of David. Instead, he came as the lowly servant, a peasant on a colt, the foal of an ass. This action of Jesus was in itself a rejection of their acclamation. The Jews were accepting him as their Messianic king, while by his very actions, he was rejecting them as his Messianic kingdom.

Matthew made special note of this, not in so many words of explanation, but by a simple omission of certain parts of the text quoted from Zechariah 9:9. Note this vital omission by comparison with the passage in Zechariah:

Stanzas: 1. *Rejoice greatly O Daughter of Zion,*
2. Shout O Daughter of Jerusalem:
3. *Behold thy King cometh unto thee,*
4. He is triumphant and victorious
5. *Lowly, and riding upon an ass,*
6. *Even upon the colt, the foal of an ass.*
7. I will cut off the chariot from Ephraim.
8. And the horse from Jerusalem
9. And a battle bow shall be cut off,
10. And he will speak peace unto the Gentiles...

Matthew quotes only stanzas one, three, five and six. He omits:

Stanzas: 2. Shout [rejoice] O daughter of Jerusalem
4. He is triumphant and victorious
7. I will cut off the chariot from Ephraim,
8. And the bow from Jerusalem,
9. And the battle bow shall be cut off,
10. And he will speak peace to the Gentiles.

There was nothing for Jerusalem to shout (rejoice) about. Shortly thereafter, when he was going to Golgotha, the daughters of Jerusalem followed him weeping. He turned to them and said: "Daughters of Jerusalem, weep not for me, but weep for yourselves and for your children." He knew and had foretold that by the time these daughters of Jerusalem had children his age, Titus would have come and destroyed the city and nation. He knew that his Roman cross was a projection of what would happen to Jerusalem and to Israel some forty years later. Matthew omitted "He is triumphant and victorious." This was not a triumphant entry; it was an entry of humiliation. His entry was not as that of a king on a great white horse, but was as the meek and lowly peasant, the Suffering Servant. He would not cut off the chariot against Israel (Ephraim or the Northern Kingdom) nor the bow against Jerusalem, for he had not come to be their Redeemer. Jerusalem was to lament, not shout. Yet, according to the last stanza of Zechariah's prophecy, "...He will speak peace unto the Gentiles."

Matthew is almost totally silent in his testimony about the strong popularity of Jesus among the Jewish people. Yet he is very verbal about Jesus' avoidance of popularity. He had smothered any flame of Messianic intent on the part of the Jewish people. John the Kabbalist, on the other hand, is very verbal about the popularity of Jesus among his people, and he is almost silent about Jesus avoiding popularity and smothering his fame. In Matthew, the popularity of Jesus is assumed; in John, the flavor of withdrawal of popularity is shadowed by his renown because of his miracles.

In our interrogation of the question of the riddle of the King and Kingdom, "Did the Jews reject Jesus as their king vs. Did Jesus reject Israel as his kingdom," we have called upon three witnesses—Mark, Luke and Matthew. Now we summon our fourth and final witness and hear his deposition about the matter. The ten questions in the inquisition must now be answered by John.

John, as no other writer, spells out vividly what he and the other disciples expected of Jesus as their Messianic king. No other witness is so emphatic in his deposition concerning the motive and purpose of Jesus as the Savior of the Gentiles instead of as the king of Israel.

The level of John's presentation is surrounded with the aura of the Zohar. In almost all the narratives of John, there are the vague and misty elements about his words which suggest a mystical interpretation. Only in the area of mysticism can one fully apprehend the strength of John's metaphors.

From the very beginning of Jesus' ministry, what did John record of his absolute statement concerning the ninth question of the purpose of Jesus' life? This required reference can be found on the occasion of his very first public statement in Jerusalem. Jesus was in the Temple during the feast of Passover, when he loudly proclaimed, "Destroy this Temple and in three days I will raise it up." The people of Judaea answered, "Forty and six years was this Temple in building and will thou rear it up in three days?" But he spoke of the Temple of his body. (John 2:19-21) The Temple in Jerusalem had already been destroyed once by the Babylonians on the ninth day of the Hebrew month of Av in the Jewish year 3338. The thirty-third day of the fifty days in the counting of the *OMehR*, between Passover and *SHahVoUoHt*, or Pentecost was the day Jerusalem was put under seige.

The name of the fast day on the thirty-third day of *OMehR*, is called *LaG B'OMehR.* This name is derived from the Hebrew letters that have the numeric value of thirty-three. The Hebrew letter *Lamed,* ל, is thirty. The Hebrew letter *Gimel,* ג, is three. Thus, *Lamed Gimel,* ל'ג is thirty-three in numeric value, but spells the word *LaG.* So, *LaG B'OMehR* tells not only the name of the fast, but also tells the day of the counting of the *OMehR.*

It might be interesting to note that in the Jewish year 3828 on the ninth day of the month of Av, the Romans destroyed the Temple for the second time. This was forty years after the crucifixion of Jesus. Again, Titus, like Nebuchadnezzar, put Jerusalem under seige on *LaG B'OMehR.*

This statement by Jesus of the seige of the Temple on *LaG B'OMehR,* or the thirty-third day of the counting of the *OMehR,* was with reference to the Romans' destruction of the earthly house of his own bodily tabernacle when he was a *LaG B'OMehR* in years of age; that is, thirty-three years old. This statement by Jesus was made on the first day of his public ministry in Jerusalem. On that day, he predicted the accomplishment of his decease for which cause he came into the world. Not only did he predict that the purpose of his life was to die, but he also prophesied the age at which he would die, a *LaG B'OMehR* in years, or in his thirty-third year of life. This announcement was made before there was ever an opportunity for Israel to accept or reject him as their Messiah.

This was repeated many times during John's deposition of Jesus' ministry: "For this cause came I into the world and to this end was I born." In acting out Israel's national drama, it was necessary for him to suffer the destruction of his own bodily Temple forty years before Israel should suffer the destruction of their sanctuary. There is a suggestion in the words of Jesus, "... to this end was I born," that the manner of his death was related to Eternal Purpose and not to object of circumstances.

Each Christmas there is a certain spirit of boo-hoo among Christians "because the poor little baby Jesus had to be born in a manger." Where else would one expect the Lamb of the Sacrifice to be born?

To accuse the Jews of the crucifixion or rejection of Jesus takes away much color from the narratives. The Good News through the cross to the Gentile nations was no accident or second choice. If he had accepted the kingdom offered him on numerous occasions to be the king of Israel, his purpose for coming into the world would have been aborted.

Rabbi Greenberg of Greensboro, North Carolina, said, "How can the Christians accuse the Jews of deicide when the only way the death of Jesus can be explained according to the New Testament is by the word 'sacrifice.'" Dr. David Flusser adds somewhat of a stunning statement concerning the purpose of Jesus, as set forth by Jesus himself and the New Testament writers:

> "Never in the New Testament is it the claim of Jesus, nor the belief of those who followed him as their Messiah, that his total mission and purpose was to suffer, die and be raised again to ascend back to the heavens. Christianity has made that the purpose and mission of Jesus. On this they are wrong! Such a statement is not found anywhere in the New Testament.
>
> "Christianity has made the purpose of Jesus totally soteriological and has ignored the eschatological content of his purpose, as stated in the New Testament. According to the New Testament, Jesus is a Messianic pretender, and it is believed that he *will* fulfill the original Jewish Messianic task when he will return. Otherwise, the idea of the Second Advent is more or less senseless. That eschatological concept is shared by both the Jew and the Christian."

In the context of his thirty-three years in a human tabernacle and a *LaG B'OMehR* destruction by the Roman execution at the age of thirty-three, there is another thought of significance. Israel was forty years in the Sinai wilderness. G-d had shown Moses the Heavenly Tabernacle, or Temple, and had instructed Moses to make a tabernacle in the desert about the order of the one shown him in the Holy Mount.

It took one year to build the Tabernacle of Israel, which Israel used as the meeting place of G-d with them for that remaining thirty-nine years. During those thirty-nine years, Israel spent six years moving about with the Tabernacle dismantled and unused. *The Tabernacle of*

Israel was in use as the meeting place for G-d and his people for thirty-three years of the forty years Sinai experience.

The deposition of John continues to answer the ten questions: "How did the people of Israel respond to the message of Jesus at this Passover in Jerusalem?" The answer is emphatic!

"Now when he was in Jerusalem in the Feast of Passover, many believed in his name when they saw the signs which he did. But Jesus did not commit himself to them [he did not reciprocate to their belief], because he knew all [the real purpose of G-d for him] and needed not that any [of the people of Israel] should testify concerning his Adamic purpose." The people of Israel *were responding* to him; yet, Jesus did not respond to their belief.

In the excitement of his rejection of Israel's response, John relates the narrative of the occasion when Jesus was visited by Nicodemus, president of the Sanhedrin Court (John 3:1-21).

"Oui! !אי Aiyy! There was a man sent out from the Pharisees, Nick-Dimon Ben-Gurion was his name. He was the president of the Jewish Sanhedrin. He came before the night of Passover and said to Jesus, 'Ravi, my great exalted rabbi, we, the Sanhedrin Court, know that you are from G-d, the coming teacher like unto Moses, the Messiah, who will answer all questions, for nobody has the power to perform these signs that you are working. No, not maybe, except G-d be in him."

"Amen! Amen!" Jesus replied to Nick-Dimon. "I say unto you, no! and not maybe! Those outside, the Gentiles, must be born from above. Otherwise, they are not able to see the Kingdom of G-d."

" איך ?eiYhK!" answered Nick-Dimon to Jesus. "How can one of these things on the outside, a Gentile, have the power to be becoming born from above when he is old? For no one has the power to enter again into the womb of his mother the second time and come again being reborn! [How can one without a Yiddisha Mamma have the Jewish soul which comes from above?]"

"Amen! Amen!" Jesus replied to Nick-Dimon. "I say unto you, no! and not maybe! Those on the outside will be born out of heaven, even by the spirit, otherwise they are not able to come into the Kingdom of G-d. For that which is generated out of the flesh is flesh because out of the flesh it came. Don't be bewildered that I say this to you. As you know, it is objectively through you, the Jewish people, that those on the outside will be born from above.

"As the breeze blows universally where it wills, and the sound of it we hear but cannot know where it is coming and where it is going, so also is everyone which is being born out of the breath of G-d."

Yet bewildered, Nick-Dimon Ben-Gurion answered Jesus and said, "How are these things, these Gentiles, to be so born?"

Answering him. Jesus said, "You, Nick-Dimon, are the greatest teacher of Israel and do not know that these things, the Gentiles, will be born from above. Amen! Amen! The knowledge we have received and the testimony which we have witnessed, even that witness concerning the salvation of the Gentiles, we all [Israel] are not able to receive [comprehend], for if the earthly things [the Gentile salvation] I have spoken to you and you are not able to believe it, how then could you see if I had told you of heavenly things [about the mystery of the church, the economy of the heavenly people]? For not one is able to ascend up that heavenly sphere except he that came out of the heavenly sphere, even the son of Adam [the Adam Kadmon], the one which is now in that heavenly sphere.

"Even as Moses lifted up *NaKhaSH*, נחש, the brazen serpent, in the wilderness, likewise must Ben Adam be lifted up in order that all the ones believing in him [the Gentiles] may have life into the ages. This is because G-d so loved the Gentile world that his son, his only son, the only begotten, he dedicated [as Isaac was bound by Abraham] in order that everyone of the Gentiles who are believing in him would not perish but have life into the ages. For G-d did not send his son into the Gentile world for the purpose of judging the Gentile world [as is expected of the Messiah, king of Israel] but in order to be a savior of the Gentile world through him. . . ."

Jesus never said, ". . .except a man be born of water and the spirit. . . ." The Greek construction *anaghudatos*, which is usually translated "of water," is very vague, even to the Greeks. The *anag* is dropped in most editions of the Greek texts. When the word *anaghudatos* is transposed back to the original Hebrew, it becomes מהשמים, *MehHaSHaMiYiM*, which means "from the heavens."

There is a relationship between "water" and "the heavens." One would point to the firmament of water in the sky (Genesis 1:4) and say: שם, *SHahM*, "there is," and מים, *MiYieYM*, "water." So the phrase שם-מים, *SHahM-MieYiM* became the word השמים, *haSHaMiYM*, for heaven which means "there is the water firmament."

What Christians call the "new birth," or "born again," finds its origin in the Jewish concept of נפש-יהודי, *NehFehSH-Y'HoUDieY*, or the "Jewish Soul." This "Jewish Soul" is also called נפש-נשמע, *NehFehSH NiSH'MaG*, or the "soul of listening," and "soul of hearing." It is also called נפש-מהשמים, *NehFehSH Meh Hah SHahMaYieM*, or the soul out of heaven.

The concept of the new birth was in Judaism long before Jesus. He, and only he, could translate that concept of Judaism into a vital experience for the Gentiles.

Nick-Dimon Ben-Gurion was acquainted with the mystical relationship between the Brazen Serpent and the Messiah. The Hebrew word for brass is נחש, *N'KHSH*. The same letters spell the word serpent, *NahKHahSH*, and are written the same. According to rabbinic tradition, Moses fulfilled both meanings by making a serpent, *NahKHahSH*, from brass, *N'KHSH*. The mystical rabbis made yet another interpretation. *NahKHahSH*, the Brazen Serpent, spoke of the Messiah, they said, because according to the Gematria, they both have the same numeric value of 358.

Upon the miracle of the feeding of the five thousand in John 6:14-15, the men said, "*This is* of a truth *that prophet* that should come into the world. When Jesus therefore perceived that *they would come and take him by force, to make him King*, he departed again into a mountain himself alone." These are the Jews of Galilee. They not only accepted and put their faith in him as their King Messiah, they purposed to force him to accept them as his Kingdom.

They were not offering a mere "Bread Crown," as the replacement people suggest. The crown they offered him was the majestic crown of prophetic expectation. What they meant by the use of the terms, "that prophet," "king," and "Messiah" is spelled out in John 7:25-31: "*And many of the people believed on him*, and said in answer to those who sought to destroy him, 'Do the rulers know indeed that this is the very Christ?'" They challenged Herod's rulers with a question, "When the Messiah comes, will he do more miracles than these which this man hath done?" These are the words of the Jews, the people of Jesus' day. The people who went to the synagogues and the Temple. Those who accuse the Jews of the rejection of the king consider all these who hailed Jesus as Christians. They were not Christians, and never converted from Judaism to Christianity.

It was near Qumran where the Sons of Zadok lived. John 10:42 states emphatically that "many believed on him there." Their belief and trust in him was not in any way related to the experience of faith of the Christians today. They believed in him as their promised King.

Back in Jerusalem, in John 11, Jesus had raised Lazarus. "Then gathered the chief priest and the Pharisees a council, and said, 'What do we? For this man doeth many miracles. If we let him thus alone, all men will believe on him . . . .'" In John 11:45-48, because of Lazarus, "Many of the Jews went away, and believed on Jesus."

Now, in this context, invert the situation. Assume that none of the Jews believed in Jesus. Let us make a hyperbolic assumption that he had no following at all among the Jewish people. If this were the case, he would not have been a threat to anyone. He would have been a soapbox prophet. There would have been no need for Herod and Pilatus to attempt to extinguish him.

The people in power under Herod and Pilatus feared Jesus because all the people outside the ruling strata believed he would overthrow the system and reestablish the Davidic throne. If he did, they would be doomed. Then there were those who feared that if his *coup d'etat* was a failure, "the Romans shall come and take away both our place and nation." (John 11:48b) That also meant their doom. If Jesus won the revolt, they lost! If Jesus lost the revolt, they lost! The final conclusion was that someone had to be destroyed—either Jesus or themselves. Out of more than political expediency, yea, with them it was a question of their lives or his life—their own executions or his execution. They made the same decision each of us would probably have made if it had been ourselves in their situation under the same circumstances at that time and place in history.

One man there in that council had prophetic foresight—Caiaphas, the high priest. He addressed the council thusly in John 11:49: "Ye know nothing at all, nor consider that it is expedient for us, [Israel] that one man should die for the [Gentile] people, even that all the [Gentile] nations perish not."

John became very excited and did his own commentary on Caiaphas' words: "And this he spake not of himself: but being high priest that year, he prophesied that Jesus should die in behalf of the [Gentile] people. Not for the [Gentile] nations only [at that time] but that also he should gather together in one the children of G-d [of the Gentiles] that were scattered abroad [in time to come]." One might wonder if Saul of Tarsus was not in that council. What Caiaphas said became the heart and core of Paul's writings.

The conclusion of the seventh question, "What was the general attitude of the people of Israel toward him?" is that they did not reject him as their Messianic King. Although he never made himself available for such, they believed and trusted he would be their expected deliverer. They even tried at times to force it upon him. Yet, he rejected them; they did not reject him.

In the deposition of John, we find almost no reference that Jesus covered his popularity and restricted his fame. The reason, no doubt, is in John's statement of purpose for his book in John 20:30-31: "...Many other signs truly did Jesus in the presence of his disciples, which are not written in this book: But these are written that ye might believe that Jesus is the Christ the Son of G-d; and that believing ye might have life through his name." If John presented the miracles and signs of Jesus as Messianic credentials to the Gentile world, it would be against his purpose to include the "tell no man" phrases.

The restriction of Jesus' fame was only to Israel. To the Gentiles, it was to be proclaimed to the ends of the ages. John's book was not so much a history of the life of Jesus as it was an evangel to the Gentiles. Only once, in 6:15, did he record: "Jesus departed and *did hide* himself from them." In John alone occurs the single statement by Jesus that he was the Messiah, and that was made to the Samaritan Gentile woman in John 4.

John only recorded seven miracles. Five of those seven are not mentioned by the other writers. The two which are, the feeding of the five thousand and his walking on water, omit the statement that "Jesus charged them to tell no man."

Each requirement of Hillel's seven laws is satisfied in this conclusion. The inference from the entire context of the four gospels has been considered. Thirteen texts and contexts attest that the Jews did accept Jesus as their promised Messianic king. It was he who rejected them, not they who rejected him.

Jesus' restriction of his fame in Israel was an overt effort on his part to avoid being proclaimed as their king. His purpose was not to be the king of Israel.

The fifth question, "If Jesus did not come to be the king of Israel (he avoided that title, despite the efforts of tens of thousands of the Jews to make him their king; he rejected them) what did he state that his purpose and mission of life was?" is asked.

As has already been shown, at the synagogue in Nazareth, and in the words of Caiaphas, Jesus' mission and purpose was to be a Messiah, one sent and anointed G-d, to be the Messianic savior to the Gentiles.

Mark makes only three allusions to this purpose. It is significant that it was at the very end of his ministry that he began to reveal what his purpose was, according to Mark's account. "And they departed thence, and passed through Galilee; and he would not that any man should know. For he taught his disciples, and said unto them, 'The son of man is delivered into the hand of men [Gentiles] and they shall kill him; and after that he is killed, he shall rise the third day.' But they [his Jewish disciples] understood not that saying and were afraid to ask him." The message of the death of Jesus has no meaning or dimension to the Jews; no, not even to his own disciples. There is no expectation in Jewish Messianic speculation for their Messiah to die. That was a strange saying in the ears of those who had "forsaken all" to follow him. They expected that he should put the Romans to death, not that the Romans should put him to death. They had placed all their stakes on him as the Messianic king of Israel. They had seen him reject the crown repeatedly. Now he told them he would die and rise again. Their aspirations were shattered by the thought of such an end to their hopes.

When Mary of Bethany anointed Jesus with the alabaster ointment, he said it was "to anoint my body to the burying, Amen! I say unto you, wheresoever this Good News shall be preached throughout the whole world...this shall be a memorial to her."

There was no *good news* to Jesus' followers that he should die. It was *bad news*. The Jews did not then see and have never yet seen any *good news* in the death of Jesus. Except for the very few in the Herodian syndicate whose positions and even lives were threatened by the regal suppositions imposed upon Jesus, no Jew would consider it good news that the Romans had nailed another of their family to the execution stake. No, not even the casual, apathetic Jewish by-passer could see a brother Jew nailed up by the Romans and consider it *good news*. The death of Jesus by Roman execution was *bad news* to those who had forsaken all to follow him. The aspirations of the hundreds of thousands of Israelis that Jesus, the Son of David, would fulfill the Jewish expectation of deliverance from the alien Romans and Herodian dynasties was shattered by the ignominy of the cross. The cross had no meaning of reconciliation for Israel. They were already reconciled to G-d. The preaching of the cross to the Jews was "an offense" because the cross is a brother to the guillotine, the gallows, and, in modern vernacular, the gas chamber and the electric chair. The trinkets that Christians wear symbolizing their faith—crosses of silver, gold, wood and plastic—hold no spiritual aura for the Jews. No! No more than would an electric chair or a hangsman's noose. Not only has the cross meant *bad news* for the Jews, but the shadow of the cross of Jesus shrouds multiplied millions of Jews who have died in the holy wars, the Inquisition, the pogroms, and the Holocaust.

The cross was bad news for the Jews, even before the crucifixion of Jesus. When Jesus was only fourteen years of age, the Romans put down a revolt in Galilee. The road leading to Nazareth was picketed with over two thousand Roman crosses on which were executed Jewish rebels. The Rabbi from Nazareth was nailed to the same type of Roman stake upon which thousands of Zionistic Jews had met their deaths. Jesus was executed for the same reason his brothers were: he was a threat to the alien Roman rule in Israel.

Jesus never wore a trinket cross dangling from his neck! On the contrary, it was the Roman cross that wore Jesus dangling from its impassionate arms. "The offense of the cross" to the Jews, spoken of by Paul, was not an offense to the ideas of Christianity. The offense is that the cross was and is a cruel, bloody, sadistic execution rack upon which many, many thousands of the people of Israel have died. The cross Gentiles wear to symbolize their faith reminds the Jew that it was there that their own kinsman died by Roman execution. Neither have they forgotten the enigma that cross meant to them throughout history. For this reason, the cross of Christ has held and will hold only disillusionment, confusion, and frustration for the Jew.

If Jesus had no Messianic inclination to be the king of Israel, what was his stated purpose and motive of life? How does that affect the Jewish people: The good news is the Gospel of the death and resurrection of Jesus for the Gentile world.

Dr. David Flusser stated, "The cross as presented by Paul was not a lateral bridge to bring the Gentiles into Judaism or to replace Judaism. The cross Paul preached is as the cross was—not lateral, but a vertical span to bring the Gentile into a direct relationship with the G-d of Israel, outside the gate of the Jewish economy." The reader might find a new dimension in his faith by reading Doctor Flusser's book, *Jesus*, which deals with these questions.

The good news in the Gospel of Jesus Christ is that the pagan Gentiles, who are by nature outlaws and enemies of G-d and Israel, could be more than mere "fearers of G-d" who acknowledged the one and true G-d of the Patriarchs. They could have a more vital relationship than to be Jewish proselytes or "strangers in the gates" of Judaism. Through faith in the risen Messiah to the Gentiles, they could enter into a new economy and relationship with the G-d of Israel through a simple faith in Jesus Christ. Having been "called out" from among the Gentiles into a heavenly citizenship, the Gentile Christian is no longer a pagan, but is a member of the household of faith, the body of Christ.

Since this vital relationship of the Christian is purely an experience of faith, it defies logic and philosophical explanation. The Christian is not an ascetic or stoic in the self-debasement of "touch not, taste not, and handle not." Neither is he a liberated epicurean of "eat, drink and be merry." The only moral code is the observance of the Noahic Covenant and "doing those things pleasing unto him."

The Gentile Christian is, above all, not a Jew in any sense of the word. Ritual circumcision and keeping of the

Laws of Torah given to Israel are explicitly forbidden in the Pauline epistles. Christians are not "spiritual Jews." Nor are they "true Jews," as some have referred to themselves. The church is not spiritual Israel, nor is it a replacement of Israel. Israel's salvation is national in scope and is premised on the Abrahamic Covenant. The Christian's relationship is solely through Jesus Christ and his salvation is wrapped up in faith in him. The eschatological promises to Israel are earthly and involve a real estate portion in the Middle East. The eschatology of the Christian is heavenly and has no worldly dimension. The Christian is "born out of heaven," a "citizen of heaven," has a "heavenly hope," a "heavenly calling," and "heavenly walk." Nowhere in the Jewish scriptures is there any mention to Israel about heavenly possessions; they are all earthly. Heaven in an eschatological sense is absent from the Jewish scriptures. Life in the world to come is to the Jew *Eretz* Israel.

The critical error of dispensationalism is the unceasing attempt to intercollate the eschatology of the church into the eschatology of Israel. Or to derail Israel between the cross and the rapture. The replacement theologian's error is in replacing Israel with the church. Both Israel and the church have their economies. They are separate and apart, an earthly people and a heavenly people. But, though Israel and the church are two valid but separate economies, they should be complementary and never aggravate each other.

If the Christian comes to G-d by faith in Jesus and then turns to keep the Torah given to Israel, he has stepped out of bounds into a perimeter where "Christ availeth him nothing." Likewise, the Jew who rejects his own tradition and heritage and becomes a "Jew for Jesus" has stepped out of his bounds into a perimeter where "Abraham availeth him nothing." The average person, in either case, who attempts to change his economy has many personal problems in identity. Not always, but generally speaking, he is frustrated as a bird swimming submerged in an aquarium, hoping not to get his fur wet.

If Jesus avoided and rejected the Messianic kingship of Israel in order to be the savior of the Gentiles, how does that Gospel to the Gentiles affect the Jews? The Gospel to the Gentiles is just as binding on the Jew as the 613 commandments, given exclusively to Israel, are binding on the Gentile Christian. Paul said of himself, "I am a

Jew...a Hebrew of Hebrews...a Pharisee of Pharisees," but Paul never referred to himself as a Christian. In the context of intermarriage between Jews and Christians, Paul's advice in I Corinthians 7:17-20 is: "But as G-d hath distributed to every man, as the Lord hath called everyone, so let him walk, and so I ordain in all churches. Is a man called being circumcised [Jewish]? Let him not become uncircumcised [as a Gentile Christian]. Is any man called in uncircumcision [a Gentile Christian]? Let him not be circumcised [become Jewish]. Circumcision is nothing, and uncircumcision is nothing, but [rather] the keeping of the commandments of G-d. Let every man abide [continue] in the same calling wherein he was called."

In the plural economies of G-d, his earthly people Israel, have their purpose as do the Christians. The RaMBaM, Maimonides, affirmed that the message of Jesus did more to bring the Gentiles to faith in the One True and Living G-d than Judaism could have ever done. It was not the purpose or objective of Israel to convert the Gentiles; Israel's purpose was only to carry the witness to them.

Rabbi Gamaliel's words concerning the message of Jesus were: "...if this counsel or this work be of men, it will come to naught; but if it be of G-d, ye cannot overthrow it, lest haply ye be found even to fight against G-d. And to him they [the Sanhedrin] agreed... ."

What Gamaliel said of the message of Jesus and Christianity can also be said of the Jew and Judaism. If it were of man, or if Christianity had replaced Judaism, it would have long ago come to naught. The very survival of the Jew, Judaism and Israel is the verification of G-d's perseverance of the people of his earthly economy. All the efforts by Christianity to thwart Judaism and the Jewishness of Jesus have been, by the same formula of Gamaliel, "to fight against G-d."

It is not easy for the traditional Christian to reorient himself and his thinking so that he realizes that the Jewish people have a vital relationship with G-d. One evangelical leader said, "My head tells me that it is wrong because it contradicts everything I have learned. But in my heart, I know it is true... . Perhaps this concept, that Judaism is still valid, is like many other truths that were dormant in Christian teaching for many centuries—

truths such as the Holy Spirit and the Second Advent of Christ."

Another Christian leader from Princeton University stated: "To understand that Jesus rejected Israel as a kingdom to be the savior of the Gentiles in a separate economy answers all the Pauline problems I have struggled with about Jews for twenty years. While the plural covenant concept answers all those problems, it creates new problems which have never existed. Namely, since the Jews have a valid relationship with G-d through the Abrahamic Covenant, what is the purpose in trying to convert the Jews to Christianity?"

That question answers itself. Since the Jews have a vital relationship with G-d through the Abrahamic Covenant, there is no purpose in trying to convert the Jews to Christianity!!!

The riddle of the Kingdom, "Did the Jews reject Jesus as their king or did Jesus reject Israel as his kingdom," is now concluded. The case rests with you, the reader. The Seven Laws of Rabbi Hillel have been applied in the "sample of the material" *Kal VHomer*

This examination claims to be no more than that: "only a sample of the whole." The ten questions in the interrogation have been answered, but not completely. You the reader are invited to continue your own interrogation.

The intent of this chapter and this entire book has been to make the reader think. Yea, even to make him argue in a holy sense. There is no harm in a challenge or in an argument. The author warmly welcomes it, and hopes that he has sufficiently provided both for the reader.

Epilogue:
THE RIDDLE OF HOLY CONTROVERSY

Rabbi Nachman was a rabbi, the son of a great rabbi, the grandson of an even greater rabbi. Rabbi Lachish was a sinner until he was in his forties. He received the *Nefesh Yehudi* (Jewish Soul) and began to study with Rabbi Nachman in the yeshivah.

Oui Vey! All the time Rabbi Nachman taught, the Talmid (student or disciple) Lachish would argue or demand that the teacher prove each statement he made. Despite his age and attitude, Lachish finally earned his rabbinic title.

Oui-oui Vey! Then the trouble really began. Everyday, on every question, at each word and at each letter of each word, Rabbi Lachish would challenge Rabbi Nachman. Rabbi Nachman always met the challenge of Rabbi Lachish, but it was not easy. As time went on, Rabbi Lachish's arguments became stronger and stronger. With wisdom and learning, Rabbi Lachish began to win a point now and then. Soon it was nip and tuck as to who would win the issue at hand. Rabbi Nachman found himself weighing carefully each word he spoke. He studied each section with discreet care before his lectures. The very thought of that gleam in the eyes and sharp fingers of Rabbi Lachish at the slightest point of challenge spurred Rabbi Nachman to a nervous frenzy and made him work much harder to be without error.

Finally the day came when Rabbi Nachman could bear it no longer. In the heat of an argument, Rabbi Nachman thought, "Who is this upshot Lachish to dispute with me?" In his anger, Rabbi Nachman drove Rabbi Lachish from his house. "Ah," thought Rabbi Nachman, "what a peace it will be to get rid of this son of contention, Lachish!"

The next morning Rabbi Nachman came to his yeshivah with great relief. "No Lachish today," he mused. Upon entering the room of study, Rabbi Nachman was met with a shocking surprise. Most of his students were gone. Benches which had been crowded with students were empty. Some of the rabbis who had assisted him in the study of Torah were also absent.

"Where are the teachers? Where are the students? What has happened?" inquired Rabbi Nachman.

"They have all followed Rabbi Lachish," shamefully replied one of the few remaining rabbis.

"All gone with Lachish!" cried Rabbi Nachman. In a mood of crushing despair, he sat down and prayed, "O Lord our G-d, King of the universe, judge between me and this man Lachish! If he be more just than I—more understanding than I of your Torah—if he have more wisdom and his case be right before thee—take, I pray you, my life from me this day. Yet, if my case be right before thee, O Lord, judge this day this man Lachish and take his life from him."

So melted inside was Rabbi Nachman that he opened the doors of his soul to let his spirit depart if it so be the will of Ha Shem. The whole assembly sat in solitude. In the stillness, the presence of the angel of death could be felt. Whoever Rabbi Nachman blessed was blessed; whoever he cursed was cursed; and he had now made himself the subject of his own mouth.

In that very hour a student came running into the house of Rabbi Nachman with a ghostly stare in his eyes.

"Rabbi Nachman! Rabbi Nachman! The angel of death just touched Rabbi Lachish—he is dead!"

Soon others returned. After the mourning, all who had followed Rabbi Lachish returned to the house of Rabbi Nachman. They returned and continued to learn from Rabbi Nachman, who had been vindicated by his righteous prayer.

Yet, there was no spirit of triumph in Rabbi Nachman. No air of victory, no strength of the champion. The days of mourning passed for everyone but Rabbi Nachman. It seemed that the sage was in awe of the words of his own mouth.

After the seasons passed, once and again the revered Rabbi Nachman continued to teach. The atmosphere was now so very different. Each movement of Rabbi Nachman's lips was scrutinized by everyone in the house.

Every word was given weight and measure as he taught. Only the greatest difference—no one ever dared question what he said; no one disagreed with him even in the most minute fashion.

Finally, the Rabbi, in somewhat of a frustration, began trying to pump questions about his teachings from his students. But not one came. Then he turned to the other rabbis and asked if there were not another interpretation on such and such a point. All he could get from the other rabbis was a nod and an amen to all he said. No one would question; no one would dare to disagree, nor even offer a complimentary similar interpretation to what Rabbi Nachman had said. The yeshivah lost its *pil-pul* so characteristic of a proper house of learning. Nobody disagreed!

Rabbi Nachman heard of a great teacher of the Torah who lived far away and was a master of debate, or *pil-pul*, in interpretation. Rabbi Nachman sent for this great Talmudist to come to his yeshivah. He thought that to bring in a new man who did not know of Rabbi Lachish would revive the spirit of learning in the house of study. So came the stranger into the house of Rabbi Nachman, but no sooner had he arrived but he learned of the fate of Rabbi Lachish. In the house of study, the master Talmudist sat quietly and listened to Rabbi Nachman. When Rabbi Nachman turned the chair to the new teacher, all he got was the great words of commendation about his teaching.

The next day Rabbi Nachman deliberately made mistakes in his teaching, hoping to draw out the new master. All the master would say was, "Rabbi Nachman, you are right! Who am I to disagree with one such as yourself? You are the master; I am the student!"

In time, Rabbi Nachman brought another, then another, and another; but no one ever again disagreed with him. In the end, Rabbi Nachman repented that he had asked the life of Rabbi Lachish.

"The day Rabbi Lachish died," said he, "was the day I ceased to learn."

The Riddle of the Shepherds

On this planet—any city
There's an avenue, and a street.
The avenue is Ignorance,
And the street—they have named it Hate.

Diagonal 'mid this crossing
Stand two shrines of Holy Elite.
One is Christendom's cathedral
Across — Temple Beth Israel.

When once I stood at this crossing,
Next the spiral cathedral walls;
Dusk of day had fled from 'round me,
Each congregation filled its hall.

Then I saw two Ancient Shepherds
Descending from two cloud step case.
First the Elder, six score in years
The Younger, Bar-Mitzvah score one.

The Elder bore two etched tables
The Younger, etched palms, feet and side.
So met they mid-intersection,
of IGNORANCE, and street named HATE.

Then I ebbed a little closer,
To hear each creed and his debate;
But Holy Awe swept that notion,
As suffering love filled each face.

And the Younger, in obeisance,
Bow'd deep with Serephonic grace,
With the voice of many waters;
"Shalom Aleychem, Ben Levi!"

"Ali-Shalomkah, Ben Yehuda!"
Was the Elder's responsive cry.
As they sat 'fore each other,
Embraced in faith and kindred ties.

And Seraphim filled the heavens
And with Cherubim forward flew
Singing anthems Hallelujah!
Now one sheepfold and no more two!

But a sound of earthly discord
Pierced the air, and the heavens too,
As the Church played loud her prelude
And the Temple her Shofer blew.

While one congregation chanted,
The other congregation sang.
But Cherubim fled the heavens
For neither knew they said the same.

Then the Elder with the Younger,
Arose and stood there face to face;
While their eyes became tear fountains
Moistened beards joined their tears in tide.

And the Younger, bending over,
As the Servant, the Son of Man;
Took and bore the stone-etched tables,
That matched so well his Yod-etched hands.

And the Elder led the Younger,
Through the ages and through the times;
On this planet, any city,
'Twixt the Synagogue and the Shrine.

'Til the Cross and the Menorah
'Til the Shofer and organ sound
Blend as did the Mogen-David
And Shepherd's Star of Beth-Lehem.

"Shalom-Aleychem! Jacob's sons!"
"Aleychem-Shalom! Christendom!"
Let us move, Rabbi and Reverend,
Let our people not here dwell!

On this planet, any city,
On this Avenue, on this Street,
Fall flat these walls as Jericho's,
Walls of "IGNORANCE," walls of "HATE."

Postscript

"So ends the episode...I shall bring my own work to an end here too. If it is well composed and to the point, that is just what I wanted. If it is trashy and mediocre, that is all I could manage. Just as it is injurious to drink wine by itself, or again water, whereas wine mixed with water is pleasant and produces a delightful sense of well-being, so skill in presenting the incidents is what delights the understanding of those who read the story. On this note I will close."

II Maccabees 15:37-39
Jerusalem Bible

Select Bibliography

Compiled by Kenneth R. Cooper

The following bibliography is designed to provide the reader with a broad background for grappling with the issues in this book. No one work teaches the "Plural Covenant" position espoused by Vendyl M. Jones. But a surprising number of them appear to teach it at least in part. At the very least, they do not contradict it. The works marked with an asterisk contain material in support of the "Plural Covenant" although none identifies with this term. All the rest help fill in the academic, cultural, theological, and Biblical background.

K.R.C.

*Aland, Kurt. *Synopsis Quattuor Evangelorium.* Würtemburgische Bibelanstalt, Stuttgart, 1964.

Albright, William F. *Archaeology and the Religion of Israel.* 5th ed., Baltimore: Johns Hopkins University Press, 1956.

Albright, William F. *From the Stone Age to Christianity.* Garden City, New York: Doubleday and Co., 1952.

Avi-Yonah, Michael. *The Jews of Palestine: A Political History from the Bar Kokhba War to the Arab Conquest.* New York: Schocken Books, 1976.

*Baeck, Leo. *Judaism and Christianity* tr. by Walter Kaufmann. New York: Athenaeum, 1958.

*Baron, David. *Rays of Messiah's Glory.* 1886 rpt. Winona Lake, Indiana: Alpha Publications, 1979.

*Baum, Gregory. *Is the New Testament Anti-Semitic?* Rev. Ed., Glen Rock, New Jersey, Paulist Press, 1965.

*Beecher, Willis J. *The Prophets and the Promise.* 1905 rpt., Grand Rapids: Baker Book House, 1975.

*Ben-Yehuda, Eliezer. *Dictionary and Thesaurus of the Hebrew Language.* 8 vol., Cranbury, New Jersey: A. S. Barnes and Co., 1972.

Brown, Francis, Driver, S. R., and Briggs, Charles A., eds. *A Hebrew and English Lexicon of the Old Testament.* 1929 rpt., Oxford: at the Clarendon Press, 1974.

*Buber, Martin. *Two Types of Faith.* tr. by Norman P. Goldhawk. New York: Harper and Row, Pub. Torchbooks, 1961.

*Bultmann, Rudolph. *Primitive Christianity in its Contemporary Setting.* tr. by Reverend R. H. Fuller. New York: World Publishing Co., 1956.

Chafer, Lewis Sperry. "Dispensationalism," *Bibliotheca Saera.* 93 (October, 1936), 390-449.

Chafer, Lewis Sperry. *Systematic Theology.* 7 vol., Dallas: Dallas Theological Seminary Press, 1948.

Cooper, David L. *The God of Israel.* Los Angeles: Biblical Research Society, 1945. (Vol. 1 of Cooper's Messianic Series.)

Cooper, David L. *Messiah: His Final Call To Israel.* Los Angeles: Biblical Research Society, 1962. (Vol. 7 of Cooper's Messianic Series.)

Cooper, David L. *Messiah: His First Coming Scheduled.* Los Angeles: Biblical Research Society, 1939. (Vol. 4 of Cooper's Messianic Series.)

*Cooper, David L. *Messiah: His Glorious Appearance Imminent.* Los Angeles: Biblical Research Society, 1961. (Vol. 6 of Cooper's Messianic Series.)

Cooper, David L. *Messiah: His Historical Appearance.* Los Angeles: Biblical Research Society, 1958. (Vol. 5 of Cooper's Messianic Series.)

*Cooper, David L. *Messiah: His Nature and Person.* Los Angeles: Biblical Research Society, 1933. (Vol. 2 of Cooper's Messianic Series.)

*Cooper, David L. *Messiah:His Redemptive Career.* Los Angeles: Biblical Research Society, 1935. (Vol. 3 of Cooper's Messianic Series.)

Daily Prayer Book. tr. by Philip Birnbaum. New York: Hebrew Publishing Co., 1949.

*Dallas Theological Seminary. *We Believe...: Doctrinal Statement.* Dallas: Dallas Theological Seminar Press, n.d.

de Vaux, Roland. *Ancient Israel: Its Life and Institutions.* 2 vol. New York: McGraw-Hill Pub. Co., 1965.

Dimont, Max I. *Jews, God and History.* New York: New American Library, 1962.

*Douvenoy, Claude. *Le Prince et Le Prophete*. 2nd ed., Jerusalem: Central Press, 1967.

*Edersheim, Alfred. *The Life and Times of Jesus The Messiah*. 1886, rpt., 2 vol., Grand Rapids: William B. Eerdman's Pub. Co., 1962.

Edersheim, Alfred. *Prophecy and History*. 1901 rpt., Grand Rapids: Baker Book House, 1955.

*Edersheim, Alfred. *Sketches of Jewish Social Life*. 1876 rpt. Grand Rapids: William B. Eerdman's Pub. Co., 1950.

Edersheim, Alfred. *The Temple: Its Ministry and Services*. Grand Rapids: William B. Eerdman's Pub. Co., 1950.

*Edwards, Jonathan. "An Humble Inquiry into the Rules of the Word of God Concerning the Qualifications Requisite to a Complete Standing and Full Communion in the Visible Christian Church," *The Works of Jonathan Edwards*. 2 vol. Edinburgh: Banner of Truth Trust, 1974, vol. 1, pp. 431-484.

*Ellison, H. L. *The Centrality of the Messianic Idea in the Old Testament*. London: Lyndale Press, 1953.

*Ellison, H. L. *The Mystery of Israel*. Grand Rapids: William B. Eerdman's Pub. Co., 1966.

English, E. Schuyler., ed. *The New Scofield Reference Bible*. New York: Oxford University Press, 1967.

"The Epistle of Barnabas," *The Ante-Nicene Fathers*. tr. by Alexander Roberts and James Donaldson. 2 vol. Grand Rapids: William B. Eerdman's Pub. Co., 1975, Vol. 1, pp. 137-149.

*Epstein, Isador. *Judaism: A Historical Presentation*. Baltimore: Penguin Books, 1959.

*Fellman, Jack. *The Revival of a Classical Tongue: Eliezer Ben Yehuda and the Modern Hebrew Language*. The Hague, Netherlands: Mouton & Co., 1973.

Flannery, Edward H. *The Anguish of the Jews*. New York: MacMillan Co., 1965.

*Flusser, David. *Jesus*. tr. by Ronald Walls. New York: Herder and Herder, 1969.

*Fuller, Daniel P. *Gospel and Law: Contrast or Continuum?* Grand Rapids: William B. Eerdman's Pub. Co., 1980.

Gade, Richard E. *A Historical Survey of Anti-Semitism.* Grand Rapids: Baker Book House, 1981.

Gaer, Joseph. *The Legend of the Wandering Jew.* New York: New American Library, 1961.

Ginzberg, Louis. *The Legends of the Jews.* 7 vol. Philadelphia; American Jewish Society, 1937.

Glatzer, Nahum. *Franz Rosenweig.* New York: Shocken Books.

Graetz, Heinrich. *History of the Jews.* 6 vol. Philadelphia: Jewish Publication Society of America, 1898.

Greenstone, Julius H. *The Messiah Idea in History.* Philadelphia: Jewish Publication Society of America, 1906.

*Griffith-Thomas, W. H. *St. Paul's Epistle to the Romans: A Devotional Commentary.* 1946 rpt. Grand Rapids: William B. Eerdman's Pub. Co., 1974.

Haas, N., and Nathan, H. "Anthropological Survey of Human Skeletal Remains from Qumran." *Revue ve Qumran.* 6 (February, 1968), 345-352.

*Hertz, J.H., ed. *Pentateuch and Haftorahs.* London: Soncino Press, 1972

*Heschel, Abraham J. *Between God and Man: An Interpretation of Judaism.* ed. by Fritz A. Rothschild. New York: The Free Press, 1959.

*Heschel, Abraham J. *God in Search of Man: A Philosophy of Judaism.* New York: World Publishing Co., 1955.

Heschel, Abraham J. *Israel: An Echo of Eternity.* New York: Farrar, Straus, Giroux, 1967.

*Heschel, Abraham J. *The Sabbath: Its Meaning for Modern Man.* New York: Farrar, Straus, Giroux, 1951.

Heschel, Abraham J. *Theology of Ancient Judaism.* 2 vol. New York: Bloch Pub. Co., 1973.

Jacobs, Louis. *Jewish Biblical Exegesis.* New York: Behrman House, Inc. 1973

*Josephson, Elmer A. *Israel: God's Key to World Redemption.* Hillsboro, Kansas: Bible Light Publications, 1974.

Josephus, Flavius. *Complete Works of Flavius Josephus.* tr. by William Whiston. Grand Rapids: Krego Pub., 1963.

*Kac, Arthur W., ed. *The Messiahship of Jesus: What Jews and Jewish Christians Say.* Chicago: Moody Press, 1980.

Kadushin, Max. *The Rabbinic Mind.* 3rd ed. New York: Bloch Pub. Co., 1972.

*Klausner, Joseph. *From Jesus to Paul.* tr. by William F. Stinespring. New York: MacMillan Co., 1943.

*Klausner, Joseph. *Jesus of Nazareth: His Life, Times, and Teaching.* tr. by Herbert Danby. Boston: Beacon Press, 1925.

*Klausner, Joseph. *The Messianic Idea in Israel.* tr. by William F. Stinespring. New York: MacMillan Co., 1955.

*Ladd, George Eldon. *The Pattern of New Testament Truth.* Grand Rapids: William B. Eerdman's Pub. Co., 1968.

Leach, E. Frank. *The Hebrew Concept of Corporate Personality.* New York: Vantage Press, 1925.

*Longenecker, Richard. *Biblical Exegesis in the Apostolic Period.* Grand Rapids: William B. Eerdman's Pub. Co., 1925.

*Mindel, Nissan. *The Commandments.* New York: Kehot Publication Society, 1971.

*Mindel, Nissan. *Rabbi Schneur Zalman of Liadi.* 2 vol., New York: Kehot Publication Society, 1969, 1973.

The Mishnah. ed. by Herbert Danby. New York: Oxford University Press, 1933.

Moore, George Foot. *Judaism in the First Centuries of the Christian Era.* 2 vol. New York: Schocken Books, 1958.

*Nixon, R. E. *The Exodus in the New Testament.* London: Lyndale Press.

Oxford Annotated Apocrypha. ed. by Bruce M. Metzger. New York: Oxford University Press, 1965.

Pedersen, Johannes. *Israel: Its Life and Culture.* 4 vol. London: Oxford University Press, 1953, 1964.

Pentecost, J. Dwight. *Things to Come*. Findlay, Ohio: Dunham Pub. Co., 1958.

Peters, George N. H. *The Theocratic Kingdom*. 1884 rpt., 3 vol., Grand Rapids: Kregel Pub. Co., 1952.

*Ponce, Charles. *Kabbalah: An Introduction and Illumination for the World Today*. San Francisco: Straight Arrow Books, 1973.

Robinson, H. W. *Corporate Personality in Israel*. Philadelphia: Fortress Press, 1967.

Rosenzweig, Franz. *On Jewish Learning*. New York: Schocken Books.

Scholem, Gershom G. *On the Kabbalah and Its Symbolism*. tr. by Ralph Manheim. New York: Schocken Books, 1969.

*Scofield, C. I. *The Scofield Reference Bible*. New York: Oxford University Press, 1917.

*St. John, Robert. *Tongue of the Prophets: The Life Story of Eliezer Ben Yehuda*. No. Hollywood, Calif.: Wilshire Book Co., 1952.

*Strack, Hermann L., and Billerbeck, Paul. *Kommentar zum Neven Testament*. 6 vol. Munich: C. H. Beck, 1961.

Waxman, Meyer. *Judaism: Religion and Ethics*. New York: Thomas Yoseloff, 1953.

*Weiner, Herbert. *9½ Mystics: The Kabbalah Today*. New York: Collier Books, 1969.

*Weiner, Herbert. *The Wild Goats of Ein Gedi*. New York: Athenaeum, 1954.

Wiesel, Elie. *A Beggar in Jerusalem*. tr. by Lily Edelman and the author. New York: Avon Books, 1970.

Wiesel, Elie. *Messengers of God: Biblical Portraits and Legends*. tr. by Marion Wiesel. New York: Random House Pub. Co., 1976.

*Wiesel, Elie. *Souls on Fire: Portraits and Legends of Hasidic Masters*. tr. by Marion Wiesel. New York: Random House Pub. Co., Vintage Books, 1972.

Wright, G. Ernest, ed. *The Bible and the Ancient Near East*. Garden City, New York: Doubleday and Co., 1961.

*Zalman, Schneur. *Likutei Amarim [Tanya].* tr. by Nissan Mindel. 5 vol., New York: Kehot Publication Society, 1975.

Additional Bibliography

*Buber, Martin. *I and Thou.* New York: Charles Scribner's Sons, 1970. tr. by Walter Kaufmann.

Cook, Walter. *Introduction to Tagmemic Analysis.* Washington, D.C.: Georgetown University Press, 1969.

Cross, Frank. *The Ancient Library of Qumran and Modern Biblical Studies.* Garden City, New York: Doubleday & Co., 1958.

DeHaan, M.R. *Five Blunders of Paul.* Radio Bible Class Broadcast, Grand Rapids, Michigan.

*Eban, Abba. *My People: The Story of the Jews.* New York: Behrman House, 1968.

Eusebius. *Ecclesiastical History.* Grand Rapids: Baker Book House, 1974. tr. by Christian Frederick Cruse.

*Jukes, Andrew. *Four Views of Christ.* 1853 rpt. Grand Rapids: Kregel Pub. Co., 1982. Original Title: *The Characteristic Differences of the Four Gospels.*

Lindsey, Robert L. *A Hebrew Translation of the Gospel of Mark.* Jerusalem: Dugith Pub. Baptist House, n.d.

Longacre, Robert. *An Anatomy of Speech Notions.* Lisse, Belgium: Peter de Ridder Press, 1976.

*Michener, James. *The Source.* New York: Random House, 1965.

Milik, J.T. *Ten Years of Discovery in the Wilderness of Judaea.* Naperville, Illinois: Alec R. Allenson, 1959.

Pike, Kenneth Lee and Pike, Eunice. *Grammatic Analysis.* Dallas: Summer Institute of Linguistics, 1977.

Pike, Kenneth L. *Phonemics.* Ann Arbor: University of Michigan Press, 1947.

Yadin, Yigael. Bar Kochba: *The Rediscovery of the Legendary Hero of the Second Jewish Revolt Against Rome.* New York: Random House, 1971.

	Ezra Script	Modern Script	Archaic Script	Tagmemic Transposition	Hebrew Name	English Name	As In	Numeric Value	Tagmemic Phonetic Description explosive air = e/a implosive air = i/a flowing air = f/a See further Bibliography: Cook Longacre and Pike
1	א			? or A	אָלֶף	?ahLehF	honest	1	un-voiced e/a avelar glottal stop =? or if voiced inside the word is e/a velar fricative = "A"
2	בּ			B	בֵּית	BaeYT	bait	2	post-voiced e/a bilabial
2a	ב			V	בֵית	VaeYT	vase	2	post-voiced f/a labial-dental
3	גּ			GG	גִּימֶל	GGieY-MehL	gong	3	pre-voiced e/a harsh velar
3a	ג			G	גִימֶל	GieYMehL	gay	3	pre-voiced e/a soft velar
4	דּ			DD	דָּלֶת	DDahLehT	dong	4	post-voiced e/a harsh aveolar ridge
4a	ד			D	דָלֶת	DahLehT	ding	4	post-voiced e/a soft aveolar ridge
5	ה			H	הֵא	HaeA	hay	5	pre-voiced f/a soft glottal fricative
6	ו			W	וָו	WahW[(v)]	German "W" vote	6	pre-voiced f/a labial-dental fricative
7	ז			Z	זַיִן	ZaYieN	zero	7	pre-voiced f/a nasal buzz dental fricative
8	ח			KH	חֵית	KHaeYT	Scott's Loch	8	un-voiced f/a harsh glottal fricative
9	ט			t	טֵית	taeYT	sting	9	post-voiced e/a soft aveolar
10	י			Y	יוֹד	YoHD	yo-del	10	pre-voiced f/a open total cavity expanding fricative
11	כּ			K	כָּף	KahF	coal	20	post-voiced e/a harsh velar
11a	כ			hK	כָף	hKF	as German ch	20	un-voiced f/a soft velar trill
11b	ךְ			K	כָּף סוֹפִית	KhF final	K or Kh	500	pre-voiced f+e/a soft or harsh velar terminal ךְ ךּ
12	ל			L	לָמֶד	LahMehD	learn	30	pre-voiced f/a bilateral dental/aveolar ridge fricative
13	מ			M	מֵם	MaM	matter	40	pre-voiced f+e/a nasal labial
13a	ם			M	מֵם סוֹפִית	MaM final	matter	600	pre-voiced e/a nasal labial
14	נ			N	נוּן	NoUN	noon	50	pre-voiced f/a nasal aveolar ridge
14a	ן			N	נוּן סוֹפִית	NoUN final	noon	700	pre-voiced f/a nasal aveolar ridge terminal
15	ס			C	סָמֶךְ	CahMehKh	cider	60	un-voiced f/a fricative closed bi-dental open labial hiss
16	ע			G	עַיִן	GaYiN	EL-AL	70	un-voiced i/a expanding glottal fricative

17	פ			P	פֵּא	PaeA	pay	80	post-voiced e/a harsh bilabial
17a	פ			F	פֵא	FaeA	fat	80	pre-voiced f/a soft labial-dental
1	ף			F	פֵא סופית	FaeA final	fat	800	pre-voiced f/a soft labial-dental terminal
18	צ			TS	צָדֵי	TSahDaeY	tzar	90	post-voiced e/a soft aveolar ridge
18a	ץ			TS	צָדֵי סופית	TSahDaeY final	tzar	900	post-voiced f/a soft aveolar ridge terminal
19	ק			Q	קוֹף	QohF	cough	100	post-voiced e/a soft velar
20	ר			R	רֵישׁ	RaeYSH	race	200	pre-voiced f/a soft aveolar ridge trill
21	שׁ			SH	שִׁין	SHieYN	sheear	300	un-voiced f/a harsh aveolar ridge labial puckered hiss
21a	שׂ			S	שִׂין	SieYN	seen	300	un-voiced f/a soft closed dental fricative labial open hiss
22	תּ			TT	תָּו	TTahW	battle	400	post-voiced e/a harsh aveolar ridge
22a	ת			T	תָו	TahW	the	400	post-voiced e/a soft bi-dental fricative

VOWELS OR VOCOIDS OF HEBREW TEXTS

SYMBOL	TRANSLITERATION	HEBREW	ENGLISH	AS IN	LINGUISTIC DESCRIPTION	DURATION
⊠	ah	קָמָץ	QaMahTS	father card	voiced glottal vocoid	long — open
⊠	a	פַּתַח	PaTahHK	hot cot	voiced glottal vocoid	medium — half
⊠		שְׁוָא	SHWA	pop sop	indicates non-vocoid	shortest
(SHWA X is used un-voiced to indicate non vowels between contoids *or* to divide a vocoid in half)						
⊠	'a	פַּתַח קָטָן	PaTahHK QahTaN	fall ball	(also ֳ and ֱ)	one-half joint vocoid
⊠	eh	סֶגוֹל	SehGol	egg	voiced velar vocoid	long
⊠י	aeY	צֵירֵי	SaeRah	aim pain	voiced aveolar vocoid	long
⊠	ae	ibid חסר	SaeRah half	say day	voiced aveolar vocoid	medium
⊠י	ieY	חִירִיק מלא	KHiRiQ full	neigh fly	voiced aveolar ridge vocoid	long
⊠	i	חסר	KHiRiQ half	it fit		short
⊠	oh	חוֹלָם חסר	KHoHL-ahM half	ocean oh!	open labial glottal vocoid	long open
⊠ו	oH	ibid מלא	ibid full	ibid	ibid	long open
⊠ו	oU	שׁוּרוּק	SHoUR-ouQ	fool	restricted labial glottal vocoid	long closed
⊠	ou	קֻבּוּץ	QouBo-UTS	ibid	ibid	ibid closed

See next page ©

A GUIDE TO THE TRANSLITERATION FROM HEBREW TO ENGLISH

1. There are twenty-two consonants or contoids in the Hebrew alphabet.

2. Five contoids have a different form or shape when they occur at the end of a word. They do not, however, change in sound value. The reason for this was that the ancient writing did not have spaces between words. Hence these five letters which most commonly ended words took a special shape to signal the end of the word. The final form is designated as "*sofit*" letters.

Regular Letters כ מ נ פ צ

Sofit Letters ך ם ן ף ץ

3. Six letters take hard or double sounds. They are designated by a dot or *NiKKud* inside the letter as:
בּ גּ דּ כּ פּ תּ
They usually occur at the beginning of the word and the softer
ב ג ד כ פ ת
usually occur inside the structure. Either may form the final sound. *Double or hard sounds are not designated in this transliteration unless there is a phonetic change.*

4. The alphabet letters are consonants or contoids only. The vowels or vocoids are not considered letters. Vocoids occur as punctuation points under the contoid letters. Neither ancient nor modern Hebrew were written with the contoid vowel marking. *This transliteration transposes the consonants or contoids as UPPER CASE CAPITAL LETTERS and the vocoids or vowels in the lower case small letters. The exception is the tet* ט *is in lower case "t" and the Tav* תּ *is in the upper case "T".*

5. *Tagmemic transliteration usually occurs only when Hebrew is used in the text. Otherwise, Hebrew terms are given in ordinary English spelling as consistently as possible.*